Utility Computing Technologies, Standards, and Strategies

Utility Computing Technologies, Standards, and Strategies

Alfredo Mendoza

ARTECH
HOUSE

BOSTON | LONDON
artechhouse.com

Library of Congress Cataloging-in-Publication Data
A catalog record of this book is available from the U.S. Library of Congress.

British Library Cataloguing in Publication Data
A catalogue record of this book is available from the British Library.

ISBN-13: 978-1-59693-024-7

Cover design by Yekaterina Ratner

© 2007 ARTECH HOUSE, INC.
685 Canton Street
Norwood, MA 02062

The following terms are trademarks of International Business Machines Corporation in the United States, other countries, or both: DB2, Lotus, Tivoli, PowerPC, Power PC Architecture, S/390, pSeries, zSeries, xSeries, System p, System z, System x, System i, WebSphere, Rational, POWER Hypervisor, Micro-Partitioning, Virtualization Engine, Tivoli, IBM.

Java and all Java-based trademarks are trademarks of Sun Microsystems, Inc., in the United States, other countries, or both.

Microsoft, Windows, Windows NT, and the Windows logo are trademarks of Microsoft Corporation in the United States, other countries, or both.

Intel, Intel Inside (logos), MMX, and Pentium are trademarks of Intel Corporation in the United States, other countries, or both.

UNIX is a registered trademark of the Open Group in the United States and other countries.

Linux is a trademark of Linus Torvalds in the United States, other countries, or both.

Other company, product, or service names mentioned herein may be trademarks or service marks of their respective owners.

Information is provided "as is" without warranty of any kind.

10 9 8 7 6 5 4 3 2 1

I would like to dedicate this book to my wife, Lynn, who supported me throughout the writing process. I thank you for being patient and for being there when I needed your guidance the most. I also dedicate this book to my son, Justin, who is growing up so fast. I hope you attain all the goals you set for yourself this year and for all the years to come.

Table of Contents

Preface

Businesses have relied on information technology (IT) to achieve their objectives ever since the invention of computers. While new advances in information technology influence business processes, it is really the business that drives advancement in information technology. Businesses demand an IT infrastructure that enables them to be more responsive, adaptive, and flexible.

Service-oriented organizations (SOOs), simply defined in this context as internal or stand-alone organizations whose purpose is to provide IT computing or business-service functionalities to other organizations or companies, are faced with the dilemma of doing more with less in a constantly changing environment. (Examples of SOOs are internal IT departments that provide data management functions to their companies, customer support centers from independent software vendors that publish licensed enterprise software, and human resource or accounting organizations within large corporations.) On one side, chief information officers (CIOs) of enterprise companies continuously have to balance IT requirements such as costs and risk management and the ever-increasing demand for higher levels of service. On the other side, independent software vendors that develop and supply enterprise application software struggle constantly to find new ways to gain market share.

In the last few years, large companies like IBM, HP, and Sun have spent millions of dollars in marketing, developing and implementing their strategies to help the SOOs with their problems which will only get worse if not alleviated today. Economic downturns, as well as other environmental uncertainties, have escalated the need for strategies that will create a more responsive, adaptive, and flexible SOO. Terms like *on-demand business, adaptive enterprise, organic computing,* and *Sun N1* have surfaced in the last few years from these large companies. SOOs have been inundated with these terms, which have only resulted in more confusion for all but a few.

Today, SOOs need more help than ever. Utility computing technology, in its broadest sense, calls for collaboration between customers, vendors, and standards organizations. But with so many different views as to how one needs to implement utility computing, how does a customer proceed? Customers are asking, How can I integrate utility computing technologies within my organization? This book will help answer this question.

WHOM THIS BOOK IS FOR

This book is for *business executives, technical executives* (CIOs and CTOs), and *professionals* (including application architects, application programmers, and business analysts) of companies of any size who wish to understand utility services and applications. It focuses on the three main components that support an enterprise business–the infrastructure layer, enterprise applications and business processes. The book discusses utility computing standards and technologies that can be used to build a utility hosting infrastructure. The book lays down the foundation for an advanced Web services enterprise application architecture and framework that fits well within utility hosting centers. Last but not least, the book touches on make-or-buy decisions for utility computing, as well as the need for exact IT measurements that can form the basis of utility computing adoption and implementation within the organization.

HOW THIS BOOK IS ORGANIZED

Chapter 1, "Advancing Toward a Utility Model," introduces the reader to historical events leading up to the emergence and resulting implementations of the utility computing model within the IT infrastructure and in software applications. It also introduces the reader to the continuum of utilities, which will serve as a topic guide for the rest of the chapters.

Chapter 2, "Standards and Working Groups," describes the different standards bodies and working groups that are involved in creating standards for use in varying technology implementations. Different vendors collaborate to create these standards so that different technology implementations can easily integrate with each other.

Chapter 3, "Utility Computing Technologies," introduces the reader to the different technologies that exist today to support utility computing initiatives. It covers hardware and software technologies that can be used within the IT infrastructure. Among the technologies mentioned are virtualization, blades, hyperthreading, automated provisioning, and policy-based provisioning.

Chapter 4, "Data Center Challenges and Solutions," focuses on the data center and the current problems of inefficiencies and overcapacity. The chapter discusses different vendor products and solutions that can help CIOs regain control of their data centers.

Chapter 5, "Automating the Data Center," presents the reader with a plan to create an automation agenda. This agenda serves as a blueprint for implementing automation strategies in a step-by-step process. Automation eliminates manual processes that can be considered big contributors to inefficiency and human errors.

Chapter 6, "Software Utility Application Architecture," switches the focus from hardware used within the IT infrastructure to software applications. This chapter introduces the reader to software as a service (SaaS) applications and its architecture. It discusses the attributes of an SaaS and lays out a plan for independent software vendors (ISVs) looking to rearchitect their traditional enterprise applications to SaaS and eventually a software utility application (SUA).

Chapter 7, "Software Application Services Framework," describes a framework that provides common services that contribute to the development of SaaS applications. The framework is based on a premise where SaaS applications will themselves use services from other providers as they contiue to provide services to consumers.

Chapter 8, "Designing Multitenant Applications from a Database Perspective," delves into the technical details of designing a multitenant application. As one of the attributes of SaaS, multitenancy has become an architectural necessity for developing an application that can serve multiple companies on a single instance. This chapter describes the pros and cons of different database design implementations that future SaaS providers can learn from.

Chapter 9, "Other Design Considerations," touches on other SaaS attributes, such as metering, monitoring, update and notification system and a utility computing tool based on current model driven architecture (MDA) tools.

Chapter 10, "Transforming to Software as a Service," describes a process for transforming traditional enterprise applications to an SaaS. The chapter presents a mythical case study of an ISV that has decided to transform its licensed enterprise application into an SaaS. With SaaS applications becoming more mainstream, an ISV looking to expand its business by offering its applications as an SaaS will get a glimpse of what it needs to do next.

Chapter 11, "Virtual Services for Organizations," provides a brief description of how businesses can improve their organizations through componentization. It gives the reader a futuristic view of a business services marketplace that is supported by utility computing technologies and standards.

Chapter 12, "The Future," provides a look at what it will take for utility computing to succeed. It describes how vendors will need to adjust to provide solutions that target not only the few that are willing to try out new technology but the majority that are on the sidelines waiting for technologies to mature before implementing them in their own environments.

The Appendix provides a comprehensive checklist for ISVs who want to transform their applications into SaaS. It can serve as a self-assessment to evaluate their application architectures and find out what help they will need to start the process.

Technologies and the standards that have been introduced to support the utility computing model has advanced rapidly in the last five years. Within those five years, we have seen implementations improve from a user's perspective. As the technology matures, we should see more utility computing technologies implemented and used within the IT infrastructure.

Acknowledgments

This book would not have been written without the help of a number of people. I'd like to thank Anthony Dasari for contributing Chapter 8 of the book and Kay Chang for contributing several sections of Chapter 11.

Several people in IBM also deserve thanks for reviewing select chapters of the book: Aleesa Talmadge, Marg Pond, and Terry Owings. Other people from IBM also deserve mention: Franck Barillaud, John Falkl, Lori Larson, Phil Chang, Virgil Albaugh, John Mims, Hari Madduri, Cheryl Linder, Marilyn Stemper, and David Lubowe.

Special thanks go to Craig Fellenstein for encouraging me and giving me the positive feedback I needed to write the book.

I'd like to thank my wife, Lynn, for reviewing the chapters and correcting my English grammar throughout the book.

Lastly, I'd like to thank Wayne Yuhasz and Barbara Lovenvirth and the copyeditors at Artech House for their patience and support.

Chapter 1

Advancing Toward a Utility Model

Times have changed. Business has changed. Computers have changed.

Over the last 40 years, businesses growth and technological advancement have spurred each other on. With each new business need, technology has stepped up to the plate and provided a solution for the problem at hand. Businesses have invested large amounts of money in new hardware and software, resulting in an information technology (IT) infrastructure that gave them a competitive advantage. Yet, while this technology boosted productivity and enabled faster and more efficient business processes, the net result has been the creation of a complex IT infrastructure that is not only hard to manage but also inflexible. After the Internet boom in the early 2000s, companies began to reexamine their infrastructure resources and found them to be mostly underutilized [1].[1] Today, companies are more cautious in their infrastructure investments – more focused on trimming down excess and reducing risks. It is clear that the companies that will be most successful in sustaining growth are those that will take advantage of new innovations while reducing cost, complexity, and overcapacity.

In recent years, a more dynamic and flexible paradigm for transforming the delivery of IT and business functionalities has taken shape. This new model, called *utility computing*, is supported by technology that will enable companies to serve and consume IT resources and business functionalities as needed. Utility computing promises to bring down costs, reduce overcapacity, and increase levels of service. So, how does the promise of utility computing differ from all other solutions that came before it? A look at recent history within the IT industry will provide the answer.

1.1 EVOLVING IT INFRASTRUCTURE

In 1989, Kodak became the first major corporation in the United States to outsource a significant part of its IT department. Kodak outsourced its data center

---

[1] Contributing to unnecessary hardware support cost and software license cost per CPU.

operations, desktop management, and network, as well as voice networks. Back then, outsourcing a strategic asset such as the IT department to third-party providers was unheard of. But, despite much controversy and doubt, Kodak soon became a role model for how to structure and manage outsourcing relationships. Soon both large and small companies found it acceptable to outsource their IT assets and staff to outsourcing vendors.

In the early 1990s, when the Internet was in its commercial infancy, several internet service providers (ISPs) formed to provide Internet access to private individuals and companies. In the mid-1990s, the commercialization of the Internet paved the way for a new means of conducting business, known as *Internet e-commerce*. As more Internet companies reported their successes in doing business electronically, traditional companies began looking at supplementing their bricks-and-mortar-based businesses with ones that were Internet based.[2] While some companies had the ability to provide e-commerce capabilities from within, several others did not have the ability to do so. These customers turned to outsourcing services that provided them with Internet hosting capabilities. ISPs like UUNET (now a Verizon company) and PSInet (now a Telstra company) created offerings called *colocation* and *managed hosting* services. In both services, customer-owned servers were, and still are, colocated on the ISP's premises. In these scenarios, the ISP provides the power, network and bandwidth required to operate the server and connect it to the Internet. The only difference between the colocation and managed hosting services is the party that manages the servers. In a colocation service, the company who owns the server manages the server themselves; in a managed hosting service, the server is managed by the ISP.

As we can see, advancements in technology and business requirements paved the way for the creation of the different types of infrastructures. Overall, there are three types of managed infrastructures, according to who owns and manages them, as well the consumers of their functionalities.

- Type 1 is an IT infrastructure that is privately managed by the internal company's IT department and that resides within the company firewalls. The infrastructure is privately owned and consumed by the corporation.
- Type 2 is a dedicated outsourced infrastructure that is solely for back-office use. It is managed by outsourcing providers. The data center is owned by the outsourcing provider. The IT resources, like servers and storage, are owned and consumed by the client company.
- Type 3 is a shared hosting infrastructure used by companies with Internet facing requirements. It is managed by ISPs. Data center facilities, including Internet connectivity, are owned by the provider. The IT resources, like servers and storage, are owned by the client company.

---

[2] Later known as *clicks and mortar*.

In the case of new technology like the Internet, reasons like lack of knowledge, complexity, and the difficulty of managing the resources played a role in moving the resources away from the corporate data center. As the difficulty and complexity of maintaining and managing the IT resources increased, so did the tendency to move the resources away to a managed outsourcing service. Figure 1.1 shows this phenomenon.

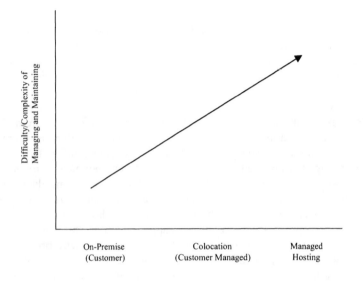

Figure 1.1 Management of IT resources tends to move away from customer premises as management complexity rises.

In the early 2000s, companies began to examine their IT spending in reaction to rising costs in a brewing economic downturn. Companies started to question the return on investment for capital expenditure and their outsourcing activities. While complexities in managing IT resources in both in-house and outsourced data centers continued to rise, underutilization of these resources also became apparent.

To help solve this problem, large server companies like IBM, HP, and Sun introduced solutions aimed at alleviating hardware management complexities concurrent with curbing underutilization. The solutions included technologies like server partitioning which allowed several individual servers to be consolidated into one large server; workload partitioning manager software, which helped manage different workloads to share resources within a single server; and capacity on demand, which provided the ability to buy CPU power by turning on a spare CPU within the server, providing CPU resources as needed.

Today, newer technologies have been introduced to help create a more flexible IT infrastructure. These technologies can be configured to provide IT resources as needed. The technologies include hardware virtualization[3] and management software that automates provisioning based on business policies. Whether these technologies are used within the data center or by the outsourcing provider, they have become the building blocks of what is called utility computing. Utility computing transforms the way IT organizations deliver IT resources, paving the way for a fourth type of infrastructure–a utility infrastructure.

- Type 4 is a utility infrastructure whose purpose is to provide IT infrastructure services as needed when needed. A utility infrastructure can be implemented in-house or by an outsourcing provider. In the case of an outsourcing provider, hardware resources within the provider's utility infrastructure are owned by the provider himself.

While utility computing can be easily mistaken for a form of outsourcing,[4] the confusion can be cleared up by remembering that outsourcing refers to where the resource resides and who manages it, and utility computing refers to how the resource is managed, consumed, and utilized. Utility computing is a model that can be used within the corporate data center or at the outsourcing data center. Utility computing helps break down the monolithic IT infrastructure into separate pieces. The physical resources are broken down and classified in relation to specific business processes that they support. With this arrangement, infrastructure resources that become idle because the business process they support has become obsolete can be diverted to other business processes that need the physical resource or simply turned off. Unlike *one big giant robot* performing several tasks, not allowing its parts to be turned off or easily diverted to other tasks, utility computing can bring about an environment that allows breaking down IT infrastructure into discrete pieces that can perform different and separate business functionalities, can be measured independently, and can be turned on and off as necessary.

1.1.1 Utility-Type Billing for Hardware

For a long time, companies have invested in IT to give them a competitive edge. Today, as IT becomes more commoditized, businesses are looking hard to find the benefits IT brings to their company. While IT remains an essential part of an organization, its strategic value is diminishing over time. As a result, demand for higher levels of service continues to grow, while IT budgets shrink. An infrastructure that meters resource usage and employs a utility pricing strategy can

---

[3] This includes servers, storage, and network.
[4] Most probably because utilities like water and electricity are provided by utility providers.

ensure that users continue to get the levels of service they need while creating an environment that minimizes cost by having customers pay only for what they need. Different hardware vendors have introduced different methods for utility-type billing. Here are some examples:

- HP Pay per Use [2] is part of the HP Utility Pricing Solutions program. It is implemented on HP9000 and Integrity servers. It consists of metering software that monitors CPU utilization and transmits this report through the Internet to a usage database situated at an HP location. The usage information is aggregated and later used to bill the customer.
- Sun Grid Compute Utility is a pay-per-use facility available over the Internet in the United States. This service does not require any purchase of hardware and is offered with no outsourcing contracts at a price of $1/CPU-hour.
- IBM Capacity on Demand[5] is a fast, nondisruptive method of activating processor and memory capacity that is built directly into IBM Series I and P servers. It offers temporary or permanent activation of additional capacity based on user requirements. It provides a way to utilize and pay for resource capacity as needed.

Metering the use of components within the IT infrastructure will likely become the norm in future utility hosting and data centers. Later chapters discuss in more detail the technologies making utility computing a reality.

1.2 EVOLVING SOFTWARE APPLICATIONS

The evolution of how hardware resources are managed and consumed within the different types of IT infrastructures is not an isolated incident; software applications are going through similar changes as well. Software applications are evolving from being developed in-house to being delivered as a service. Just like the hardware components of the IT infrastructure, software applications started out as simple and easy-to-use tools that helped businesses in their activities. Early on, business organizations used software applications that were mostly developed in-house. They were simple and easy to maintain. In 1983, only 23% of major applications came from purchased software [3]. As time went on, more functionality was added to the applications in response to varying needs within the organization.

With more functionality added, software applications became more complex and harder to develop and maintain. As a result, software development that was once done internally began to shift toward being done externally. Independent software vendors (ISVs), as we now call them, took over most of the software development and created standard software applications that could be customized

---

[5] www.ibm.com/servers/eserver/iseries/ondemand/cod/index.html.

and configured to individual company needs. In 1988, the number of applications purchased went up to 44% [3]. This was good news not only for the software vendors but also for the customers who bought the applications. As demand grew, software vendors were able to capitalize on the economies of scale, bringing down development cost, which was then passed on as reduced application cost to customers. In a short time, we saw the "make" model (the era of developing software in-house) turn to a "buy" model (the era of acquiring software applications from external software vendors).

In the mid to late 1990s, applications sold by vendors were once again becoming more complex, this time in terms of application management and upkeep. In addition, customers of these applications were paying ever-increasing licensing fees and maintenance contracts. Although numbers may vary,[6] a conservative estimate of enterprise application software expenditure around this time amounted to approximately 30% of the entire IT budget [4].[7] It was during this time that a new breed of outsourcing providers, called application service providers (ASPs), emerged. The ASPs proposed to take *ownership* of the application including management and maintenance, in exchange for a minimum two-year contract that included a low startup cost and a regular monthly service fee. This arrangement would rid the customer of expensive application expenditure in return for signing a *lease* contract with the ASP.

Just like the hardware infrastructure, the complexity, high cost, and manageability of software applications played a role in moving software application development and maintenance away from organizational confines. Figure 1.2 shows this phenomenon.

While ASPs flourished during the Internet boom, most if not all of them suffered huge loses when the economy went sour. As a result, a lot of them went bankrupt or consolidated. While the ASP concept was a good one, the business model was flawed. The model relied on offering the same hard-to-manage software applications back to the customer. Customizing the application to suit different client needs proved expensive. And while ASPs may have been able to spread the costs of managing multiple instances of the same application for different customers, the ASPs still had to deal with the same maintenance and management headaches experienced earlier by their clients.

While the problems of the ASPs were unfolding, a few innovators were developing software applications that offered capabilities similar to those that enterprise applications offered. The difference was that these new applications were written to be delivered over the Internet and were designed to accommodate multiple companies within a single instance. This gave the provider of these applications, who very often was the developer, the distinct advantage of being

---

[6] Due to the fact that enterprise application expenditure is always grouped with the rest of IT expenditures.
[7] This includes cost to acquire, maintain, and upgrade existing applications.

able to offer the application with little up-front configuration.[8] In addition, the application's single instance design made maintenance and management much simpler than managing multiple instances of traditional enterprise applications offered by the ASPs. The most important advantage of all was that the provider did not have to pay licensing fees, as the application was developed by the same company. This savings could then be passed on to customers.

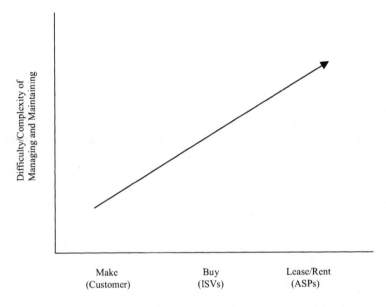

Figure 1.2 Software development and management tends to move away as it becomes more complex.

Today, we know these applications as software as a service (SaaS) applications. They are offered to companies on a per-user subscription basis. Most of them do not require long-term minimum contracts. They started out catering to small and medium-sized business but are now used by large firms as well. Due to their rising popularity and the steady revenue decline of traditional ISVs, traditional ISVs are now slowly adopting the SaaS model in their own line of business. In later chapters, we will discuss the architecture of the SaaS model and how an ISV can turn its traditional enterprise application into an SaaS application.

1.2.1 Software Delivered as Services

Customer demand and competition within the software industry has evolved the pricing models of enterprise software applications over time. When ISVs first

---

[8] Because the application is already installed and configured for use, the only thing needed is to configure for new user access.

came into existence, the most common pricing model used was a fixed-term license (FTL). An FTL grants the company exclusive use of the enterprise application for a specific length of time (term). When the license expires at the end of the term, the company must either stop using the product or obtain a new license. Although the company purchasing the application only needed to pay this amount once for the term specified, in most cases, an FTL can cost a large sum of money. In an effort to attract businesses that might not be able to afford large up-front costs, some ISVs based their pricing to a variable annuity model. A variable annuity model offered IT organizations the use of a software application without incurring a high up-front licensing cost. In lieu of an FTL fee, these vendors charged a monthly licensing fee. A typical variable annuity contract would last for three years and be bundled with maintenance and software support as incentives. Early cancellation could cost the company a fee.

While the pricing model continues to evolve, so does the delivery model. From a consumer's point of view, the evolutionary path of the delivery model for application software has been from a "make to a buy" to a "rent" model. From an ISV's perspective, however, the delivery model is viewed as on-premise or off-premise delivery. The on-premise model is the traditional way of delivering the enterprise application. In an on-premise model, the application is installed within the customer's premises and maintained by local IT personnel. With the introduction of distributed computing and the Internet, the delivery model has evolved to an off-premise model. In the off-premise model, the enterprise application is deployed and hosted in a managed hosting environment outside the organization. The customer accesses the software functionalities through a privately owned leased line or the Internet. Figure 1.3 shows the evolving models of a software application.

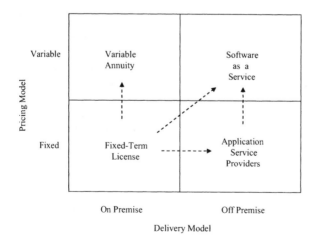

Figure 1.3 Evolving models of software applications.

Today, we are seeing the pricing model for software applications evolving to a more granular level–pay as you use. This pricing model allows customers to access enterprise-level software functionalities on a monthly subscription basis without long-term contracts. As customer demand for different types of pricing and delivery fuels the evolution of software applications, software vendors and providers will continue to monitor these changes to drive new strategies for their future success.

1.3 CONTINUUM OF UTILITIES

The continuum of utilities shows the progression of technological advancements responsible for evolving different parts of the organization[9] into utilities. Each level in the continuum represents new innovations driven by customer needs and made possible by the introduction of a new technology or method. The continuum will serve as a topic guide for the rest of the book. In addition, the continuum stresses that to attain the highest level of cost savings that the utility model can bring about, higher levels of standardization and sharing need to exist. The levels of the continuum are as follows:

- *Level 1*—Utilitylike functions in the IT infrastructure as discussed in this chapter. At this level, new technology enables utilitylike functionalities and pricing in servers within the infrastructure. This is made possible by technologies such as the following:

  - *Capacity on demand* (COD)—A purchasing option that allows companies to receive a server equipped with one or more extra CPUs on top of what the company ordered. The extra CPUs are not turned on until the company needs them. The company pays to turn on the CPUs for a certain amount of time as needed.
  - *Workload partitioning*—A software application that works with the operating system (OS) to control resource usage of processes running on the server. Processes are granted CPU and memory resources according to specified rules thereby limiting resources used by a particular process and enabling more processes to run on the server.
  - *Logical server partitioning*—The ability for a multiway server to be partitioned into several distinct servers running their own OSs.

- *Level 2*—Infrastructure utilities discussed in Chapter 4. At this level, a utilities infrastructure begins to emerge as new technologies enable

---

[9] Both IT infrastructure and business functions.

operations of virtualized operating environments. This is made possible by technologies like:

- Virtual servers, storage, and networks with advanced partitioning and management technology;
- Automated provisioning and policy-based management software used to allocate resources as needed.

- *Level 3*—Application utilities discussed in Chapter 6. At this level, architectural changes to enterprise software applications transform single instance applications into multitenant applications served through the Internet. This is made possible by technologies such as

  - Service-oriented architecture (SOA) implemented as Web services;
  - Metering and account software for enterprise applications.

- *Level 4*—Shared business functionalities and processes discussed in Chapter 11. At this level, companies identify business functionalities that are nonstrategic. Businesses deconstruct processes within siloed organizations and componentize business processes. The purpose is to find similar functional components within different processes to externalize or share with other organizational entities within the company. It is included in the continuum to show that the utility model also applies to business processes. This is discussed in more detail in Chapter 11.

- *Level 5*—Virtual infrastructures. At this level, infrastructure utilities begin to share free resources with each other. Communications between utilities are done through industry-standard protocols and formats.[10] This is made possible by:

  - Grid and an infrastructure utility economy,[11] which is established to automate the sharing of virtualized resources within the disparate IT infrastructures.

An inherent characteristic of the utility model is the potential cost savings that it can bring to an organization. But for costs savings to be realized, producers and consumers of utility services and processes need to know that each level in the utility continuum requires an increasing degree of standardization and sharing. Hardware and software vendors can increase levels of standardization in a new technology by implementing accepted industry standards in their products that

---

[10] An example of this is the data communications markup language (DCML) from dcml.org.
[11] See Chapter 5, Section 5.40.

enable different hardware and software components to interact with each other, regardless of vendor origin. This eliminates the need for customers to implement different methods of integration, curtailing complexity within their IT infrastructures. Figure 1.4 shows the different levels of the continuum of utilities.

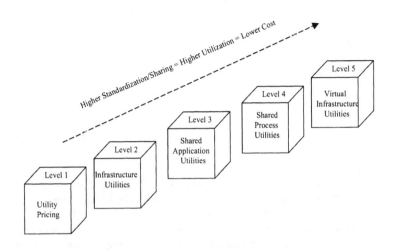

Figure 1.4 Different levels in the continuum of utilities.

Businesses can help increase levels of sharing within their organizations by letting go of an outdated company culture that promotes resource control on an individual or departmental basis. Resources can be consolidated to form a pool of resources utilized by different business units within a company. This increases resource utilization, thereby lowering cost through shared resource management and upkeep.

1.4 SUMMARY

As was mentioned earlier, businesses implemented technologies that gave them a competitive advantage. With that came the challenges of increased IT infrastructure complexity and rising IT management cost. Today, these challenges still exist, along with new challenges like rapidly changing market conditions and increased need for better business collaborations in a globally competitive economy. It is clear that any new technology introduced today must be able to:

- Reduce IT complexity;
    - o Simplify IT through infrastructure management;
    - o Reduce unnecessary consumption of IT resources within the infrastructure through shared and virtualized infrastructures;

- Increase IT flexibility;
    - o Help enterprise customers design and architect the IT infrastructure to align better with their changing business;
    - o Bring flexibility to an organization in the face of volatile demand shifts and changes;
    - o Create business flexibility through integration of application and business processes to produce a seamless flow of information;
- Increase integration ability;
    - o Integrate, automate, and virtualize IT environments through hardware and software services;
    - o Make business processes and technology work in lock step with each other;
    - o Combine the robust nature of the traditional IT computing model with an industry standards-based computing model that enabled the Internet and the World Wide Web;
- Promote new ways of doing business;
    - o Reach new levels of innovation while continuing to deliver improvements in productivity to improve the bottom line;
    - o Create the ability to respond to any customer demand;
    - o Use only best practices that are a result of years of working experience with enterprise customers, helping them to be more flexible and adaptive to changes in their respective markets.

The introduction of utility computing technologies and the utility computing model is already transforming the way IT resources are managed and consumed. It is already helping businesses reduce IT complexity and increase IT flexibility. The technology is changing the way IT infrastructures are designed so that incremental implementations can take place and leave room for changes that may happen in the future. Next, we look at existing and emerging industry standards helping shape the utility computing model.

References

[1]   IBM, "A Taxonomy of the Actual Utilization of Real UNIX and Windows Servers," IBM white paper, 2003.

[2]   HP, *HP Pay Per use (PPU) User's Guide for Version 8.x*, 1st ed., June 2006, http://docs.hp.com/en/5991-5361/5991-5361.pdf.

[3]   Hartog, C., and R. Klepper, "Business Squeeze Pushes Software Sales Up 184%," *Computerworld*, August 22, 1988, p. 55.

[4]   "IT Industry and Management Outlook," *Computer Economics*, 2003, available at http://computereconomics.com.

Chapter 2

Standards and Working Groups

In the early-to-mid 1980s, personal computers existed in the realm of science fiction—Star Trek tricorders and the like. At that time, the concept, never mind the definition, was amorphous. Yet, a few companies were entering into this brave new territory–Apple, Commodore, and IBM among them. One of the things IBM did was to release and make public the specifications for its IBM personal computers (PCs), and in a stroke of luck and genius, it set the standard for designing future generations of PCs. Due to standards, about four in ten homes in the United States have personal computers and one-third of these have a modem, enabling them to be connected over telephone lines.

In 2001, more than 20% of households in the United States that own personal computers connected their computers to the Internet. Like the proliferation of PCs, the proliferation of the Internet was due in part to the introduction of standards. For the Internet, the standards were based on Web technologies. Without the introduction of standards, technologies like the PC and the Internet may have not become as ubiquitous as they are today.

Today, several working groups and organizations involved in developing technical specifications are hard at work developing and promoting standards that will help the advancement of data center interoperability. These standards will pave the way for technology that will help alleviate data center management concerns, like increasing cost and complexity brought about by growth. This chapter introduces the main working groups associated in the development of these technical specifications and standards, as well as current and emerging standards that will be used by infrastructure management applications to create a truly automated and interoperable data center.

2.1 STANDARDS BODIES AND WORKING GROUPS

In relation to today's Internet and Web services standards, a standard originates from the collaboration of work efforts by leading-edge companies that have the common goal of providing their customers with solutions to problems of portability and interoperability between their products and other vendor products. Once the standard gains acceptance from a wider range of vendors, the standard eventually becomes the accepted standard. Often the original standard specification is handed over to a standards body that assumes responsibility for further developing and refining the original standard to accommodate a wider set of requirements set forth by other members of the standards body. This section describes the main standards bodies responsible for developing Internet and Web services standards that will be used to provide software and hardware vendors the ability to interoperate and thus eliminate proprietary-based interfaces that have caused inefficiencies in the management of data centers.

2.1.1 Internet Engineering Task Force (IETF)[1]

The IETF is an organization that creates standards for the operation of the Internet infrastructure. Formed in 1986, it has evolved into an active standards organization involving thousands of people from the international community of academia, research, and industry. The IETF has no formal membership; any individual may participate in mailing lists or attend meetings. When defining a standard, the actual technical work of the IETF is done in its working groups, which are organized by topic into several areas (e.g., routing, transport, security).

Standards originating from the IETF will have a higher impact on utility computing solutions as these solutions assume computer networking as a base capability. As requirements for highly scalable, dynamic, and secure networking become common, the IETF is leading the transition of the Internet infrastructure to a new base protocol, known as Internet Protocol Version 6 (IPv6), which will dramatically increase the number of Internet addresses available and simplify address management. In addition, the IETF continues to evolve security and routing protocols that enable dynamic creation of more secure networks.

2.1.2 World Wide Web Consortium (W3C)[2]

W3C was created in October 1994 with the goal of leading the World Wide Web to its full potential by developing common protocols that promote the Web's evolution and interoperability. As of this writing, W3C has developed more than 80 technical specifications for the Web's infrastructure. Recent technical specifications include the Web Ontology Language (WOL), resource description framework (RDF), and simple object access protocol (SOAP), all of which are or will be in used to advance the concept of utility computing. W3C has over 350 member organizations from all over the world.

---

[1] www.ietf.org.
[2] www.w3.org.

2.1.3 Global Grid Forum (GGF)[3]

The GGF is a community-initiated forum of thousands of individuals from industry and research that promotes and supports grid technologies and applications. They create specifications, user experience documents, and implementation guidelines to help organizations in developing, deploying, and implementing grid technologies.

In addition, they promote the development of a broad-based integrated grid architecture to support emerging grid communities. Such architecture can advance the grid agenda through the adoption of fundamental basic services and through the sharing of middleware code among different applications with common requirements. The following are a few GGF recommendations that relate to utility computing:

- Open grid services architecture (OGSA)–The alignment of Grid and Web services technology to realize a truly open and interoperable system of applications and services framework;
- Open grid services infrastructure (OGSI)–A base set of distributed computing specifications that defines standard interfaces, behaviors and schemas for grid computing in support of OGSA;
- Distributed resource management application API (DRMAA)–An application programming interface specification for the submission and control of jobs to one or more distributed resource management (DRM) system.

Like the IETF, the GGF organizes its working groups into topic areas like applications and programming, architecture, data, security, and resource management, to name a few.

2.1.4 Distributed Management Task Force (DMTF)[4]

The DMTF is an industry organization that helps in the development, adoption, and interoperability of management standards and initiatives for enterprise and Internet environments. DMTF standards aim to streamline integration and reduce cost when enabling end-to-end, multivendor interoperability in management systems through the exchange of management information, regardless of platform or technology. The common information model (CIM) and Web-enterprise management (WBEM) are examples of standards that the DMTF has developed.

---

[3] www.gridforum.org.
[4] www.dmtf.org.

2.1.5 Organization for the Advancement of Structured Information Standards (OASIS)[5]

Founded in 1993, OASIS produces more Web services standards that any other standards organization. OASIS is a not-for-profit, international consortium that drives the development, convergence, and adoption of e-business standards. Among the Web services standards that OASIS developed are service provisioning markup language (SPML); universal description, discovery, and integration (UDDI); and Web services security (WS-Security). It has more than 4,000 participants representing over 600 organizations and individual members in 100 countries.

2.1.6 Web Services Interoperability Organization (WS-I)[6]

The WS-I promotes interoperability between Web services across platforms, applications, and programming languages. The organization includes a diverse group of software vendors, enterprise clients, and others interested in Web services to aid the development of interoperable Web services with guidance, recommended practices, and resources. The WS-I provides resources to help developers create Web services that are interoperable and compliant with WS-I guidelines and industry standards.

The WS-I Basic Profile 1.0 specification describes ways in which diverse Web services specifications can work together to create interoperable Web services. The WS-I is also working on a profile to cover the implications and workings of the OASIS WS-security standard.

2.1.7 Open Group[7]

The Open Group is an international vendor- and technology-neutral consortium that is committed to delivering greater business efficiency by bringing together buyers and suppliers of information technology to lower the time, cost, and risk associated with integrating new technology across the enterprise. The Open Group's vision is to create a boundaryless information flow achieved through global interoperability in a secure, reliable, and timely manner. Two of its missions relating to the development of interoperability standards are:

- To work with customers and to capture, understand, and address current emerging requirements, establish policies, and share best practices;
- To work with suppliers, consortia, and standards bodies to develop consensus and facilitate interoperability and to evolve and integrate specifications and open-source technologies.

---

[5] www.oasis-opcn.org.
[6] www.ws-i.org.
[7] www.opcngroup.org.

The Open Group is responsible for developing standards such as the application response measurement (ARM), the single UNIX specification, and the common information model (CIM; in cooperation with DMTF), to name a few.

2.1.8 Java Community Process (JCP)[8]

In 1998, Sun Microsystems formed the JCP for companies and Java developers to participate openly in developing and maintaining the Java technology. The JCP provides specifications, reference implementations, and technology compatibility kits that guide the evolution of Java technology to support other emerging standards like Web services. The JCP works to ensure the stability and cross-platform compatibility of Java. Anyone can join the JCP, but membership is not required to participate and contribute.

2.1.9 Object Management Group (OMG)[9]

The OMG is an open membership, not-for-profit consortium whose mission is to produce and maintain computer industry specifications that facilitate interoperability between enterprise applications. The OMG is well known for specifications for model-driven architecture (MDA), the unified modeling language (UML), the common object request broker architecture (CORBA), and more recently the emerging reusable asset specification (RAS).

2.2 SERVICE-ORIENTED ARCHITECTURE (SOA)

As more and more technologies and resources become Web based, a single architecture has emerged to make the concept of interoperability within the Internet a reality. This architecture is called *service-oriented architecture*. From IBM's viewpoint,[10] SOA is a component model that interrelates the different functional units of an application, called *services*, through well-defined interfaces and contracts between these services. The interface is defined in a neutral manner that should be independent of the hardware platform, the operating system, and the programming language the service is implemented in. This allows services, built on a variety of such systems, to interact with each other in a uniform and universal manner.

Within the service-oriented architecture, there exist three components: the service provider, the broker or registry, and the requestor or consumer. Each performs a role described as follows.

---

[8] www.jcp.org.
[9] www.omg.org.
[10] www.ibm.com/developerworks/webservices/newto/.

2.2.1 Service Provider

The service provider creates a service or function and publishes its interface and access information to the broker. If the access information is for private consumption only, the service broker may chose to publish the information on a private Web site instead. The publicized functionality is known as a service.

2.2.2 Service Broker or Registry

The service broker or registry is responsible for making the service interface and implementation access information known and available to any potential requestor or consumer. In a sense the broker is acting as the middleman between the service provider and the requestor.

2.2.3 Service Requestor or Consumer

The service requestor is the consumer of the service or functionality. It locates these services from the service broker and binds or implements their service's access interfaces in order to use the services through Web communications protocols. Figure 2.1 is a visual representation of an SOA.

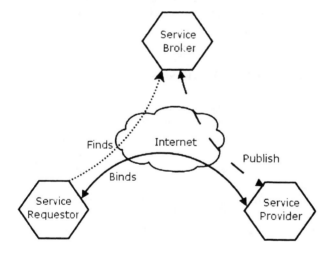

Figure 2.1 Representation of an SOA.

2.2.4 Web Services Technologies

Today's Web services model comprises technologies that form the building blocks of an SOA (discussed in the last section). Within the Web services model resides a service-oriented distributed computing framework in which Web services interact through the exchange of XML documents. Web services are modular applications that are mapped to programs, databases, or business functions and are described, published, located, and invoked over a network [1]. The framework that Web services operate in represents an implementation of a service-oriented architecture. This section provides a bird's eye view of Web services technologies that are in use today.

2.2.5 Extensible Markup Language (XML)

Data and documents in a Web services environment are expressed and described by a family of technologies known as XML. XML was developed by the XML Working Group formed under the auspices of the W3C in 1996 and provides the foundation for many of the open standards of today. XML was created to form a standardized format for representing data and documents, concentrating on structure and thereby making it independent of the delivery medium; thus, XML is the perfect standard for today's utility computing needs. This is particularly true of needs that relate to interoperability between applications and components.

Following is an example of an XML document:

```
<?xml version="1.0">
<PhoneDirList>
        <Person>
                <Name>Jane Doe</Name>
                <Phone>123-123-1234</Phone>
                <Address1>1234 Green St</Address1>
                <City>Austin</City>
                <State>TX</State>
                <Zip>78758</Zip>
        </Person>
</PhoneList>
```

From an application standpoint, the XML sample above can be a representation of data stored in a database expressed as an XML document. This XML document can then be used for Internet-type operations such as producing documents that can be browsed by a Web browser, transferring data to a legacy database for processing, or merging the data with other data to form the input to a new database.

Figure 2.2 shows how XML can be used for transferring data between Web browsers and software applications. A Web client using browser technology requests data from an application server. With the appropriate software application, data from the database is queried and represented as an XML document and transferred through the Internet to the client browser. In the same fashion, the legacy server can request data from the application server as would the client Web browser. Only this time, instead of the XML data being displayed in a Web browser, the data is used by the application running at the legacy server as input that is processed and later merged into the legacy database.

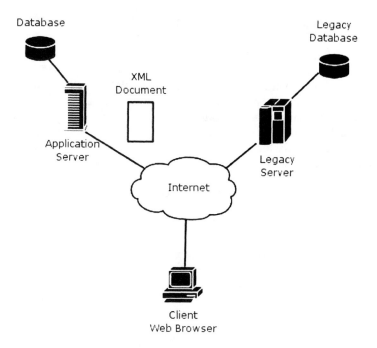

Figure 2.2 Application exchanging an XML document over the Web.

2.2.6 XML Schema

XML schemas express shared vocabularies and allow applications to carry out sets of predefined rules. XML schemas provide one means for defining the structure, content, and semantics of XML documents. They also allow the entities within the XML data to be bound to user-defined-type information. Taking our example above, an XML schema for our sample XML document describes the structure of the XML document in such a way that both the application server and legacy server know how to parse and validate the document for use within their respective environments.

Given the `PhoneDirList` XML example above, the XML schema that predefines that example document might look like the following:

```
<xsd:schema
xmlns:xsd="http://www.w3.org/2001/XMLSchema">
      <xsd:element name="PhoneDirectory"
type="PhoneDirType"/>
      <xsd:complexType name="PhoneDirType">
            <xsd:sequence>
                  <xsd:element name="Person"
            type="PersonTypc"/>
            </xsd:sequence>
      </xsd:complexType>
      <xsd:complexType name="PersonType">
            <xsd:sequence>
                  <xsd:element name="Name"
type="xsd:string"/>
                  <xsd:element name="Phone"
type="xsd:string"/>
                  <xsd:element name="Address"
type="xsd:string"/>
                  <xsd:element name="City"
type="xsd:string"/>
                  <xsd:element name="State"
type="xsd:string"/>
                  <xsd:element name="Zip"
type="xsd:integer"/>
            </xsd:sequence>
      </xsd:complexType>
</xsd:schema>
```

The preceding example schema shows how elements would be defined to produce XML documents as shown in the previous example. An element can also contain subelements. In this case, the subelements for Person are Name, Phone, Address, City, State, and Zip. Also notice that the XML schema follows the form of an XML document.

2.2.7 Simple Object Access Protocol (SOAP)

To facilitate the transfer of XML data from one place to another in a standardized manner, a Web-based technology named SOAP was created. SOAP is an XML-based protocol for applications to send and receive messages over the Internet. It is a W3C recommendation and specification that defines the XML-formatted data for the exchange of structured information in a decentralized and distributed environment. It is the main communications protocol used by the three components within the Web services implementation of a service-oriented architecture. SOAP was designed to be simple, extensible, and independent of any particular platform or programming model.

In relation to the Web, SOAP recognizes that the Internet provides a good medium for client/server communications. SOAP extends the HyperText Transport Protocol (HTTP), specifically intended for human consumption, into one that supports XML messaging. In practice, SOAP messages are encapsulated and sent through HTTP request and response messages. In a simple HTTP message exchange where a client is able to read HTTP messages through a browser that knows how to encode HTTP documents, clients that receive SOAP messages must know how to validate and understand the XML documents as defined by the SOAP specifications.

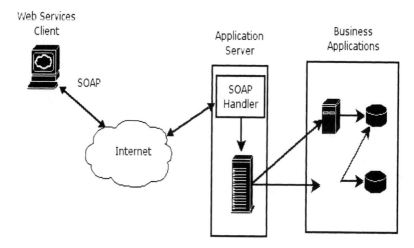

Figure 2.3 High-level view of Web services interaction using SOAP.

Figure 2.3 shows a high-level SOAP message exchange between a Web service provider and consumer. Within an SOA environment implemented through Web services, SOAP transports XML documents across the Internet to facilitate communications between a service provider and the service consumer. Both service provider and consumer employ a SOAP processor to decode the SOAP message and map it back to the underlying software implementation of the service.

2.2.8 Web Services Description Language (WSDL)

WSDL is an XML-based specification that provides a method for describing characteristics of a Web service. These characteristics provide information necessary to integrate a Web service and include the following:

- Name and addressing information of the Web service;
- Protocol encoding used by the Web service;
- Functions, parameters, and data types used by the interface of the Web service.

The WSDL XML definitions may be published either through registries called universal description, discovery and integration (UDDI) or through a static Web link that can be located by a Web locator such as Google. The UDDI or static Web link entries can be thought of as directory entries for finding available Web services.

2.2.9 Universal Description, Discovery, and Integration (UDDI)

UDDI is a business-registry specification that forms the technical foundation to support the description and discovery of Web services providers within and between enterprises.

UDDI is a specification for indexing Web services that allows Web services consumers to connect dynamically and use other services from external providers. Entries in the UDDI registry make use of several standards, including SOAP, XML Schema, and WSDL, which describes information about the business offering a Web service, the capabilities of the services offered, and technical details about how to invoke and use the service.

Figure 2.4 shows the functional representation of Web service technology as implemented for an SOA. The service provider (1) publishes the description of a service in the form of a (2) UDDI entry in the UDDI repository as the service is made available for use. The service requestor represented by an application or another Web service (3) finds the service by seeking functionalities it needs through the UDDI registry. Once a service is found, the requestor (4) binds to the service by implementing its access information interface from (5) WSDL to use the service functionalities from the service provider. All interactions and information exchanged between the service provider, service broker, and service requestor are done through SOAP.

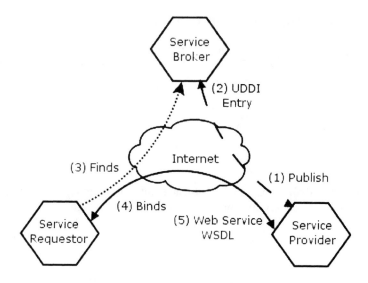

Figure 2.4 The implementation representation of Web services for SOA.

While some standard specifications have been released as formal specifications, some may still be in their draft state. These final and draft standards all contribute to the advancement of utility computing initiatives and define common description formats for describing physical resources within the data center. Further, they specify encoding protocols to facilitate better communications between management software that promotes best practices in integrating technology implementations without the need to replace current working implementations. Next, we describe some of the standards specifications coming from the previously named working groups.

2.3 BUSINESS PROCESS EXECUTION LANGUAGE (BPEL)

A *business process* is a collection of interrelated work tasks, initiated in response to an event that achieves a specific result for the customer of the process [2]. In the past, most of these work tasks were done manually. Today, with the proliferation of Web services standards and technologies, the same work tasks within the process are becoming automated. As work tasks become more automated, companies will find ways to create a truly automated process—one that is initiated in response to an event and carried through until a specific result is achieved for the customer of the process entirely in an automated fashion.

To facilitate the automation of business processes within a Web services environment, the BPEL specification was created. Based on the Web services standards mentioned in the last section, BPEL defines a model and grammar for integrating complex work tasks within business processes. BPEL provides the ability to integrate individual tasks, going beyond the simple exchange of data in a stateless environment to a peer-to-peer, synchronous and asynchronous messaging exchange between two or more parties with long-running interactions in a stateful environment. Figure 2.5 shows how BPEL is used to create an automated travel-reservation workflow.

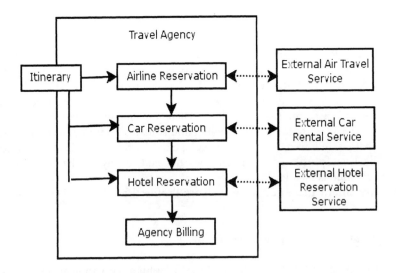

Figure 2.5 Travel agency reservation business process flow.

In our example, a customer initiates an itinerary reservation request through the travel agency's Web site. Once initiated, the process begins by making airline, car, and hotel reservations. The reservations are done through external services made available by the air travel, car rental, and hotel reservation Web services. Once reservations are completed, the workflow ends with an automated billing process to bill the customer.

2.4 INTEROPERABILITY STANDARDS FOR DATA CENTER MANAGEMENT

Data center management has become a hot topic in the last few years. Lowering costs and increasing efficiency within the data center have been the driving forces for innovative advances in task automation and choreography. A data center is composed of servers, storage, and software applications that support a business in providing value to its customers. Within a data center are system administrators tasked to maintain the servers, storage, and applications using software management tools that may or may not be well integrated with each other. As businesses are subject to the ups and downs of the economic and political climate, system administrators continually have to maintain the data center accordingly. To keep up with changing customer and business needs, automating tasks within the data center becomes an increasingly more important factor for businesses in providing value to their customers. This section discusses the standards that are bringing about this vision of an integrated and automated data center for the future.

2.4.1 WS-I Basic Profile 1.0a

The WS-I Basic Profile Version 1.0a, which was released on August 8, 2003, describes a manner in which four key Web services specifications (namely, XML Schema 1.0, SOAP 1.1, WSDL 1.1, and UDDI 2.0) can be implemented to achieve a consistent measure of interoperability. This standard provides Web services implementers with a set of rules to follow when implementing their company's Web service. The WS-I basic profile specification contains a set of constraints and guidelines that, if followed, can assist developers in writing interoperable Web services. The basic profile specification does not add to any of the other Web services specifications mentioned.

For more information, see www.ws-i.org/Profiles/BasicProfile-1.0-2004-04-16.html.

2.4.2 Data Center Markup Language (DCML)

DCML is a proposed XML-based standard for describing the various components running in a data center and how they interoperate. DCML provides the ability to describe the state of the environment, the blueprint for managing the environment, and the policies and standards used in managing the environment. The DCML standard makes use of other defined and emerging standards, such as the resource description framework (RDF)[11] and the web ontology language (WOL).[12] The following are the design goals of DCML:

- *Interoperability*–DCML provides a common language that can be used by different management systems, allowing them to interoperate.
- *Visibility*–DCML provides a common data format that will improve the quality of information and means of acquiring information, allowing improved manageability of physical resources.
- *Extensibility*–DCML defines how new schemas are created to describe the information necessary to manage new entities.

---

[11] www.w3.org/TR/rdf-concepts.
[12] www.w3.org/TR/owl-guide.

- *Flexibility*–DCML provides flexibility in syntax and semantics to allow management systems to better describe resources in a physical and logical manner. DCML flexibility also means DCML processors can run on multiple platforms.
- *Security*–DCML provides facilities for portions of information to be encrypted and/or signed.
- *Adaptability*–DCML incorporates the existing installed technologies and standards and then builds on them to introduce new functionality.
- *Automation Capability*–DCML provides a vocabulary that describes the managed environment in a way that enables tools to automate the data center.

In general terms, DCML will provide a set of specifications that the IT vendor community can utilize to address customer concerns with their data centers. By having a standard set of specifications to describe, manage, and interoperate resources within the data center, customers will be able to manage disparate systems better.

For more information, see www.dcml.org.

2.4.3 Common Information Model (CIM)

CIM is a DMTF standard that provides a conceptual framework for describing the definition of management information for systems, applications, networks, and devices in the Internet, enterprise, or a service-oriented environment, such as a utility computing infrastructure. CIM is based on an object-oriented model that provides management systems with the ability to represent management information about multiple, unique objects and the relationships between them, independent of methods used for their implementation.

CIM facilitates interoperability between different management applications by creating a standard that allows access to data and the controlling of devices independent of the operating platform. This can be particularly useful in a heterogeneous environment where different servers from different vendors may exist. Using CIM, information such as serial number, device model number, location on the network, and even the relationship of these devices to applications and users can be viewed.

For more information, see www.dmtf.org/standards/cim.

2.4.4 The Web-Based Enterprise Management (WBEM) Initiative

The WBEM initiative is an effort by the DMTF to design a set of management and Internet standard technologies to unify the management of enterprise computing environments. WBEM enables the industry to deliver a well-integrated set of standards-based management tools leveraging the emerging Web technologies. The DMTF has developed a core set of standards that make up the WBEM. These include a data model, the common information model (CIM) standard, an encoding specification called the xmlCIM encoding specification, and a transport mechanism called CIM operations over HTTP.

Members of this working group include BMC Software, Cisco Systems, Inc., Compaq, Intel, and Microsoft.

For more information, see www.dmtf.org/standards/wbem.

2.4.5 Web Services Resource Framework (WSRF)

WSRF defines a set of standard specifications for operating on stateful resources through Web services. Stateful resources are defined as resources whose state may change in the course of interacting with other Web services. For example, a hotel reservation system must maintain state information concerning room availability, customer reservations, and system state, such as load and performance. WSRF provides the specifications based on which other Web services can query, create, and change reservations and manage the reservation system. The following are the standards that make up the WSRF specification:

- WS-Resource properties define how the data, also known as properties, associated with a stateful resource can be added, removed, changed, and queried using Web services technologies. The specification defines how the properties are defined in the WSDL file and the form of request messages and receive messages for changing or querying these properties.
- WS-Resource lifetime specifies how a WS-Resource is destroyed–whether they are allowed to expire or must be explicitly destroyed. This specification enables application developers to clean up resources when the Web services are no longer needed.
- WS-BaseFaults defines a means of error notification within a Web services environment using the WSRF specifications. The WS-BaseFaults specification enables Web services designers to express application error messages in a common form, enhancing problem determination and fault management.
- WS-ServiceGroup defines a means of grouping or aggregating Web services and WS-Resources for an application-specific purpose. Requestors of a service can direct a request to a specified group, essentially directing a single request to the collection of Web services.

For more information, see www.globus.org/wsrf.

2.4.6 Web Services Distributed Management (WSDM)

The WSDM working group is a part of OASIS whose goal is to define a Web services architecture for managing distributed systems. There are two specifications under the umbrella of the Web services distributed management technical committee: management using web services (MUWS) and management of Web services (MOWS).

2.4.6.1 Management Using Web Services (MUWS)

MUWS defines how IT resources connected to a network provide manageability interfaces enabling the IT resource to be managed from remote locations using Web services technologies.

2.4.6.2 Management of Web Services (MOWS)

MOWS defines how Web services endpoints used to manage IT resources are managed. In reference to the MUWS specification, MOWS specifies how Web services endpoints are managed in terms of status and state.

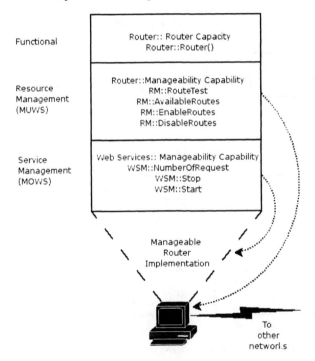

Figure 2.6 The relationship between MOWS and MUWS specification.

Figure 2.6 shows the relationship between MOWS and MUWS in the WSDM specification. It shows a physical router that implements MUWS and MOWS. MUWS provides endpoints as Web services that can accept request messages to get status or change router configuration. The MOWS implementation changes the MUWS endpoint status to either a start or a stop status.

As of this writing, both the MOWS and MUWS specifications are in the draft stage. Members of the working group include Actional Corporation, BEA Systems, Inc., BMC Software, Computer Associates, Dell, Fujitsu, Hewlett-Packard, Hitachi, IBM, Novell, Oracle, Tibco, and webMethods, Inc.

For more information, see www.oasis-open.org/committees/tc_home.php? wg_abbrev=wsdm.

2.4.7 Service Provisioning Markup Language (SPML)

SPML is an XML-based framework for exchanging user, resource, and service provisioning information. In the context of IT systems, service provisioning means the preparation beforehand of materials or supplies required to carry out a defined activity [3]. SPML will be implemented in provisioning systems within an IT data center to automate initial configuration and setup of users, network, servers, and storage. Figure 2.7 shows a service provisioning setup where a controlling authority kicks off a provisioning request to the server provisioning system.

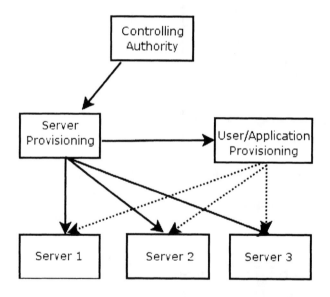

Figure 2.7 An example implementation of a service provisioning system.

After the servers are configured, the server-provisioning system kicks off a request to the user and application provisioning system. The server provisioning may be responsible for configuring the minimum required memory, storage, and services requested. The user and application provisioning systems may provision users, access rights, and entitlements for software applications like Web servers and databases. As of this writing, the latest version of SPML is Version 1.0 released on June 3, 2003.

For more information, see www.oasis-open.org/committees/tc_home.php? wg_abbrev=provision.

2.4.8 Application Response Measurement (ARM)

The ARM specification was developed to enhance the application monitoring capabilities of complex and distributed client/server or Web applications. Over the years, business enterprise applications have evolved from stand-alone hostcentric applications to distributed client/server applications. Traditionally, application monitoring tools have been put in place to monitor the overall health and performance of these mission-critical enterprise applications. These monitors track transactions and application resource usage by monitoring external activities displayed by the application. As client/server enterprise applications have become more complex and distributed, it has become harder for application monitoring tools to monitor the transactions, operations, performance, and health of the applications.

To overcome the shortcomings of application monitoring tools for distributed applications, the approach of letting applications participate in the monitoring of their own processes has been proposed. As a result of this proposal, the ARM working group of the Computer Measurement Group (CMG) published its ARM Version 1.0 API specification in June 1996. Later, CMG submitted the ARM Version 2 API to the Open Group which subsequently approved it for publication. ARM Version 3.0 added new capabilities and specified interfaces in the Java programming language and was released in 2001. ARM Version 4.0, released in 2003, added more capabilities and provided equivalent functions for both C and Java programs. The current release of the ARM specification as of this writing is Version 4.0.

Figure 2.8, using a travel reservation as an example, shows how a distributed application can be monitored better through the use of ARM APIs. A vacationer or business person logs on to a travel reservation system to make reservations for the following: airline, hotel, car, and other miscellaneous activities. The parent transactions, shown as P1 through P2, kick off other transactions at the back end, which may or may not be monitored. Some transactions may come back faster than others, and some may be delayed or fail completely. In a multitransaction scenario where hundreds of transactions are made each day, it will be hard for anyone to track the health of transactions unless measurements for each of the segments are taken. If transaction P3 is delayed or late, is the cause a failure at the car reservations entry point or is it at one of the Q transactions behind it? By ARMing the application and taking appropriate measurements, problems encountered during the operations of applications can be diagnosed more quickly and easily.

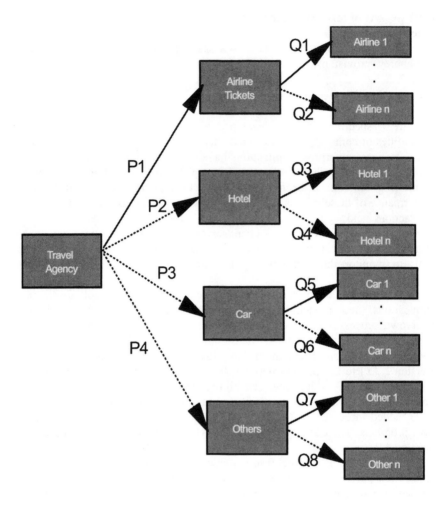

Figure 2.8 A typical travel agency reservations flow where the application is ARMed to measure and monitor transactions between endpoints.

As customers demand better levels of service, monitoring the health and performance of applications will be as important as keeping mission-critical servers up and running 24 hours per day.

For more information, see www.opengroup.org/tech/management/arm.

2.4.9 Reusable Asset Specification (RAS)

RAS is an XML-based specification that addresses the engineering elements of reuse. In particular, RAS is a set of guidelines and recommendations that deals with the structure, content, and description of reusable software assets.

A reusable asset is defined as an asset that provides a solution to a problem for a given content. That reusable asset may contain work products from a software development life cycle such as requirements documents, models, source-code files, test cases, or scripts.

The RAS specifies how to bundle the reusable asset in such a way that its contents are described externally and can be examined easily through what it calls an RAS manifest. In this manner, projects needing similar components can find assets from searchable asset repositories that can be customized to fit the needs of the current project.

In the future, RAS can be implemented inside computer-aided software engineering (CASE) tools so that it can automatically go to an RAS repository service. The tool can specify the parameters it needs to search for and send a request to search the repository. The repository service can come back with a reply similar to the replies one gets when searching something on Google. Figure 2.9 shows a conceptual view of a CASE tool implementing RAS to search for reusable assets.

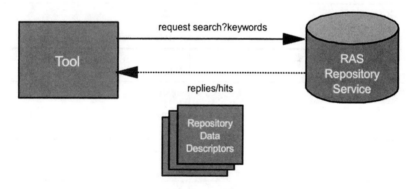

Figure 2.9 A conceptual model of a tool that implements RAS searching for reusable assets in an RAS repository service.

Since utility computing is also about reuse, RAS can be extended beyond being just a software reuse specification to cover data center components and reuseable business process service components.

For more information, see www.omg.org/cgi-bin/doc?ptc/2004-06-06.

2.5 SUMMARY

This chapter provided an introduction to the standard working groups and the standards they are developing to help achieve the vision of a true automated data center. Table 2.1 provides a summary of the working groups and their related standards. The chapter introduced Web services as an SOA implementation and discussed how a Web services standard like BPEL provides a model for integrating business workflow exposed as Web services inside and outside an organization. As business processes become more automated, the need for faster and more efficient ways of managing the data center becomes apparent. In the future, infrastructure technology that supports business processes will have to become flexible and resilient to changes in the business environment. One way to become flexible and resilient to change is to implement automation geared toward streamlining the data center.

Table 2.1 Standards Organizations and Related Standards

Organization	Related Standards
IETF	IPv6
W3C	XML family SOAP WSDL
GGF	OGSI OGSA DRMAA
DMTF	CIM WBEM
OASIS	SPML WSDM WSRF DCML
WS-I	Basic profile 1
OG	ARM
JCP[13]	Java compatibility
OMG	RAS

To provide automation within a data center, software management tools that interface with hardware equipment need to be able to provision the hardware equipment automatically. As with all large data centers where equipment can be heterogeneous, providing automation that controls these disparate systems from one

---

[13] Not a standard working group.

single point of management can be problematic. Today, system administrators have to use different management tools that often duplicate tasks, contributing to inefficiency. Both hardware and software vendors of data center equipment and management tools will have to work together to implement these standards in their products if they are to fulfill the needs of today's and tomorrow's data centers.

References

[1]   Newcommer, E., *Understanding Web Services*, Boston, MA, Addison Wesley, 2002.

[2]   Sharp, A., and P. McDermott, *Workflow Modeling*, Norwood, MA, Artech House, 2001.

[3]   "Service Provisioning Markup Language," Version 1.0, OASIS, June 3, 2003, available at www.oasis-open.org/committees/provision/docs.

Chapter 3

Utility Computing Technologies

Proven technologies, like virtualization, advanced application accounting, and dynamic partitioning, that have long existed in mainframes are now available in similar implementations on newer server architectures. Other technologies like the Internet, grid, Web services, and hyperthreading (HT), are all new. Today, these technologies are contributing to create an infrastructure based on the utility model. When combined, these technologies are changing the way IT resources are managed and consumed, alleviating low utilization rates and increasing levels of service. Let's explore the technologies and concepts that are being applied in improved ways to the emerging infrastructure resources of today and tomorrow.

3.1 VIRTUALIZATION

The first virtual machine (VM) technology made its debut in the early 1960s when IBM brought out its System/360. For the first time, hardware resources were divvied up and handled as though more than one machine were available. Programs previously requiring dedicated machines could now be run simultaneously on one set of hardware. Making this all possible was the virtualization of servers, CPUs, storage, network resources, and input/output (I/O.) Today, the same virtualization technology concept introduced by IBM some decades ago has been adopted and implemented in the latest hardware and computing environments.

3.1.1 Server Virtualization

In the context of servers, virtualization is the technology that allows a server with multiple CPUs to be partitioned into smaller logical partitions, each looking and operating like a stand-alone CPU. Each partition can run an independent instance of an operating system. Each partition is also assigned its own memory and storage that is not shared by any other partitions within the same physical machine. As an example, an eight-way multiprocessor machine with server virtualization implementation can be subdivided into a maximum of eight logical machines with one CPU, each running its own instance of the operating system. Physical memory and I/O resources can be divided up between the logical machines as needed.

3.1.2 CPU Virtualization

CPU virtualization is the technology that allows for the virtualization of CPU to the subprocessor level. It is akin to server virtualization, but it allows for more granular partitioning. Usually the sub-CPU virtualization and scheduling is handled by a *hypervisor,*[1] which sits between the hardware and the operating system. Figure 3.1 shows the difference between server and CPU virtualization. An implementation of this technology was first introduced on IBM's S/360 mainframe and more recently on its new IBM Series p servers based on POWER5 processors running Version 5.3 of the AIX operating system. On AIX 5.3 running on POWER5 architecture, each CPU can be virtualized to 1/10 of a processor. This means that an eight-processor server can be partitioned to run as many as 80 virtual machines.

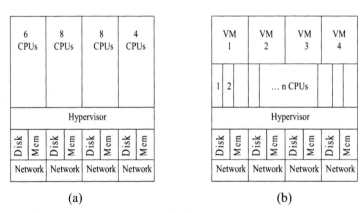

Figure 3.1 Difference between (a) server and (b) CPU virtualization.

With both server and CPU virtualization, a single multiprocessor machine represents a pool of resources that can be partitioned logically according to resource and capacity needs. With the addition of monitoring and automated configuration software, this pool of resources can be allocated and shared among many different organizations needing varying workloads in an automated fashion, in essence handling the task of adding or subtracting resources to match workload as needed.

---

[1] Use of a hypervisor allows multiple operating systems to run on a host computer at the same time.

3.1.3 Grid Virtualization

A grid computing environment is made up of clusters of physical servers connected through a variety of network connections. Servers within the grid are utilized in a manner that harnesses unused processing capacity to complete varying workloads. A grid environment can be viewed as the "pooling" of physical server resources into one homogeneous entity that can handle workload in a distributed manner.

Within a grid environment is a job scheduler that monitors and distributes workloads onto servers within the pool. Application programs written to take advantage of the pools of servers within the grid are specifically written to take advantage of the available grid resources. In this environment, the tasks are brought to the resource to handle needed capacity, as opposed to the single physical server scenario discussed in the server and CPU virtualization sections, where the resources are brought to match needed capacity.

3.1.4 Storage Virtualization

Physical storage can be classified as direct-attached devices known as disk arrays or network-attached devices known as host-level storage. Both of these are available today. Disk array and host-level storage virtualization come from companies like EMC and Network Appliance, while others like Verities offer virtualization at the host level only. Two well-known host-attached technologies currently exist that can accommodate storage virtualization methods:

- *Storage area networks (SAN)*–These are high-speed switched networks designed to allow multiple computers to have shared access to many storage devices.
- *Network-attached storage (NASs)*–These come in the form of NAS appliances or NAS gateways. NAS devices are virtual file servers that support NFS-type protocols. A NAS is a device that directly attaches to the network and has file-sharing capabilities

Table 3.1 shows a comparison of these storage technologies.

Table 3.1 Differences Between SAN, NAS, and Direct Attached Devices

Direct Attach	SAN	NAS
Low configuration and flexibility	Highly scalable	Low scalability
High administration cost	High IT skills needed	Lower IT skills needed; filesystem managed by NAS head unit
No data sharing	Limited data sharing unless virtualized.	File sharing over TCP/IP using CIFS/HTTP/NFS

Table 3.1 Differences Between SAN, NAS, and Direct Attached Devices (Continued)

Direct Attach	SAN	NAS
Performance depends on direct-attached technology	High performance	Limited performance
No scaling	Scales up	Scales down
Quick inexpensive deployment through direct-attached cable	Lengthy, expensive initial deployment; most SANs utilize fiber channel	Quick inexpensive initial deployment; uses TCP/IP Networks: Ethernet, FDDI, ATM (perhaps TCP/IP over fiber channel someday)
Limited reach through direct-attached (SCSI) cable	Limited reach (Only server class devices with fiber channel can connect to the SAN. The fiber channel of the SAN has a limit of around 10 km (6.25 mi) at best.)	WAN reach

The advantage of applying virtualization software to disk devices is that a single physical storage unit can be made to appear as multiple physical disks to different hosts that use them. In essence, a single large physical disk can be divided up into smaller chunks of logical disk storage that is accessed by different hosts either through the network or a direct-attached method.

3.1.5 Network Virtualization

Today, network virtualization is achieved by using a virtualization switch (like Inkra's Virtual Service Switch). This technology divides available network bandwidth into separate, distinct, and secure channels and devices. This allows for internal network security zones on the one hand, and consolidated security for network connections to several business partners on the other. Just like virtualization on other layers of the infrastructure, network virtualization is designed to virtualize the facets of the network fabric–examples are virtual private networks (VPNs), firewalls, load balancers, and voice over IP.

Another type of network virtualization is that used within servers whose virtual machines can share a single network interface card (NIC). Each VM can configure its own virtual IP address using the same physical NIC. IBM's AIX operating system and Veritas's VMware implement this type of network virtualization.

3.1.6 I/O Virtualization

The IBM AIX 5L Version 5.3 running on a POWER5 platform is an example of an operating system that introduces I/O virtualization in the form of small computer system interface (SCSI) virtualization. This allows virtual partitions to share one physical SCSI adapter between different logical CPU or server partitions.

Virtualization may bring a slighty higher overhead compared to nonvirtualized settings. Still, the advantage of having the flexibility to virtualize resources allows system administrators to plan for peak and low CPU, storage, network, or I/O usage.

3.2 HYPERTHREADING (HT)

Intel first introduced hyperthreading technology in its Intel Xeon processor family in 2002. HT technology allows the operation of two simultaneous threads of execution on a single CPU. This is possible by having two logical CPUs on one physical processor. According to Intel, the technology allows one physical CPU to present itself to modern operating systems as two virtual processors. Although a single CPU with HT technology does not perform as well as two physical CPUs overall, Intel benchmarks show that it can boost performance by 30% in some server applications.

Today's operating systems have hooks to low-level hardware that control HT technology. This allows system administrators to control the use of HT technology, turning it on or off as needed. This affords performance-tuning engineers the ability to create baseline measurements easily, using regular CPU technology that can be used to compare these measurements with measurements made using CPU with HT technology turned on.

3.3 BLADE SERVERS

Blade servers are an evolution from traditional big bulky servers to what IDC[2] calls "an inclusive computing system that includes processor and memory on a single board." These boards reside in a cabinet and access power, network, and storage services through the chassis backplane. According to IDC, customers who demand that information systems be variable, available, and efficiently managed have contributed to the evolution of servers into blade technology.

Blade servers may come in uni-, dual-, or multiprocessor configurations. With its modular architecture, blade servers offer tremendous space savings and ease of management (server deployment, reconfiguration, tuning, upgrades, and platform migration) in data centers. All server vendors, like Dell, HP, SUN and IBM, offer their own brand of blade servers.

---

[2] International Data Corporation, www.idc.com.

3.4 AUTOMATED PROVISIONING

Automated provisioning will completely replace manual provisioning and make all previously mentioned technology implementations more worthwhile for CIOs and hosting providers. Manual provisioning of resources, on a large scale, is often expensive, time-consuming, and error prone.

The use of automated provisioning software can speed things up by eliminating tedious, labor-intensive, and repetitive tasks, for instance, the configuration or reconfiguration of servers. Configuring servers consists of getting the right hardware and software installed. Adequate storage, memory, and I/O adapters need to be put in place. After configuring the right hardware, the server is run through several tests to make sure the hardware is sound. Then, the operating system and other additional software are installed. Only then can the machine be ready for use. All these may take anywhere from 6 to 72 hours, depending on hardware, software, and other resource availability. With virtual technology and automation, all of this can be done in a matter of hours.[3]

With automation, the risk of injecting human errors into repetitive tasks is minimized.[4] Once a process is programmed for automation, the task is performed consistently every time. New standards for interfacing hardware resources to management software are being developed as this book goes into production. Slowly, each hardware resource will have its own standards-based interface that will allow management software to check its status, bring it online or offline, and redirect its use to organizations that need it.

Today companies are retooling their infrastructure to incorporate virtualization technologies to work with management software geared toward automated provisioning. As the need for a more flexible IT increases, we will see a move to a more consolidated and automated infrastructure environment.

3.5 POLICY-BASED AUTOMATION

As more companies retool for automated provisioning, the interaction between administrators and the management software that provides resource provisioning control for the physical resources they support (that has interfaces allowing them to control these resources) remains mostly manual in nature. Human interaction is done through the use of a management console. As an example, when the system administration sees, through its monitoring utility, that a server running an application has 90% CPU utilization and the service level agreement (SLA) is set at 85% CPU, the system administrator initiates the provisioning of another server, which in turn will start a workflow to configure a server, install the software

---

[3] Refer to the case study in Section 3.7.
[4] Automation may also magnify errors. A program with an error will inject the error every time.

stacks needed by the application, configure the necessary network connections, and then install and possibly configure the application on the new server.

Newer management software that incorporates policy-based automation software, which is mostly available now as separate plug-in modules to existing management software, will take over human-initiated provisioning. By making use of monitoring software in cooperation with automated provisioning, policy-based automation can be achieved. Monitoring rules that adhere to SLA policies will trigger provisioning workflows when needed. Deprovisioning policies will provide the ability to recycle resources for future reuse.

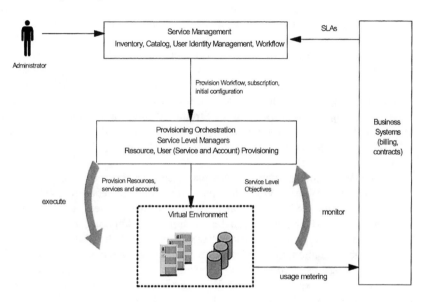

Figure 3.2 A conceptual view of how policy-based automation works.

Figure 3.2 shows a conceptual view of how policy-based automation works. After the initial configuration and SLA requirements are fed into the service management engine, initial hardware resources, including user provisioning, are done. After that, the policy-based provisioning engine takes over. The policy engine has service level objectives set for the configuration. The configuration is monitored for any objectives that are likely to be exceeded or not met, and the provisioning engine is triggered to reprovision resources as needed. Sometimes, resources may be needed by two virtual environments at the same time. In this case, the provisioning engine decides which environment request to satisfy.

Policy-based automation is the next step toward full automation of the IT environment. As it stands today, policy-based automation cannot take place until the infrastructure is tooled and configured for automated provisioning.

3.6 APPLICATION MANAGEMENT

Application management systems today consist mainly of patch management, operating system and software provisioning, configuration tracking, and application deployment. While all are meant to streamline application management to save on cost, Gartner Group believes that most large enterprises will continue to underestimate the ongoing cost of applications by 50% (0.8 probability). Companies like Opsware (www.opsware.com) and Appstream (www.appstream.com) provide products that help in this market segment.

In a different light, applications today are evolving into componentized business functionalities. These business functionalities will be represented as Web services functions in the future. In the context of Web services, application management is called Web services management (WSM). WSM deals with life cycle management of Web services, just like application management deals with the life cycle management of applications. Several companies are working on standardizing interfaces for WSM. The companies work together under the Organization for the Advancement of Structured Information Standards (OASIS). Among the standards that are emerging are Web services distributed management (WSDM) and Web services resource framework (WSRF).

- *WSDM*–Defines a Web services management system to manage distributed resources. Within WSDM exists the Management of Web Services Specification, which basically addresses management of Web services endpoints. Management can be as simple as knowing if the endpoint is available or unavailable. The WSDM covers more than just Web services as business functionalities; it can also cover other resources whose capabilities are exposed as Web services. An example is a storage device whose storage metrics are exposed through Web services. In the context of application management, WSDM will be applied to Web services that are componentized business functionalities.
- *WSRF*–Defines a framework for modeling and accessing stateful resources using Web services. WSRF addresses the relationship between the Web service and stateful resources, particularly WS-Resource life cycle. WS-ResourceLifetime specifies when a WS-Resource can be destroyed and defines a way that it can be monitored. WS renewal references provide policy information to allow versioning of endpoint references, enabling resolution of time and versions in discovery and access.

As of this writing, both specifications are new and still in draft phase. They will need more iteration before they are considered to be in final form. Without Web services management capabilities, deployment of Web services will be limited.

3.7 EVALUATING UTILITY MANAGEMENT TECHNOLOGY–A CASE STUDY

Although some pundits are silent about it, there is no doubt that there are a lot of questions being asked about the viability of virtualized technologies, especially those that pertain to sub-CPU virtualization. Customers looking into virtualized technologies are concerned about performance considerations when they deploy their applications to a virtualized platform. The concern is valid since virtualization technologies in most modern platforms have only been released in the latest operating systems for enterprise servers. Virtualized platform technologies from VMWare and Microsoft for Windows Servers exist but may be limited in their capabilities and lack additional support from external workload management components. In today's environment, the main points for evaluating virtualization technology are scalability, CPU utilization, and affinity. The following study shows how to evaluate virtualization implementations.

3.7.1 The Setup

While this study was done using a particular brand of software partitioning technology, it has universal appeal to anyone wanting to evaluate future server and CPU virtualization technologies. The study is only meant as a guide or a model to build on when evaluating virtualization technologies.

The setup consists of a single, generic, four-way CPU (2-GHz CPU speed) server with 4 Gb of total memory. The server had more than enough network cards (six to be exact) and more than ample local storage for use. A Web benchmarking tool, which was similar to Web Bench,[5] was used in the study to drive the load on each virtual machine configured.

Client machines were configured such that each client sent HTTP requests to a specific virtual machine on the server. To start off, one VM was configured and turned on. The first client (C1) would then send an HTTP request to VM1 until the test was done. Next, a second VM, VM2, was configured and turned on. A second client machine (C2) was added to the test environment to send an HTTP request only to VM2 while the first client sent an HTTP request to VM1. This procedure was repeated until six configured VMs and six clients were simultaneously sending HTTP requests to their VM counterparts. Figure 3.3 shows the test setup used in the study.

---

[5] A free tool for Web benchmarking available on the Internet.

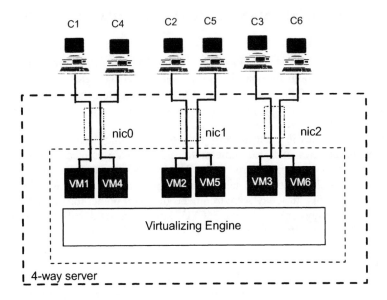

Figure 3.3 Test setup used to study virtualization technology.

To spread the load equally, the VMs were configured in such a way that they had a one-to-one mapping to a CPU. In other words, when VM1 was turned on, it was mapped directly to CPU1, then VM2 was mapped to CPU2, and VM3 was mapped to CPU3. When VM4 was turned on, it was mapped back to CPU1, and so on for the rest of the VMs. The VMs also were given 512 Mb of memory for their own use. Each of the VMs were assigned their own virtual IP addresses, and, for the purpose of testing virtualized network I/O, a network interface card was shared between two VMs.

3.7.2 Scalability

In the context of virtualization, scalability is a measure of how well the load of the VMs can be spread within processors. In essence, it shows how well the sub-processor sharing algorithm performs. In the study, the test for scalability for the virtualization technology faired well, as shown in the Figure 3.4.

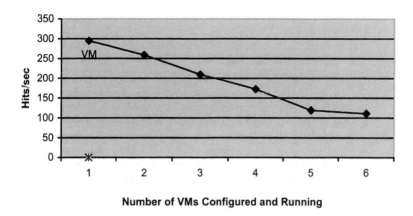

Number of VMs Configured and Running

Figure 3.4 The capacity to process hits gradually decreases as the number of VMs configured is increased.

Figure 3.4 shows that as the number of client-VM pairs increased, the number of hits per second for VM1 showed a constant decrease. The gradual reduction was seen as a positive attribute since it showed that the product had excellent scaling abilities. The constant decrease of hits per second can be expected for a constant gradual increase in load.

3.7.3 CPU Utilization

In any hardware implementation, it is important to know how the hardware will perform as the load on it is increased. In a virtualized CPU implementation, the question is, how many virtual machines can one configure on each CPU?

CPU utilization was recorded during test runs. Figure 3.5 shows a graph of the CPU utilization of the four-way machine with two CPUs turned off versus the number of VMs configured. In the test configuration with only two CPUs turned on, as the number of configured and active VMs went up, the CPU utilization went up as well. The graph also shows how many VMs can be configured before a certain CPU utilization threshold is reached.

Hosting architects can use this graph to help them decide how many VMs to configure per CPU. In other words, if an application provider can tolerate 50% to 70% CPU utilization on the servers, then the hosting architect can look at the graph and configure between 3 and 4 VMs on the server, or about 1.5 to 2 VMs per CPU (4 VMs/2 CPUs at 70% CPU utilization).

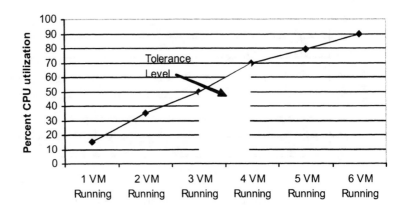

Figure 3.5 A graph that can be used to configure the desirable number of VMs for a particular type of server installed with the virtualization engine. The tolerance level may represent the customer tolerance level, shown here at the 70% server-utilization level.

While some implementations offer dynamic reconfiguration[6] of virtual machines, best practices suggest that configuration settings on such implementations be capped.[7] This prevents processes that demand more CPU from taking resources away from other VMs exposing the need for more hardware resources.

3.7.4 Affinity Test

One of the VM resource configurations is an option to specify which CPU a particular VM has affinity with. This specifies which CPU within the CPU set a VM will run on. In many modern time-sharing operating systems that support running on a multiprocessor machine, the scheduler carefully schedules a thread to be on a CPU it deems less utilized. This is called initial load balancing. After the scheduler picks the initial CPU to run on, the scheduler will try to keep the process running on the same CPU it started on for performance reasons. Switching a process from one CPU to another can be expensive in terms of cache misses, which can translate to performance degradation. Some modern operating systems also allow the permanent binding of kernel threads to a particular CPU so that even if a thread is switched out, it will be queued to the same CPU on its next time slice.

---

[6] Automatically takes resources from a pool of available resources or from other VMs.
[7] Meaning to put a limit on the amount of resources that can be dynamically added to satisfy resource needs.

In the affinity study, the test setup consisted of an even number of VMs running on each of the CPUs. The test only used two CPUs on the server. The test runs had two, four, and six VMs per CPU. All of them were configured to have affinity with one of the CPUs. For example, in the first run with two VMs, VM1 was configured to have affinity with CPU1, and VM2 was configured to have affinity with CPU2. For the four-VM run, VM1 and VM2 were configured to have affinity with CPU1, and VM3 and VM4 were configured to have affinity with CPU2.

The VMs were also configured to share network interface cards (NIC) equally, just like they shared the CPU. For example, on a two-VM run, VM1 and VM2 had a NIC card each. With the four-VM run, VM1 and VM2 shared a NIC card, while VM3 and VM4 shared another NIC card.

The first set of tests was run with the binding switch on to bind particular VMs to a particular CPU. That test showed that CPU performance was constant and held steady for most of the test runs. In the configuration where CPU binding was turned off, performance for each of the VMs was erratic and all over the place.

The affinity tests showed that sharing resources equally among VMs has a positive effect on overall performance. Of equal importance is the fact that resources can be configured and limited to particular VMs. Having an affinity switch to bind VMs to a specific CPU on the server is a nice feature since this allows better granularity of limiting resources for VM use.

3.7.5 Insights and Recommendations

The study was done with a hosting environment in mind. Through the experiences learned in this study, the following insights and recommendations can be helpful to infrastructure architects deciding to implement a virtualized hosting environment.

3.7.5.1 Must-Have Characteristics of Virtual Technology

In a hosting environment, virtualization will work only if it guarantees resource limits on virtual machines. This allows hosting center architects to configure VMs with set limits on resources. This also ensures that VMs will not lose resources to other VMs that exceed their set limits.

Resources identified that need guaranteed limits are CPU, memory, and network I/O. CPU and memory limits can be measured in percentages of the total resources on the physical server. Network I/O is a factor of the rated I/O capacity of the network interface card.

In the test environment, it was found that the virtualization product used does not have a way to limit network I/O when a network interface card is virtualized, which affects the quality of service (QoS). Depending on the hosting environment and customer requirements, this can easily be worked around by avoiding virtualization of network interface cards. In the test environment, configuring the network cards as nonvirtualized cards and assigning each card for use by only one VM alleviated the QoS problem.

3.7.5.2 Must Not Exceed Maximum Virtual Machines per CPU

The question of how many VMs should be configured on the server always comes up. It is a critical question to ask because, for capacity planning purposes, one does not want to overutilize or underutilize the server. In a server consolidation project, a fast and simple way to calculate this is as follows: take the average of the total CPU compute power of all servers to be consolidated, and transpose that to how many VMs will be configured on existing servers or new servers to equal the amount of compute power as well as memory. For example, suppose there are 50 servers with a total number of 100 CPUs running at 1 GHz each, and the average utilization rate of these servers is about 50%. Simply multiplying the number of CPUs with the speed and the utilization rate gives you the approximate capacity needed for the servers to be used for consolidation.

$$100 * 1 \text{ GHz} * 50\% = 25 \text{ GHz}$$

To consolidate a 25-GHz load into servers running at 2 GHz requires approximately 13 CPUs. One blade server with 16 CPUs running virtualization technology should be able to handle n VMs running on the blade to consolidate the 50 servers into 1 (16-way) blade server with some capacity to spare.

The only problem with this method is that it will only work if the processors are identical in terms of their characteristics in handling workload. When consolidating different server platforms to a different type of server platform, it may be necessary to use conversion numbers that are available for platform-to-platform migrations. An example is consolidating Intel servers to an IBM RISC server. Counting CPU speed alone will not work for this type of consolidation effort.

Another way to determine the maximum number of VMs that can be configured on a CPU is to gather actual CPU utilization data while running test applications, gradually increasing the number of configured VMs on the CPU. Figure 3.5 shows a way of measuring CPU utilization as VMs are added. A hosting architect can use this graph to show an ISV customer how much CPU utilization to expect as VMs are added to the server. The ISV will be able to tell the architect his tolerance level for CPU utilization, and the architect can proceed to configure how many VMs that represents. In this case, the customer has said his or her tolerance level is around 70% CPU utilization.

3.7.6 Benefits of Virtualization

In 2001, expenses for hardware, software, staff, facilities, and services for servers accounted for 40% of total IT expenditure. In 1996, it accounted for only about 31% [1]. More recently, it has been reported as high as 80%.

Another study [2] has shown that server consolidation can lower total cost of ownership. The most significant savings surprisingly did not come from a smaller hardware footprint or from lower hardware maintenance cost but from software maintenance and other software-related costs. Lowering the number of CPUs by using server consolidation through virtualization saves customers from having to pay per CPU license and for maintenance costs [2].

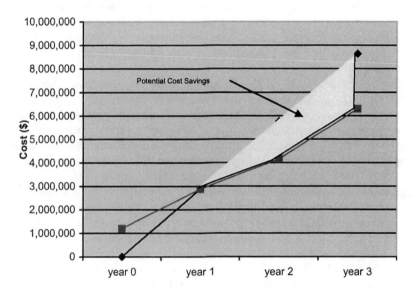

Figure 3.6 Shaded area shows the potential savings attained after the first year of implementing server consolidation through the use of virtualization technologies.

Figure 3.6 shows the potential savings over a 3-year period when servers were consolidated. Total server footprint went from 144 to 18 servers. The initial server consolidation cost was about $1.2 million. This was based on a typical cost of running a server per year at $20,000 per server [1].

3.7.7 Other Considerations Concerning Virtualization

Server, CPU virtualization, and hyperthreading technology bring to light many questions that need to be answered about performance, scalability, and licensing issues:

- *Scalability*–Will virtualized technology provide the same scalability as nonvirtualized server counterparts?
- *Performance*–What criteria will performance be based on? Since virtualization offers a minimum configuration and has the capacity to grow as capacity increases, will performance criteria be measured in terms of service levels? How will a customer know the minimum configuration an application needs to begin with?
- *Licensing*–Will the operating system be licensed based upon the number of physical CPUs installed on the server or will it be licensed based on the number of virtual machines it runs? If there are three OS instances running on the virtualized server, will the customer have to buy three separate OS licenses? What if a middleware or application is licensed per number of CPUs; how does that figure in a virtualized server? Will middleware vendors that charge for their application based on number of CPUs, count logical CPUs, or will they have a different price strategy when virtualization technology is used?
- *Application integration*–As the IT infrastructure becomes more dynamic, operating platforms that offer virtualization will need to give applications the means to integrate with the technology. This means providing APIs so that applications have a chance to react to dynamic virtual operations that may affect them. For instance, if adding an additional CPU may cause an application to violate licensing agreements, then the application needs to be able to tell the operating platform to stop the addition of the CPU.
- *Reliability*–Different virtualization technologies present different challenges in terms of reliability. Some technologies are designed to have redundancy to eliminate single point of failures, while some leave it up to the administrator to factor in redundancy within the configuration.

With virtualization, underutilized servers can be consolidated, resulting in savings on capital as well as systems management expenses. Server virtualization will be used as a core strategy within data centers because it lends itself well to easier manageability in terms of the provisioning of operating system stacks.

3.7.8 Study Conclusion

Virtualization implementations from different vendors will vary. Most, if not all, implementations will have sub-CPU virtualization capabilities. While some implementations may claim unlimited CPU virtualization, some will limit themselves to a fixed number of subpartitions per CPU. It is also important to take note of how sharing of other resources like memory, I/O, and storage is implemented. Having the ability to reconfigure these resources dynamically is also important when operating a 24x7, high-availability server–one needs to make sure reconfiguration of virtualized resources does not contribute to downtime.

Performance and scalability within a virtualized environment, specifically a distributed virtual environment, needs to be studied more carefully. Capacity planning for a virtualized and utility environment is treated differently from capacity planning for a traditional computing environment. While traditional capacity-planning techniques plan for peak capacity (i.e., the customer predicts there will be a maximum of 1,000 users doing 100 transactions every 3 hours, then the server will be configured according to those requirements), capacity planning for use in virtualized environments will not. Rather than rely on capacity planning guides based on high-water mark scenarios, capacity planning for virtualized and utility environments should be based on end-customer usage profiles on an aggregated basis.

Performance guides for virtualized infrastructures will be different. It is not enough to run load test simulations on a set of standard configuration settings to come up with a performance guide for customers to use for patterning their initial configurations. In a virtualized computing environment, different modeling techniques need to be developed.[8] As an example, within a utility data center, an enterprise application, which consists of several application modules, can be placed on several servers for scalability purposes. The enterprise customer using this application will have its own set of users who will have their own profiles which they can use only for individual modules of the application, but not by the whole application. If there are five modules to the application, each group of users may be using only 20% of the application, which translates to different patterns of use for the servers as well.

Creating a model for scalability and performance based on the application usage is crucial to getting as close as possible to the customer usage pattern. The model may evolve as application modules are added and placed on other servers. Communication of these modules with external Web services will also affect performance and scalability considerations.

By having a few standard configurations to start with and by relying upon what we know, models for performance and scalability for virtualized environments can be achieved. Although technologies are still evolving, and hundreds, maybe thousands, of system configurations can be considered for the model, we can draw upon past experience to create the future.

---

[8] Application-based performance and scalability should be considered, but a transactional system model within a distributed enterprise system should be considered in studies as well. With Web services and SOA-based transactions playing a big part in management and application layers of the utility infrastructure, work in server capacity planning needs to be done in conjunction with work that is happening within the software application arena.

3.8 VIRTUAL TEST AND DEVELOPMENT ENVIRONMENT (IMPLEMENTING SOLUTIONS)

Software application development, application system and verification tests, and performance analysis are tasks that require the latest and greatest hardware resources. With the pressure for faster time to market, software developers, testers, and performance analysts demand access to development and test machines as quickly as possible.

Software development shops, specifically ones that support multiple platforms, are in dire need of hardware that they can use to develop and test software applications needed to support the dynamic changes that happen within a business environment. A typical development cycle lasts from 12 to 18 months. During this cycle different levels of hardware needs are expressed by each organization from development to the different stages of testing (unit, functional, system tests) that need to be done on an application.

Finally, a separate performance group runs performance tests against the application to make sure it gives out the desired scalability and response characteristics. After the development cycle, the machines get little to no use until a new cycle starts.

Some development organizations solve this problem by leasing equipment to supplement what they already have in-house and returning the equipment when the development cycle ends. This can work only if the leasing company can provide them exactly what they need. Demands vary for the latest resources and hardware configurations, just like dynamic business environments are fueling the need for a virtualized computing environment today.

The development shop has peak seasonal needs for hardware resources, usually toward the end of the development cycle when everyone is finalizing implementations and trying to make release deadlines. Development shops with a few dozen developers, testers, and performance analysts can never get enough machines to do their work on.

Today's server and CPU virtualization technologies can accommodate the demanding needs of a development organization. In a virtual test and development environment (VTDE), developers, testers, and performance analysts will be able to get what they need when they need it. A VTDE will be able to accommodate different development environment organizations, providing them with resources that may otherwise be too expensive and time-consuming to maintain.

Today, the IBM Solutions Enablement Group within the Systems and Technology division runs a VTDE within the Innovation Center situated in Dallas, Texas, called the Virtual Loaner Program (VLP), which is made available to select business partners. These business partners, some of them value-added resellers (VARs)[9] avail themselves of a VTDE that provides them access to the latest IBM

---

[9] A value-added reseller is a company that sells something produced by another company after adding something of value. An example of this is a solutions package that the VAR might put together for a company—servers, networks, middleware, and specialized software that will provide functionalities.

Series p servers[10] running the latest AIX or Linux operating systems, which would have otherwise been too costly even to lease, let alone purchase. With the VLP, IBM business partners are able to develop and test on resources without having to worry about maintaining the resources themselves.

The VLP schedules different organizations on the shared environment. The VLP environment can save existing development environments as an image, which enables resource sharing among different vendors. The saved development environment image can later be restored for the same organization to continue its development work.

The VLP can serve as a model for future providers of VTDEs. Software development already occurs today within a virtual environment. And open source projects are undertaken by and coordinated among developers in different parts of the world working in their own development environments. Yet enterprise applications that still run on enterprise servers, such as AIX, HP, and Microsoft, will still need the right hardware and operating system versions to develop and test on. A virtual development environment providing the latest hardware resources and operating systems is an option that cannot be overlooked. Figure 3.7 shows a high-level view of the IBM VLP.

VLP Production 1

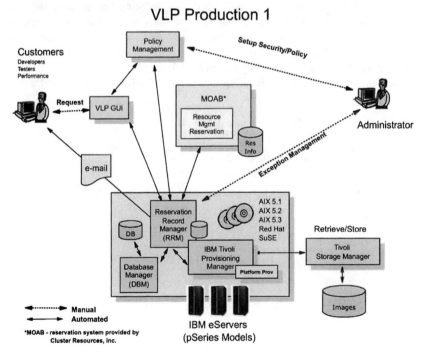

Figure 3.7 High-level architectural view of the IBM Virtual Loaner Program.

---

[10] Other platforms available are Series i and Blade platforms.

In the figure, the customer, shown on the left-hand side, initiates a request for hardware resource through a Web interface. The request is handled by the resource manager, which allocates the requested resource (if available) and sends an e-mail notification back to the customer that the resource is ready for use. Reports have shown that customers get their resources allocated within a 2-hour turnaround time.

3.9 SUMMARY

Hardware virtualization, the grid, and policy-based automation software are some of the core technologies that make up the foundation of an IT utility-based infrastructure. Using these technologies will not only lower total cost of ownership, it will also add value in the form of improved quality of service. The case study on IBM's Virtual Loaner Program clearly represents how these technologies are used today to provide server resources within 2 hours after a configuration request has been placed.

Today, companies are busy consolidating their existing servers with the help of virtualization technologies. Once that is done, they will begin the process of finding solutions that will give them the ability to automate more tasks. The ability of large vendors to make these solutions available to any size business is imperative for the success of a utility computing future. Next, we examine in more detail how utility computing is changing the current IT infrastructure model.

References

[1]   "Scorpion Update, an Evolving Method of Analyzing and Optimizing the Corporate IT Server Infrastructure," IBM white paper, January 2003.

[2]   "Sagittarius, Statistics and Analysis of the Demographics of UNIX and Windows Servers," IBM white paper, January 2003.

Chapter 4

Data Center Challenges and Solutions

At the heart of all IT operations is the data center. It is where all the hardware (servers, storage, and network switches and routers) and software resources are connected and integrated to provide IT computing functionalities for the enterprise. The data center may be situated in one central location or in several geographic locations connected via high-speed lines. Attendants are administrators specialized in network, server, database, and security administration who manage the data center either locally or remotely.

In the past, the introduction of hardware monitoring and management software proved to be effective tools for managing the data center. Hardware monitoring alerted system administrators to potential problems before they happened, while management software automated tasks like backup and restore and simple device configuration. But as data centers grew, monitoring and management software solutions became inadequate and were perceived only as stop gaps to the problems of increasing complexity. Other ways of managing and providing infrastructure services in the form of outsourcing and application hosting emerged, while CIOs faced budget cutbacks and customers demanded better levels of service. Today's data centers, whether they are owned by the enterprise or by outsourcing or application hosting providers, are complex, rigid, and underutilized. In this chapter, we examine traditional data center challenges and then explore utility-based solutions that can help alleviate these challenges.

4.1 CHALLENGES IN TRADITIONAL INFRASTRUCTURES

In Chapter 1, we described the types of infrastructures that existed before utility computing technologies came into existence. Type 1 is a privately managed infrastructure; type 2 is a dedicated, outsourced infrastructure; and type 3 is a shared hosting infrastructure. For the purpose of this section, we classify these as traditional-type infrastructures. Traditional infrastructures, today, face complexity and underutilization challenges. Complexity stems from the creation of data centers that have become large and disparate. These data centers may have

57

increased in size due to increased capacity requirements during an economic boom or through mergers and acquisitions. Underutilization, on the other hand, came about when the same resources became redundant after an economic downturn.

In the last few years, CIOs have faced the dilemma of managing large data centers with smaller budgets. These data centers have a myriad of heterogeneous servers and devices that are hard to integrate, requiring specialized skills to manage and operate. Complexity in the data center exists not only in hardware but in the entire infrastructure–networks, software packages, and the architecture itself. Complexity contributes to IT costs, implementation delays, and eventually lower levels of service, compounded by the shortage of skilled labor. Thus, CIOs have no choice but to pay dearly for required skills.

A characteristic common in the traditional infrastructure is that servers, storage, software, and networks[1] are set up to be used by a single company or organization. Utilization of resources within the different types of data centers tends to follow the business activities of whoever owns the resources—when business activities peak, utilization rates are high, and when activities slow down, utilization rates fall.

Over the course of a year, the use of hardware resources within the infrastructure can fluctuate, depending on customer usage. Take for example CPU usage; in certain months, an enterprise application may be used more, thus utilizing CPU resources more, while in other months CPU can be considered unused as use of software applications falls to nil. An example of this would be the human resources organization. Every year between the months of November and December, there is an increased use of servers that run the benefits-enrollment software application. The rest of the year, however, use of these servers may remain consistently low. In a study done on server utilization [1], aggregated daytime server utilization of Windows servers amounted to only 5%. And the corresponding aggregate daytime utilization of UNIX servers showed a utilization range of 15% to 20%. Whether the servers are utilized or not, system administrators continue to manage these resources as if they are fully utilized, contributing to an increased cost of data center management.

Like underutilized hardware, underutilized software applications need continued system administration and maintenance. Even if the software application is not fully utilized, software patches need to be installed, data needs to be backed up, and servers need to be monitored for peak performance just in case the software application is needed. A study done in 2003 [2] showed that at least 30% of the whole IT budget went to software maintenance.

In traditional infrastructures, hardware resources are planned and bought for peak capacity. This means that if expected seasonal spikes require more capacity, then the maximum resource configuration that meets this capacity requirement

---

[1] Except for type 3, where the network is shared by different organizations that colocate their equipment in the hosting center.

must be purchased. And if the demand continues to increase, then more server resources are added to scale up to the new capacity requirements. Unfortunately, when capacity demand wanes, resources become underutilized, leading to unnecessary maintenance costs.

Complexity and underutilization are the biggest concerns of CIOs today. While it may sound easier said than done, complexity and underutilization can be curbed by simplifying the data center. By eliminating redundancy and using newer technologies that will allow resources to be shared and provisioned as needed, users will get higher levels of service, even as companies cut IT budgets and face economic ups and downs as well as changing market conditions.

4.2 MATCHING CAPACITY TO DEMAND

Capacity-planning methods used in the traditional infrastructures planned for peak capacity. Hardware resources were put in place to meet normal utilization rates, as well as anticipated increase in utilization. More capacity was added as future needs were identified. Figure 4.1 shows the traditional capacity planning method. In this figure, planned capacity always exceeds demand, except in one instance where demand exceeds capacity. The time period after T5 also shows that as demand decreases, the gap between demand and capacity increases. The gap between used capacity and planned capacity represents the unused capacity.

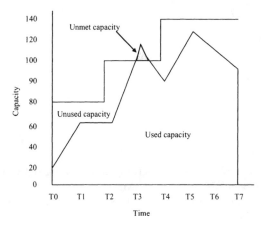

Figure 4.1 Traditional capacity-planning model.

In an improving economy, such as that experienced between 1995 and 2000, demand for resources increased, fueling the growth of hardware resources needed in traditional infrastructures. As the economy slowed after 2000, however, capacity requirements also slowed, resulting in underutilized resources. The consequence of underutilized hardware and software application is unnecessary expenses from managing and maintaining these resources. Whether resources are in a privately managed, outsourcing, or application-hosting data center, underutilized and redundant hardware resources are costly–and the cost mostly falls on whoever is managing them.

Even as the cost of hardware continues to fall,[2] all other costs, like labor in the form of expensive consultants, programmers, administrators, and project executives, as well as software license procurement, continue to rise. Once the project is done and the infrastructure is in place, maintaining and managing the data center then becomes the focus of concern.

In light of an economic downturn, capacity-planning guidelines need to be reexamined to see if they can be modified to accommodate future needs and growth in relation to the economic environment.[3] Figure 4.2 shows an ideal capacity-planning model where capacity follows demand, whether it be up or down.

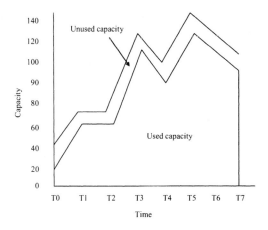

Figure 4.2 Ideal capacity-planning model.

With the problems of complexity and underutilization getting out of control, it did not take long for vendors such as IBM, HP, Sun BMC, Computer Associates, and Veritas to announce products and technologies that promised to help eliminate these problems.

---

[2] In a typical IT project involving purchase of new hardware, hardware expenditure will only constitute 20% to 25% of the total project budget.

[3] A META Group study published in September 2003 revealed that capacity planning was the top critical issue for large enterprises (that is, those with more than 1,000 people), with 33.8% of respondents identifying this as a critical issue for 2003 and beyond. The high priority of the endeavor will escalate consolidation and efficiency demands.

- IBM, HP, and Sun introduced servers that can be partitioned into smaller, discrete servers that each run a separate instance of an operating system, allowing one physical server to be shared by multiple organizations. In addition to their partitioning capabilities, the servers can be reconfigured dynamically without interruption of current running software programs, allowing the resources of underutilized servers to be redirected to organizations in need of additional capacity.
- Veritas introduced storage management software that improves disk utilization and eliminates storage-related downtime. Veritas claims that its software offers system administrators the flexibility to move data between different operating systems and storage arrays, balance I/O across multiple paths to improve performance, and replicate data to remote sites for higher availability without changing the way users or applications access the files.
- BMC and Computer Associates introduced management software that works with different Enterprise Resource Planning (ERP) vendor products such as SAP and PeopleSoft (now an Oracle company). Both vendors claim to help their customers provide in-depth performance and availability management for their client's applications, which then help in meeting capacity-planning requirements.

Technologies that help simplify the infrastructure and allow reallocation of underutilized capacity so that it can be used by other systems or another organization create an environment that closely resembles the ideal capacity model. As resources such as servers, storage, and software applications within the IT infrastructure become more utilitarian in nature, the concept of computing offered as a utility will become a reality.

4.3 UTILITY INFRASTRUCTURE

Level 2 of the continuum of utilities represents infrastructures that implement utility computing products and services. Utility computing, in its simplest form, is the delivery of IT functionality as services–just like the delivery of service utilities like water and electricity. An enterprise can tap into this utility for business as well as infrastructure services. The services are physically hosted in utility hosting centers (like utilities that can be turned on and off on demand) that are either located inside or outside the enterprise, or both. Like the traditional utility, the service is monitored or metered, allowing capacity always to meet demand–even if demand varies from day to day. It will be reliable and will cater to the on-demand nature of the enterprise organization (i.e., it will respond to the peak and low demands for capacity). Utility computing promises the following benefits [3]:

- *It will reduce cost of operating expenses*–Increased resource utilization benefits infrastructure owners by reducing hardware management expenditure through shared resources in the organization.
- *Turn IT from fixed to variable assets*–Increased ability to match resource requirements to varying capacity requirements over a period of time alleviates the need for purchasing hardware resources as a result of planned peak capacity.
- *Simplify IT by reducing complexity*–Enhanced ease of systems management and maintenance within the IT infrastructure reduces complexity.

This new utility computing environment (UCE) fulfills the IT needs of today's enterprise businesses. The UCE delivers standardized processes, application functionality, and infrastructure over the network as a service. The UCE shares the same qualities as electric or water utilities. For instance, it is:

- Sharable–Can serve many customers;
- Standardized–Requires (allows for) little customization;
- Flexible and scalable–Allows customers to use what they need, pay as they go.

From a technical perspective, a UCE is:

- *Integrated*–Allows the integration of enterprise and legacy applications transcending vertical industries through the use of open standards technologies like Web services;
- *Open*–Uses open specifications and standards to enable ease of integration of enterprise resources and applications;
- *Virtual*–Uses server consolidation and capacity on-demand technology to increase utilization of hardware resources;
- *Autonomic*–Alleviates the need for skilled technical human resources to manage the complexity brought about by the rapid advancement of technology, allowing the infrastructure to respond to customer needs for instant provisioning of resources.

Since 2004, with businesses and companies recovering from the dot-com bubble burst, CEOs have taken the first steps toward transforming their data centers into utility computing environments. CEOs have retooled their data centers with new hardware and management software capable of handling future needs. This includes replacing old hardware with new hardware that can be virtualized. Companies have started to simplify their data centers by consolidating servers to eliminate excess capacity. As companies continue to take control of their IT infrastructures, new ways of managing these virtual resources are being introduced to early adopters. Next, we describe how the new environment can be managed and provide product and service implementations from large vendors.

4.4 INFRASTRUCTURE MANAGEMENT

Server consolidation through virtualization,[4] when planned properly, can eliminate the complexity of having to manage disparate systems. Depending on the software applications and operating systems used, a company may be able to consolidate 300 servers made up of different platforms and running different operating systems into four or five servers[5] and still get the same functionality and capacity. This simplifies integration between systems, easing one form of complexity in the data center. As more server and data center consolidation gets under way, underutilization will become less of a problem and simplicity in the data center will take form.

As was mentioned earlier, scarcity of skilled professionals to maintain and manage the systems also adds to complexities in the data center. This can be alleviated by the use of management frameworks that specifically target virtualized environments to monitor server states and automate administrative tasks. Monitoring software interfaces with operating system commands that can display CPU, network, and storage usage. Depending on the sophistication of the monitoring software, monitoring capabilities may be combined with software that not only warns system administrators of impending failures but also has the programmed intelligence to take corrective actions itself.

4.4.1 Shared Resource Management

When it comes to sharing resources, the network is one resource representative of a utility computing environment. In a networking environment, there exists hardware that can monitor and control network usage. Data bandwidth can be configured in such a way that it can be limited for certain users and unlimited for some. Networking hardware also allows for dynamic reconfiguration of the network, rerouting network traffic to connections less used if the current one becomes overly congested. This level of dynamic reconfiguration eases the need for more network requirements since existing network communication lines are better utilized, resulting in less need to purchase more physical lines than are needed. In a utility computing environment, this same concept is achieved by sharing resources like servers and storage through a virtual environment.

In a virtual environment, hardware resources are monitored for usage, making sure capacity always meets demand. A group of idle hardware resources is also

---

[4] A study done by IDC [4] states that reducing cost, simplifying management, and increasing flexibility are the top three reasons why organizations are virtualizing their servers.
[5] With virtualization technology.

ready to be provisioned as needed. The provisioning component can take any hardware resource from a pool of idle hardware and configure it with the necessary operating system and software applications.

Software for the servers is provisioned by first packaging the software into specific software stacks. For example, a software stack can contain first an operating system with a specific version and fix packs, system administration command utilities like SSH (secure shell) and sftp (secure ftp) that work with the operating system, middleware (like databases, Web servers or application servers), and, lastly, specific software applications at a certain level of fix patches. Hundreds of these software stack combinations can be created and then offered on a menu to be picked and chosen from. The automated software-provisioning component, when ordered, builds one of these software stacks for a particular server platform. Once it is built, an agent deploys the stack remotely on the server and installs each of the components, starting with the operating system.

Figure 4.3 shows a hypothetical infrastructure made up of data centers situated in three different geographical locations. Users from different locations use the Web, application, and database servers in their daily activities. Monitoring agents are installed on each of the servers to monitor usage and activities and are displayed in the command console located in one of the data centers.

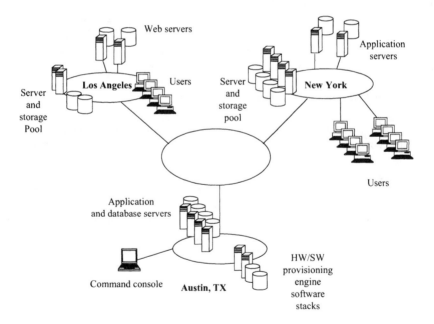

Figure 4.3 A utility computing environment implementation using automated provisioning software.

An inventory of servers and storage sits idle until the need arises for these resources to be configured and deployed to meet demand for additional resources. When demand falls, the excess capacity is decommissioned and put back into the free resource pool. Resource provisioning and deprovisioning are done with automated provisioning software, eliminating the need for manual deployment.

Take note that the server and storage pools shown in Figure 4.3 are represented by servers and storage that do not implement virtualization technology. Virtualization can still be achieved by using older server and storage technology, where servers are provisioned and deprovisioned through the use of automated provisioning software. In this scenario, unnecessary upkeep and management of idle servers and applications are greatly reduced.

If the old servers and storage are replaced with new hardware that implements virtualization technology, then the resulting diagram may look like Figure 4.4. The Web and application servers from two locations, New York and Los Angeles, are consolidated into one server that has spare CPUs. The application and database servers, including the provisioning engine located in Austin, are consolidated in a single server.

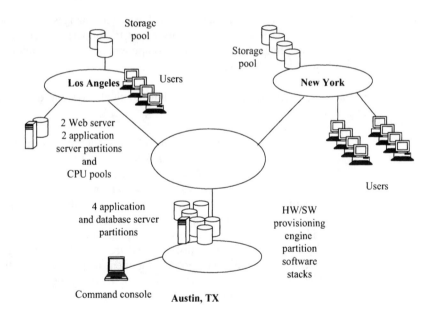

Figure 4.4 Consolidated servers using virtualization technology.

Infrastructure management complexities are reduced by simplifying the infrastructure. Automated software provisioning can be used to simplify hardware management using older server and storage technology or with newer hardware that implements virtualization technology. In this environment, higher standardization and sharing will be required, leading to higher utilization and lower management cost.

4.5 INFRASTRUCTURE PRODUCT AND SERVICES

Over the last few years, technology vendors have announced products, including hardware, software, and utility services, which will support today's utility computing initiatives. While all started with offerings based on their own product lines, they have since expanded to support heterogeneous systems.

4.5.1 Sun N1

The Sun N1 architecture promises to redefine the way people think about managing and deploying complex resources [5].

4.5.1.1 Sun N1 Technology Features

To provide support for Sun's N1 initiative, Sun has made changes to its own products, like the Sun Solaris Operating Environment to support virtualization, and made the Sun Management Center the core component providing monitoring, reporting, and container management.

- Virtualization of data center resources into a single system delivering business services;

   o This is achieved through their N1 grid container technology available for all Sun server platforms, including UltraSPARC processor-based and x86-based systems with 32-bit Xeon and 64-bit Opteron architectures. This feature comes with the Solaris Version 10 operating system. According to the Sun Solaris documentation, two components form the basis of the Sun N1 grid container–Solaris 10 Resource Manager and Solaris Zones. The resource manager allocates resources to the container at some defined limit. The zone component maps the application to server resources in a virtual fashion. Working together, these two components deliver a complete container.

- Automation of software and hardware installation and configuration for new business service deployment;

   o The N1 service provisioning system–Allows for the capture of different application models (i.e., installation, registration, configuration methods, dependency requirements) in order to facilitate automated application deployment and provisioning for various types of applications from different vendors, such as IBM (AIX), Microsoft (Windows-based applications), J2EE, and .NET Web services. The system uses a hub and spoke model that consists of (1) the N1 service provisioning master server providing for the garage or repository of the models and applications themselves, and (2) remote agents which can reside in different managed servers in a local or remote data center. The premise of the N1 provisioning server is to create a centralized pool of IT resources–servers, storage, firewalls, load balancers, and more–that can be repurposed automatically as quickly as possible.

o   The N1 system manager targets blade servers, content load balancers, and gigabit Ethernet switches (mostly all SUN branded products). The servers can be running Solaris on SPARC or x86 platforms, as well as the Linux operating system. Sun N1 system manager focuses on Sun servers, while Sun N1 Service provisioning system supports heterogeneous platforms.

- Dynamically manage the allocation of IT resources based on predefined business policies;

o   Predefined policies are handled by the provisioning managers through SLA policies that can be set within the server to automate provisioning tasks. From the Sun product description, the provisioning manager can be configured to delegate administration and managerial access to a set of hardware resource pools to a group or organization. Monitoring for free resources as well as for resources while in use so that alarms can be configured to sound when a certain threshold is met.

- Accounting and reporting on a per-service basis;

o   This is achieved by using a component within the N1 grid engine 6, called the accounting and reporting console. This feature records and monitors resource consumption on a per-task or per-process basis. With the right tools and interface, this feature can be used to create reports from collected data that can be used for planning, chargeback, and billing purposes.

For more information, see www.sun.com/n1.

4.5.1.2 Other Sun Utility Offerings

Sun also offers the following utilities:

- The Sun Grid compute utility is available to anyone at $1/CPU-hour. It is available over the Internet only in the United States.
- The Sun utility computing for high-end grid service is intended for customers who need occasional or moderate access to high-performance systems or who need access to computing resources to handle sudden spikes in demand.
- The Sun utility computing for midrange and high-end StorEdge provides storage infrastructure services at different price points depending on storage needs. Sun maintains ownership of the hardware resources and licenses installed on the customer's premises.

4.5.2 Hewlett-Packard Adaptive Enterprise

HP's utility computing strategy goes under the name of HP Adaptive Enterprise. According to HP, the Adaptive Enterprise strategy enables businesses to use IT more efficiently. To do this HP offers products and services that consist of HP hardware products implementing virtualization technology, management software, and computing services with utility pricing and features.

4.5.2.1 Virtualization Technology

HP implements virtualization technology at different product levels. They are classified as element, integrated, and complete IT utility virtualization.

- Element virtualization–Individual or element-based virtualization where resources such as storage, servers, and networking use virtualization technology on an individual basis to meet the demands of single application environments of business process. HP solutions within this category include HP servers, storage, and management software.
- Integrated virtualization–A virtualization package that incorporates service level agreement management. Integrated virtualization is achieved through;

    o   Virtual server environment—Provides a pool of virtual servers that can grow or shrink based on service level objectives and business needs. This is done through products like the (1) HP-UX workload manager which performs real-time analysis of resource usage and acts on service level objectives and business priorities; (2) HP processes resource manager which enables management of granular processor, memory, and I/O allocation that can be allocated to different processes in need of resources and; (3) flexible virtual partitions (vPars); which is a virtual technology enabling resources to be shared by other virtual partitions, increasing utilization usage of processors.

o Consolidated client infrastructure–Provides a centralized desktop and storage solution. The infrastructure uses HP blade technology with management software that dynamically creates a connection between a user and blade server as needed.

o The complete IT Utility uses grid-based software and technology that enables data centers to operate as a utility infrastructure.

4.5.2.2 Management Software

The HP OpenView management product is HP's infrastructure management software which provides management solutions to implement utilitylike functionality in the data center. HP OpenView manages servers, networks, and storage. The software also includes management services in the area of SLA management, fault management, and performance management, among others.

4.5.2.3 Utility Computing Services

HP utility computing services consists of offerings providing varying utility-type pricing options.

- Managed capacity offers a managed hosting service, managed storage, managed desktop, and managed messaging and e-mail in a utility pricing model. In this offering, resources are owned and managed by HP acting as a utility provider of IT resources.
- Metered capacity offers a pay-per-use model available for HP Integrity and 9000 servers, storage, imaging, and printing. This offering uses metering software to collect data from resources located at the customer's facility.
- Instant capacity offers reserved capacity on servers that can be turned on as needed. This is similar to the capacity-on-demand technology described in Chapter 1.

4.5.2.4 HP Utility Data Center (UDC)

The HP UDC that was unveiled in November 2001 was discontinued[6] after September 24, 2004, in favor of more modular utility computing technologies such as server virtualization and automated provisioning on modular platforms. It was created to support virtualization of networking, servers, storage, and

---

[6] Forrester Research principal analyst Frank Gillett said that one of the great obstacles the UDC had to overcome was the entry price of more than $1 million [6].

operating system and application provisioning across multiple platforms (including Windows, Solaris, HP-UX, and Linux). Software application operations such as fine-grain software provisioning, patching, and application deployment and rollback were provided by a partner vendor, Opsware, through its software application provisioning solution.

4.5.3 IBM On Demand

The utility computing offerings that IBM brings to the market are based on its on-demand strategy. IBM applies the on-demand strategy to its infrastructure, application hosting services, and business process services.

4.5.3.1 Infrastructure Products and Services

IBM products for the infrastructure include server, storage, and infrastructure management software. Products in these categories implement virtualization technology that can help create a utility-type environment.

- IBM server virtualization features partitioning technology that can be used to create pools of virtual resources within the server. The IBM POWER architecture allows the server to be partitioned to run different operating systems at the same time. It can dynamically utilize shared CPU resources within different partitions. This technology is available on all IBM platforms–System p, System i, System z, and System x.
- IBM storage products implement virtualization technology. When deployed in combination with IBM Tivoli storage management software, the solution reduces complexity in managing storage needs.
- IBM Tivoli Intelligent Orchestrator is a software management product that provides automated provisioning and policy-based operation capabilities. It can monitor servers, middleware, and applications, sense problems, and determine actions to take. It can be used to deploy a server automatically, install the necessary software, and configure the network.
- Universal Management Infrastructure (UMI) is an architectural implementation used in IBM's utility computing data center. It is comprised of IBM products that include Tivoli Intelligent Orchestrator and IBM servers and storage solutions. It is also set up to manage other platforms like Intel, Sun, and HP. The services in the UMI architecture include resource metering and automated provisioning.
- Remote management of customer data centers using UMI provides services to automate, manage, and support multiplatform data centers remotely while allowing customers to retain ownership of their equipment and IT staff. This allows customers to maintain control of their operating environment while letting customers experience what utility computing is all about.

4.5.3.2 Application Hosting Services

IBM works with different software vendors to offer their applications on demand. Examples of these applications are SAP On Demand and Siebel On Demand.

- The flexible hosting center uses UMI to help manage IBM's hosting infrastructure. Hosting customers can host their applications in the traditional hosting center or in a hosting center that offers capacity on demand and pay-as-you-go services. Through the use of its UMI technology, IBM is able to offer hardware infrastructure to its customers on an as-needed basis.
- IBM Software as Services program is intended for independent software vendors that want to host their applications on IBMs hosting data centers. A transformation process helps them transform their application to SaaS applications. A generic program is discussed in more detail in Chapter 10.

4.5.3.3 Business Process

IBM provides business and technical process services to customers who need them on demand. Examples of these services are payroll and product life cycle management.

Although Sun, HP, and IBM offer a comprehensive line of utility computing products and services, customers can choose from a wide variety of products and services from other vendors offering their own brand of hardware, software management, utility hosting centers, SaaS, and SaaS transformation services. With a myriad of products and services available to choose from, how does a customer decide which products or services to buy? The first step is to identify which utility infrastructure the customer intends to operate in. This is discussed in the next section.

4.6 UTILITY INFRASTRUCTURE CLASSIFICATIONS

In Chapter 1, we discussed a fourth type of infrastructure called the utility infrastructure. Depending on customer needs, this type of infrastructure can be further classified as private, public, or hybrid infrastructures. These classifications help identify the types of products and services a customer will need when transforming to a utility infrastructure.

Utility computing vendors know that while some large corporations have chosen to relinquish control of their data center operations to outsourcing providers, much of today's IT infrastructure remains behind corporate firewalls. This is why utility computing vendors offer products and services that can accommodate all types of customers. In general, a customer looking to transform its infrastructure to a utility computing environment will be looking for the following characteristics in vendor products and services:

- Reduced total cost of ownership;
- Simplified management and maintenance;
- Increased flexibility, scalability, reliability, and performance;
- Generation of resource utilization, faults, and performance reports;
- Provisioning of resources as needed;
- Monitoring of IT environment with more vigilance.

With the different classifications of utility infrastructures available, customers are given more flexibility to reduce the cost of infrastructure management by implementing the solutions themselves (private), having an outsourcing provider implement the solutions (public), or both (hybrid).

4.6.1 Private Utilities

Computing utilities are considered private when a company implements the services internally for the purpose of delivering IT functionalities to organizations within the company. In this type of infrastructure, the customer picks a vendor that can provide the company with a solution that may include both hardware and software management application. The solution is used to convert parts of the infrastructure into pools of free resources that can be shared and provisioned as needed. The vendor collaborates with the customer in the architectural design of the infrastructure as well as provisioning decisions that the customer may need initial help with.

Private utilities are for companies that have the resources to manage their own data centers and want to remain in control of their infrastructure. IT infrastructure and functionality stays within the confines of the company. CIOs remain responsible for all risks associated with managing and maintaining the infrastructure.

Private utilities offer companies the advantage of starting small when implementing utility computing solutions. As the company grows and gets used to the new way of providing IT resources, it can slowly convert more of its infrastructure into utilities.

4.6.2 Public Utilities

When the infrastructure grows, it becomes more complex, making it harder to manage. Outsourcing parts of or the entire infrastructure is an option some large companies take to solve this problem. But unlike traditional outsourcing, where the customer owns the hardware managed by an outsourcing provider, in a public utility solution, the hardware and software[7] are owned by the utility provider. The provider uses economies of scale to his advantage by having several customers share a common infrastructure. Although the infrastructure is shared, strict separation of customer resources and data is enforced.

Public utility offerings are for corporate customers who see the benefits of utility computing solutions but would rather have them implemented by external providers. Through a public utility offering, corporate customers can outsource their IT needs to well-established providers and take advantage of the economies of scale afforded by a shared environment.

In the case of hardware infrastructure, decisions regarding resource provisioning are made by the customer and the provider. These decisions lead to the creation of service level agreements that the customer and infrastructure provider both agree on. Customer billing is based on metered use of resources—the customer only pays for what he uses. The offering provides the customer real-time cost pricing of services that deliver results. Just like the private utility, the public utility affords the customer the freedom to pick and choose only services that he absolutely needs.

4.6.3 Hybrid or Selective Utilities

The hybrid utility offers the benefits of both private and public utility offerings. A hybrid or selective solution gives customers the option to outsource part of their IT infrastructure to a utility provider. From the customers' point of view, the offering allows them to manage strategic risks [7] associated with outsourcing. *Strategic risk* is described as misjudging strategic capabilities and losing control of them to the outsourcing provider. Customers can look at their portfolios of capabilities, identify their strategic and nonstrategic competencies, and then decide what to outsource and keep.

As with the other two types of utility offerings, the hybrid utility allows corporate customers to regain control over their IT infrastructure spending through the metering and monitoring capabilities of the utility environment. By allowing only noncore business functionalities to be outsourced initially, the customers retain control of their core business while gradually moving to a utility computing environment. Through a hybrid or selective solution, risk is minimized by giving customers flexibility in their outsourcing decisions. Table 4.1 summarizes each type and its different attributes.

Table 4.1 Different Types of Utility Infrastructures

	Public	*Hybrid*	*Private*
IT infrastructure ownership (hardware/software/people)	Vendor	Vendor/customer	Customer

---

[7] In case of an SaaS.

Table 4.1 Different Types of Utility Infrastructures (Continued)

	Public	*Hybrid*	*Private*
Infrastructure location	Vendor data center	Mixed vendor and customer data center	Customer premise
Infrastructure management delivery	Vendor delivers utility offering within its data center, which includes virtual servers, network and storage.	Vendor packages a subset of the utility offering and tailors it to customer IT infrastructure.	Vendor sells utility offering and customer tailors it to IT infrastructure.
Customization	Low: little to no optional customization	Medium: mix of vendor and customer customization limited only to utility vendor implementation	High: customer design limited only to vendor utility implementation
Infrastructure management	Vendor managed	Customer and vendor managed	Customer managed
Application management	Vendor managed	Mix of vendor and customer managed	Customer managed
Provisioning decisions	Based on vendor SLAs agreed to by customer	Based on customer and vendor SLAs	Based on customer SLAs

Once the customer identifies the class of utility infrastructure that best describes its future environment, it can start the process of making the paradigm shift.

4.7 MAKING THE PARADIGM SHIFT

In the last four decades, advancements in technologies introduced new paradigms in the context of how businesses and organizations go about their day-to-day activities. First, it was the invention of computers, which brought about increased productivity. Then, it was the introduction of the network, which increased collaboration between organizations within the company. Then, it was the proliferation of the Internet, which cleared the way for new ways of engaging with business clients through e-business markets. Today, the introduction of new technologies is once again bringing about a new shift, this time in the delivery and consumption of computing power.

This new paradigm, called utility computing, promises to transform the IT infrastructure into a utility computing environment providing computing power and services to organizations, as well as individuals, in terms of computing units. Instead of ordering physical servers, storage, or network connections, computing power will be ordered using CPU units in MIPs, storage units in giga/terabytes, and network units in mega/gigabits. The new environment will have highly monitored service levels, highly standardized integration capabilities, and highly componentized business processes, all of which are characteristics that will require changes in organizational culture and involve certain risks. For those who can overcome the changes and risks, the reward attained with this new paradigm comes in the form of reduced cost, higher levels of service, and improved flexibility.

When initiating a paradigm shift, risk-averse companies take a phased approach because it allows for better monitoring and measurement of results. Pilot projects in small areas within the company can try out new processes and methods without affecting critical business components. In relation to implementing changes toward a new paradigm, these companies also recognize that they may need to revamp their business processes to match the shift—in extreme cases, they may have to overcome antiquated business cultures.

Smart providers of this new paradigm, on the other hand, will anticipate an incremental adoption by their customers. So as not to drive away customers who are comfortable with a total paradigm shift solution, smart providers will create hybrid solutions that can be implemented in a stepwise fashion. A selective rather than a total solution will favor this paradigm as customers get used to its standardized processes and infrastructure offerings.

Companies switching to this new paradigm will need to see a list that shows them the differences between traditional and utility infrastructures. This list will contain issues that they need to overcome or know how to deal with. Here is an example of such a list:

- *Vendors*–Organizations that operate traditional infrastructures know and trust their vendors after years of building a relationship. Customers of utility computing products may have to deal with new vendors that still need to prove their reliability and viability. This can lead to vendor management problems.
- *Services*–Services provided by traditional IT infrastructures are highly customizable, while utility computing services offer less customization and are highly standardized. Some business processes may need to be changed to be more standardized.
- *Service level relationships*–Traditional infrastructures base their SLAs on availability and performance, while utility infrastructures add additional SLA based on capacity needs. Users need to be more aware of how many resources they use based on service level objectives agreed on by both the customer and IT provider.
- *Business processes*–Traditional infrastructures are set up to support organizational objectives based on individual organizational needs, while utility environments are set up to support multiple organizations in a shared environment. For a utility environment to be effective, businesses need to

know which processes can be shared by different organizations. This can lead to the creation of virtualized services supported by virtual environments.

- *Technology*–Components in traditional infrastructures are usually customer and vendor specific, which promotes high customization and vendor lock-in, respectively. Utility computing technologies are based on standardized technologies preventing vendor lock-in but they offer less customization. This may create problems for customers who require high levels of customization within their environments.

- *Organizational culture*–Traditional infrastructures cater to a culture in which individual business organizations control their own IT resources, while utility computing environments cater to a centralized and shared environment. Cultures that have been around since the organization was formed may be hard to overcome.

Table 4.2 describes some of the differences between traditional infrastructures, outsourcing, and utility computing as well as the risks associated with them. The table serves as a guide for customers thinking about migrating to utility computing as it exists today.

Table 4.2 Differences Between Traditional Outsourcing and Utility Computing and Associated Risks When Adopting Utility Computing

	Traditional Infrastructure/Outsourcing	Utility Computing	Issues Associated with Utility Computing
Vendor	Large-scale, usually single vendor outsourcing. May have the option to be selective.	More open to selective outsourcing. Potential to have multiple vendors providing infrastructure, application, and business functionalities.	Vendor management issues. Vendor viability. Vendor reliability.
Services	Standardized as well as highly customizable	Highly standardized. Low on customization options. Customization for backend purposes only.	Business process needs to adopt standardized interfaces.
Service level relationships	Service level agreements based on availability and performance. Contracts are based on customized services and out-sourcing agreements– maintenance of computers, sales tax on purchased equipment, software licenses and so forth. May be more complicated and open to interpretation.	SLA mirrors traditional outsourcing with additional SLA based on capacity needs. Outsourcing contracts may be simpler since the whole infrastructure belongs to provider. Simpler contracts cover most outsourced services.	Users need to be more aware of service level agreements in terms of agreed on capacity requirements. Users are more accountable for resources they use.

Table 4.2 Differences Between Traditional Outsourcing and Utility Computing and Associated Risks When Adopting Utility Computing (Continued)

	Traditional Infrastructure/Outsourcing	*Utility Computing*	*Issues Associated with Utility Computing*
Business process	Follows traditional business organization processes, which are mainly siloed. Processes are based on individual organizational needs, not shared.	Highly componentized processes separating core and noncore business processes. Similar processes may be shared along vertical lines of business. Eliminates duplicate IT resources.	Businesses may not recognize which processes can be shared, creating duplicate processes, which does not foster high rates of utilization for common processes and IT resources.
Technology	Mostly nonstandard. Customized to customer specifications. Subject to vendor technology, which promotes vendor lock-in.	Based on highly standardized interfaces which can prevent vendor lock-in.	Technology that may not work in customer's highly customized business environment.
Organizational ownership/culture	Individual organizations own their resources; no sharing of resources.	Shared resources among organizations.	A shared resource mentality may be hard to introduce.

While some items in the list can be addressed by the IT organization, one item in particular—organizational culture—will need to be addressed by everyone within the organization. Relinquishing control of IT resources in favor of a shared environment controlled by the IT organization may be too much of a leap for business managers. But as the company begins to embark on new projects, utility computing may be used to introduce the new environment and slowly change perceptions and raise comfort levels. For a similar perspective, read [8].

4.8 SUMMARY

In early 2004, IDC[8] issued a report saying spending on new servers for that year would be about $55 billion, while spending to manage those servers would be about $95 billion. By 2008, new server spending is expected to creep past $60 billion, and management costs are expected to soar to around $140 billion. Can companies continue to sustain the rising cost?

This chapter talked about the overall state of the IT infrastructure. It described complexities and problems such as the underutilization of resources in traditional

---

[8] International Data Corporation,www.idc.com.

data centers. Owners of traditional data centers see the need to regain control of rising cost and complexities brought about by growth and increased demand from users. The solution is to simplify, consolidate, and virtualize the environment to contain costs and facilitate more efficient use of resources. Resources within the data center need to be structured so that they can be turned on and off as needed.

New technologies are paving the way for companies to adopt a new paradigm of providing IT so that consumers can consume them like electric or water utilities. Companies can start making the paradigm shift today by examining the differences of the new paradigm from their traditional environments. They can start implementing small pilot projects to try out new technologies and measure their success, while engaging the right vendor to provide them with the proper guidance. Next, we look at implementing automation in the data center.

References

[1]   Heap, D., "A Taxonomy of Actual Utilization of Real Unix and Windows Servers," IBM, January 2003.

[2]   "IT Industry and Management Outlook," *Computer Economics*, 2003, available at www.computereconomics.com.

[3]   Thickins, G., "Utility Computing: The Next New IT Model," April 2003, available at www.utilitycomputing.com.

[4]   IDC Multiclient Study, Server Virtualization Market Forecast and Analysis, 2004-2009, September 2005.

[5]   "N1–Introducing Just-in-Time Computing," Sun white paper, 2002.

[6]   Boulton, C., "HP: UDC Alive and Well", internetnews.com, October 2004, available at www.internetnews.com/ent-news/article.php/3425591.

[7]   Ross, J., and G. Westerman, "Preparing for Utility Computing," *IBM System Journal*, Vol. 43, No. 1, 2004, p. 7.

[8]   Fisch, M. "Shining the Light on Utility Computing–A Business Perspective," The Clipper Group Explorer, October 2003, Report # TCG2003057.

Chapter 5

Automating the Data Center

Business consolidation, new government regulations, and economic uncertainties, are just some of the reasons we are seeing rapid changes and growing complexities in today's data centers. To help with these changes and complexities, both hardware and software vendors are developing innovative products to help manage cost and streamline operations. Just as most hardware vendors develop products to consolidate disparate server and storage needs through virtualization, many software vendors have announced products to automate management of data center resources from servers, storage, and software applications.

Automation is an integral part of utility computing. Without automation, serving up IT functionalities in a utility environment can be time-consuming and inefficient. It is akin to serving up water as a utility with workers manually pumping water out of a well. Automation saves time and money. It eliminates costly repetitive and manual tasks. When implemented correctly, it can also improve quality of service by reducing human errors. But what does it really take to automate a data center fully? The first part of this chapter introduces the reader to planning concepts and considerations that will get companies started on their way to automating their data centers as part of their utility computing initiatives. The second part of the chapter is a look at the future of automation beyond the data center. It references current research on grid management and proposes additional ideas for automation.

5.1 GETTING STARTED

To get started on the path to automating the data center fully, we need to break the data center down into its most basic components. The data center is made up of the following components: people (users and systems administrators), processes (workflow), data (information), and IT systems (hardware, software applications). Each of these components will have requirements or characteristics that influence the way a data center operates. Knowing what these requirements and characteristics are leads to identifying where automation can help. Figure 5.1 shows the key components of the data center.

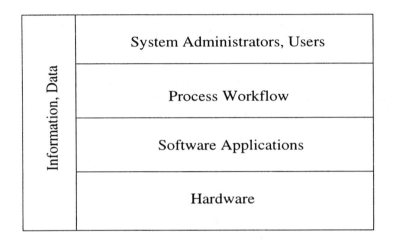

Figure 5.1 Key components of a data center.

Users of the resources within the data center require access to these resources from anywhere and at anytime. Mostly, users may not care if they use the same device or resource as long as they are able to accomplish their tasks. As with resources, access to up-to-date data and information ranks high among user requirements. Users need to be able to collaborate and transact with other users inside and outside the organization.

System administrators and managers are required to provide high quality of service in support of organizational business objectives and policies. To meet the highest level of service, the data center needs to have a well-integrated environment that provides system administrators with a unified view of the users, processes, information, and systems across the organization. With a clear view of the "big picture," an end-to-end data center process that starts with a business requirement and ends with a successful deployment of IT resources to fulfill the business requirement can be achieved.

A data center operating environment must be able to link the allocation of its IT systems to achieve its business requirements. In addition, a data center must be able to allocate its IT systems with minimal intervention. This requires collaboration within the environment, together with a flexible and dynamic workflow that makes it possible to manage growth and change within the business. Table 5.1 summarizes the characteristics and requirements of the components within the data center.

Table 5.1 Components, Characteristics and Requirements of a Data Center

Components	*Characteristics*	*Requirements*
Users	Potential access to resources 24 hours a day	Need access to resources anywhere, anytime.
Data and information	Huge, disparate	Needs to be up to date. Needs to be accessible from anywhere anytime.
System administrators	High quality of service 24 hours a day, 7 days a week	Needs to have a unified view of data center. Requires more efficient ways to provide high levels of service.
Process workflow	Based on best practices	Needs to be flexible and dynamic and linked with business processes.
Software applications	Complex	Requires minimal downtime and constant management and upkeep.
Hardware resources	Operational 24 hours a day, 7 days a week, with little downtime	Requires efficient monitoring and provisioning capabilities.

With the characteristics and requirements on hand, we can then start to visualize what processes and methods within the data center can be made more efficient through automation.

Before embarking on the path to automation, companies should realize that not all data centers are created equal. Most data centers were formed through organizational investments that differ depending on the goals and the internal political structures of the business. Automating the data center requires a business to reexamine its goals and political structures, together with the state of its data center, the company's readiness to share resources within organizational boundaries, and its long-term requirements for flexibility and agility.

5.1.1 Just in Case (JIC) Versus Just in Time (JIT)

Data centers have traditionally employed a just-in-case method for provisioning IT resources. With the JIC method, the infrastructure architect provisions new systems to support business initiatives based on maximum capacity from projected workloads. In most cases, this method results in pockets of underutilized and overutilized resources. Underutilization leads to higher cost of ownership and overutilization results in lower quality of service. In the case of overutilized resources, system administrators have to move resources manually from underutilized systems to overutilized ones to meet temporary peaks in demand, then move the additional resources back at a later time when they are no longer needed. This cycle of adding and removing resources manually is not only impractical; it is prone to human error.

A just-in-time method for provisioning IT resources fits today's dynamic data center requirements. In the JIT method, a software application implemented to support business processes is given the resources it needs, when it needs them, without overprovisioning. The JIT method also allows for the deallocation of resources when they are no longer needed (i.e., the workload decreases). The deallocated resources are sent back to a "resource pool" and made available to other workloads at a later time. The main difference in the JIT method is the availability of a resource pool that is managed and shared throughout the whole data center. While the JIC method relies on statically configured servers with manual reconfiguration requirements, the JIT method implements dynamically configured servers with some form of automation.

As mentioned previously, employing automation within the data center requires different lines of businesses, including the IT infrastructure, to reexamine their goals and the company's readiness to share resources within organizational boundaries. The JIT method requires businesses to transition from the traditional "organization-owned resources" to a "shared resource ownership" mentality. In this environment, the IT infrastructure needs to be more aligned with the business objectives of the organization. In addition, the IT infrastructure will need to be tightly integrated with business organizations and their processes.

The next section discusses an automation agenda that will employ several utility computing technologies. These technologies will allow CIOs to lower IT infrastructure costs by eliminating manual and error-prone activities. Lastly, the true value of automating the data center comes not only from lowering the cost of ownership; it comes in the form of increased efficiency and flexibility, allowing the IT infrastructure to support a rapidly changing business.

5.2 AUTOMATION AGENDA

Every organization thinking of automating its IT infrastructure should have an automation agenda. An automation agenda is a roadmap that the organization can use as a guide in incorporating automation within its IT infrastructure. Components within the data center to be included in the automation agenda are servers, storage, network infrastructure, and desktops. Each step or action to automate these components should be incremental in nature. In this way, changes in the infrastructure are perceived as an evolution instead of a disruption. Here are the steps in the agenda:

- Identifying the what and how;
- Creating asset information;
- Consolidating gathered data;
- Planning and implementing virtualization;
- Planning and implementing automated provisioning;
- Planning and implementing policy-based automation.

Each step in the agenda helps build the foundation for the next step. And although each step is an activity of its own, when using tools to accomplish the task, it is recommended to use tools that can easily integrate with other tools used in the overall automation process. Remember, automation will not happen overnight; it will require careful planning and execution.

For the purpose of this section, we will plan for automating network and server provisioning for several business units within an organization. In this example, we have a business with four departments that use different assets in their data center. These organizations include accounting, human resources, sales, and development. They each run their applications on different servers. They all have varying workloads, depending on the time of the year. In the current setup, varying workloads are handled manually by reconfiguring the network and servers to accommodate varying demand. In the next year or two, they have a chance to upgrade their servers to newer models and acquire management software that can help them implement more automation in their environment.

5.2.1 Identifying the What and How

Planning involves defining what[1] the organization wants to do and how it can be accomplished. Defining the "what" category establishes the scope and the baseline of the work. The scope of the work limits work to specific areas of the data center, and the baseline establishes criteria for measuring improvements brought about by automation. As was mentioned earlier, it is recommended to plan for incremental changes; therefore, the overall agenda for automating the data center may end up with several agendas covering different parts of the data center. As an example, agendas can be put in place for different components of the data center. Separate agendas may be established for automating desktop management and for network, storage, and server.

Here are some questions to ask in defining the "what":

- Who are the customers?
- What resources (including software applications) are these customers currently using?

---

[1] It is assumed that, at this stage, the whole organization is convinced that automating all or part of the data center will be beneficial to the business. Refer to [1] for more guidance on the value of data center automation.

- What are the server and network utilizations during peak and low times?
- What current management systems are in place?
- What is the current measure of the level of service?
- What levels of service is the customer getting today?
- What types of control is the customer willing to give up to meet the service levels expected in the future?
- What types of investments is the customer ready to commit to this agenda?

By asking these types of questions, one can establish a baseline of current levels of service and create an inventory of assets used in the present environment. No doubt, other questions need to be added to this list as different customers will have different expectations and criteria. It is important to answer these types of questions upfront, before embarking on finding a solution that best fits the overall expectations and criteria of all parties involved.

Finding how present assets are managed and how service levels are being met will also show what processes are currently in use. This helps define "how" tasks are accomplished within the data center.

Here are some questions to ask in defining the "how":

- How does the process handle peak loads?
- How do the customers plan for expected workloads?
- How long does it take to configure new servers to handle new demand in workload?
- How are current service level agreements enforced?

Finding out how systems are currently managed allows one to know the current processes and procedures used in the data center. By knowing what processes are in use, we can determine how processes can be improved, replaced, or incorporated in the processes to be used for automation. Other areas to be considered when investigating process information are software distribution and maintenance, hardware failures and maintenance, security policies, and system recovery.

5.2.2 Creating Asset Information

Organizing the asset information within the infrastructure is part of identifying the "what" from the previous section. Assets within the data center will include, but not be limited to, servers, storage, networks, switches, and load balancers. For this, you will need to create network diagrams that include information on servers, switches, and load balancers.

- *Servers and storage*–Create a diagram of servers used by each department. Included in this information are the hostname, make and model of the machine, installed operating system and version, assigned IP address, type of interface card, and number of CPUs. List all storage used by each of the servers. List the applications running on these servers.

- *Network information*–Create a diagram of your network that includes the IP network, IP subnets, and virtual LANs. Include IP address used and reserved for future use.
- *Switches*–Create a diagram that shows the physical and logical connections of the switches and routers used within the data center. The diagram should include the makes and models of the physical hardware and corresponding software. Indicate if they are SNMP capable and if they are being used.
- *Load balancers*–List the names and models of the load balancers. Include the balancing algorithm used. Create a diagram that shows the load balancers and the servers they are connected to.

Part of creating the asset information is making sure that the assets list the services they provide as well as the users of these assets. The information gathered in this section will need to be updated regularly to give a true picture of the data center utilization by the organization and users.

5.2.3 Consolidating Gathered Data

Once the assets and processes to manage the assets are gathered, the next step is to consolidate this data and organize it to get an overall view of the current environment, management systems, and levels of service. Table 5.2 shows an example of different departments within the business and their corresponding processes and data center needs. In this example, server and network utilization may vary from very low to very high, depending on the time of the month and year. Organizing process information in this way gives one a sense of how resources within the data center are utilized.

Table 5.2 Example of Different Businesses and Their Process and Data Center Needs

Customer	Applications	Service Levels	Server Utilization	Network Utilization
Accounting	Third-party accounting package	Medium to high	15%–60% (average) 85%–92% (tax season)	35% (average) 65% (tax season)
Human resources	Employee savings and insurance enrollment, employee records	Medium to high	10%–46% (average) 75%–95% (benefits enrollment time)	35% (average) 85% (enrollment season)

Table 5.2 Example of Different Businesses and Their Process and Data Center Needs (Continued)

Customer	Applications	Service Levels	Server Utilization	Network Utilization
Sales	Salesforce automation	Medium to high	15%–40% (average) 85% (2 weeks before end of sales quarter)	45%–75% Peaks between 11 am and 2 pm
Development	Source code control, QA test suite	Medium	20%–75% (average) 100% (QA testing)	50%—95% during testing cycle

Different methods can be used to get an accurate view of utilization, which can include interviewing users and taking snapshots of utilization at 30-minute intervals for a month during expected high and low usage.

Once all the "what" and "how" data is gathered, we are ready to look at how these data can be put to use within the data center.

5.2.4 Planning and Implementing Virtualization

The whole premise of the JIT method, as discussed in Section 5.1.1, is the availability of a resource pool that can be shared among different organizations. Within this resource pool are assets ready to be configured and deployed when needed. A typical resource pool may contain physical assets like servers and storage. When a department needs extra processing capacity due to high utilization, one of these servers can be installed with the required operating system and application stack, then configured with the proper network addresses. When the high-utilization requirement has passed, the server is removed from the network and put back in the resource pool. The same process is repeated for other applications as needed. In essence, we have created a virtual environment where increased workload is satisfied by resources from a virtual resource pool.

To be able to virtualize an application environment, the amenability of the applications and servers within the environment to horizontal scaling must be investigated. Horizontal scaling is a technique used in environments where the systems architecture allows the addition of similar resources to handle workload as needed. A simple example of horizontal scaling is adding an extra CPU, if the architecture allows it, to add more processing power. A more complicated example is a Web environment utilizing load balancers to route workloads to different servers to handle Web traffic. In this case, another server can be added to help handle more workload.

In a virtualized environment, we need to know when to add or remove resources. To do this, we need to gather information about system usage on a real-time basis. This information will be used to help decide what application environment needs to be allocated extra resources from the resource pool. The decision to deploy resources to application environments needs to take into consideration the service level objectives and priority (importance to the business) of each environment. Figure 5.2 shows a high-level view of tasks and resources within a virtualized environment. In the figure, utilization rates are gathered from the operating environment; the information gathered is then used to decide how to deploy resources from the resource pool.

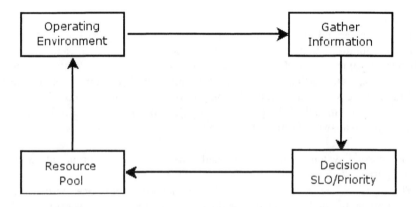

Figure 5.2 A high-level view of tasks and resources within a virtualized environment.

As we look at the high-level view of the tasks and resources in a virtual environment, we can use the data we gathered in Section 5.2.3 to start creating our own virtual environment. In our example case study, we note that within this particular data center, resources are manually moved from one environment to another depending on workload requirements. Albeit unorganized, from the high-level perspective presented in Figure 5.2, specific areas in the data center in our case study are already operating in a quasivirtual manner. We can also see from gathered data that operating systems running on the servers within this quasivirtual environment are. This allows the administrators to reconfigure and allocate the servers for use with different application environments. In this case, automated server configuration and deployment software called a provisioning manager (covered in the next section) can be introduced into the environment. Another option would be to replace existing servers with today's servers that have built-in virtualization capabilities. These servers are capable of running multiple instances of operating systems in different virtual partitions. These servers have built-in virtualization environments making allocation and deallocation of resources easier. We will assume that existing servers will be replaced by servers equipped with virtualization technology.

5.2.4.1 Planning

To take most of the guesswork out of planning the virtual environment, it is best to work with a model of the current and planned server environment. The current environment model can be created from the data gathered from the previous sections. The data should include the server model, type, configuration (number of CPUs, amount of memory), and utilization rates. This data can then be used to map the workload running on these servers to new servers that implement virtualization.

It is recommended to work with a server vendor who can assist in creating a server configuration that can best handle current, anticipated, and future workloads. In some instances, vendors even have performance centers that can be used to demonstrate particular server configurations with customer application and data. Different scenarios must be played out to test the proposed server configuration. The model of the proposed configuration using virtualized servers should be able to answer questions like:

- What current systems can be moved and consolidated to the proposed server configuration?
- What options are there to transfer workloads from one virtualized environment to another? Can this be done without stopping the workload?
- Given certain performance and utilization characteristics of different workloads, what would be the right combinations of workloads to put on virtualized partitions on one physical machine?
- How does the virtualized environment handle future growth?

The proposed configuration model should be flexible enough that different parameters of the server implementation can be varied to see if different scenarios can lead to more optimized configurations. The result of the planning stage is a hardware resource plan for current and future requirements.

5.2.4.2 Implementation

The implementation process begins with physically setting up the virtual servers in a test environment. Selected workloads from the current setup are transferred to the test environment. The selection of these workloads is based on a balance of criticality and characteristics based on potential for improvements. Workloads that meet these criteria are those on physical servers that are underutilized and are assessed as less critical to business functions. Once moved, the workloads are tested and assessed. Tests may include varying virtual server configurations while monitoring workload performance and server utilization. Once the testing phase completes and IT personnel are satisfied with the results, the environment is switched over to a production environment.

Services levels are monitored to make sure users are getting the same or better levels of service before switching to a virtual environment. At some future time, other workloads can go through the same planning and implementation process.

Operating in a virtual environment is the first step toward data center automation. From an operational standpoint, we want a data center that implements a virtual environment, requiring little or no manual intervention to move resources around.

Next, we look at the provisioning manager tool, which takes over the tasks of knowing what and how resources are provisioned in a virtual environment.

5.2.5 Planning and Implementing Automated Provisioning

Configuring a server for production requires several steps: physically configuring the hardware system and installing the operating system, together with required patches and security fixes. After the operating system and patches are installed, the server is configured for security, performance, and network connectivity. Finally, user logins are added and application software is installed and configured. The process of configuring a server for production is not only time-consuming but it is subject to human error. For instance, a single step in the process may be inadvertently omitted and leave the newly configured server vulnerable to security breaches. With use of a provisioning manager, configuring a server can be automated and much of the manual work eliminated, thus saving time and minimizing human error.

A provisioning manager is a software application that manages hardware and software provisioning within the data center based on system administrator input. Provisioning managers can be classified into two types: those that provision operating platforms and those that provision software applications. For the purpose of this chapter, we only concentrate on operating platform provisioning.

Using a provisioning manager to execute tasks considered repetitive creates an environment that requires less human intervention, thereby reducing errors in the process. Examples of these tasks are:

- Installation of operating system, applications, and middleware;
- Configuration of network ports and switches;
- Reallocation of CPUs from one server partition to another;
- Allocation of extra storage capacity.

Provisioning managers employ two methods to accomplish provisioning tasks: scripting and imaging.

- *Scripting* is the method of writing executable files called scripts to perform configuration tasks. Scripts contain commands that execute on the operating system. A script is written to wait for results returned from executing specific commands to see if the commands were performed correctly.
- *Imaging* is the method of replicating images of operating systems or applications. These operating system or application images have been preconfigured with the necessary patches and required system-level configuration. When a server needs to be deployed, these preconfigured images are installed on the server. Installing preconfigured images reduces installation time since most of the configuration work has already been done beforehand.

Both methods require that system administrators have the necessary skills to write the scripts and to create and install images. Once written, a script can be used many times over to do a repetitive task. The scripts have to be maintained to make sure changes in operating systems and configuration requirements are reflected. The same holds true for images of operating systems and software applications. Newer levels of operating systems and applications need to be reflected in the images by creating new ones.

Adding a provisioning manager enables a virtualized data center to automate repetitive tasks. Figure 5.3 shows the components in the data center with the addition of the virtualization and provisioning manager layers.

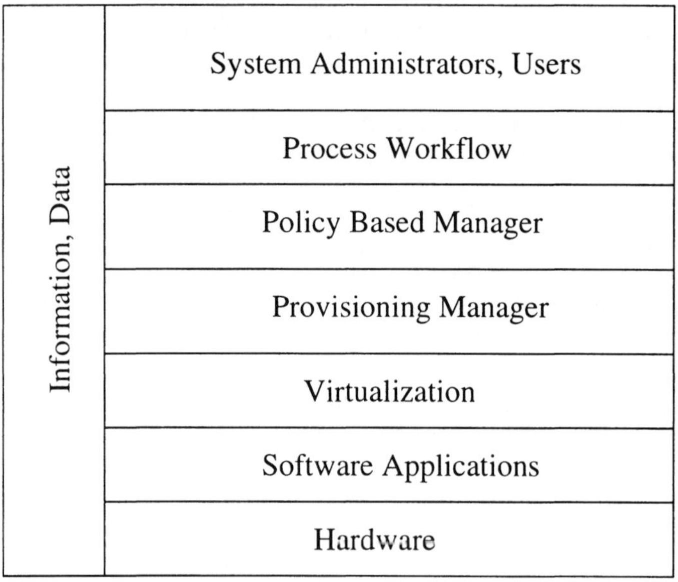

Information, Data
System Administrators, Users
Process Workflow
Policy Based Manager
Provisioning Manager
Virtualization
Software Applications
Hardware

Figure 5.3 Data center components with added automation.

Several vendors offer provisioning managers to manage specific components within a data center. The basic requirement for the provisioning manager is to provide automation support in areas such as operating system installation, network configuration, and other server provisioning tasks. Depending on the vendor, the provisioning manager will have built-in provisioning capabilities for automating different brands of routers, switches, and other hardware components, like storage and disk arrays. Some may also offer data-acquisition tools to monitor server utilizations and track software licenses and versions. Here are some guidelines for choosing a provisioning manager for a data center.

- *Operating platform support*–A provisioning manager must have support for different operating platforms in use within the data center. They must be able to support new servers that offer built-in virtualized environments. They must be able to support different kinds of servers, from blades to stand-alone servers.
- *Integration*–The provisioning manager must be able to integrate with other parts of the infrastructure. For example, it must be able to integrate with a policy manager (discussed in the next section) to enable more automation. It must be able to integrate with a configuration manager to allow for automated resource discovery and software distribution.
- *API and scripting support*–The provisioning manager should provide API and scripting support so that system administrators can extend support to other hardware not supported by the provisioning manager by default.
- *Remote support*–Since not all data centers are in one location, the provisioning manager must have the ability to support remote data centers.
- *Patch and images management support*–It must have the ability to distribute software and operating system patches.
- *Inventory and configuration management support*–It must have the ability to store network- and server-related information details, enabling IT staff to quickly view the system architecture and changes that may need to occur through automation.

5.2.5.1 Planning

The main purpose of the planning stage is to come up with a set of requirements that will help decide the specific automated provisioning system to run the environment. IT personnel must keep in mind that since utility computing initiatives are done in incremental steps, the automated provisioning system must be able to work within a virtualized and nonvirtualized environment. And, as Figure 5.2 shows, information gathered from the operating environment influences the decisions made by the automated provisioning system itself. In this respect, the automated provisioning system must be capable of integrating with monitoring systems that operate on older server technology.

For the purpose of this exercise, we will assume that workloads will not be moved from virtual to nonvirtual environments or vice versa. Begin by creating a model that can simulate "what-if" scenarios for different anticipated workload requirements based on historical utilization and performance information. Based on these "what-if" scenarios, requirements for provisioning resources can be established. For example, historical data shows that during the months of September to December, the human resources system utilization rate jumps to 95%. When this happens, extra CPUs are allocated to handle the additional workload. Therefore, allocating CPUs then becomes one requirement for allocation. Another scenario might pertain to reconfiguring load balancers to re-balance network traffic to several Web servers.

These requirements will determine what capabilities must be present in the automated provisioning system. If these capabilities are not standard, the provisioning system must allow these capabilities to be added through specially written scripts. The end result of the planning process is a decision to go with a specific automated provisioning system capable of fulfilling requirements.

5.2.5.2 Implementation

The implementation process starts by ensuring that performance and system monitoring tools are in place in both virtualized and nonvirtualized environments. These tools will alert system administrators when set thresholds are about to be breached. When an alert comes, system administrators can determine what to do next. For example, if an alert requires a system administrator to reconfigure load balancers to alleviate load from certain Web servers, then he triggers a workflow on the provisioning system to perform this task.

Establish and identify the operations that will be performed by the provisioning system. The identified operations will make up the workflows[2] that will be programmed into the provisioning system. Some examples of data center operations include:

- Configuring an IP address;
- Configuring a server;
- Installing software patches;
- Adding/removing user.

When testing the automation process, manually trigger process workflow for provisioning on a hardware test environment. Once satisfied that everything works as needed, configure the provisioning system into parts of the production environment. Iterate the process for every piece of the production environment the provisioning system needs to be implemented on.

---

[2] A workflow is a representation of the set of steps that must be followed in a data center environment in order to carry out a provisioning operation [2].

As most data center configurations and architectures change over time, it is essential to maintain strict change-control policies. The change-control policies must take into consideration hardware, workflow, processes, and other elements that may be affected by the change. The change-control process must be able to manage and track changes until they are verified to work in the production environment.

5.2.6 Planning and Implementing Policy-Based Automation

In the previous section, we described the provisioning manager, which manages the resources within the data center. It knows what resources to manage and how these resources are managed based on administrator input. In this section, we discuss the last piece of the automation agenda–the policy-based manager. The policy-based manager adds more automation by triggering provisioning tasks based on data gathered within the environment. Without a policy-based manager, decisions on provisioning are made by the system administrator based on metrics gathered and analyzed manually. The policy manager helps eliminate the manual decision-making process as well as the manual analysis of metrics data.

In addition to eliminating manual analysis tasks, the policy manager also adds efficiency to the provisioning process, contributing to higher levels of service. While in most cases provisioning is as simple as allocating an extra CPU to the environment, some tasks may require a string of tasks, depending on the need for extra resources. The knowledge of the need for extra resources will come from real-time data gathered and practices, methods, and policies established within the data center. Established practices, methods, and policies used within the data center are documented and adhered to by system administrators. Mostly, system administrators learn these practices and methods over time. But sometimes, due to turnover, these practices and methods are lost and must be relearned by new hires. A policy manager can keep track of these practices and methods, decide which practices have priority, and apply them to provisioning tasks as needed.

A policy manager allows the system administrator to manage the IT environment at a higher level; instead of having to know every single internal detail of the IT environment to configure and provision systems, the system administrator need only specify the goals and objectives that need to be met in order to manage the systems within the data center. Figure 5.4 shows the interaction between the policy manager and provisioning manager. The policy manager analyzes information gathered from the operating environment and determines when and what to provision.

Besides integrating with a provisioning manager, a policy manager can also integrate with other tools in the data center. An example of such a tool is a workload manager. A workload manager monitors workload for each application environment, making sure the servers in that environment are operating at optimum levels. The workload manager gathers data and feeds that data into the policy manager, which then decides a proper course of action.

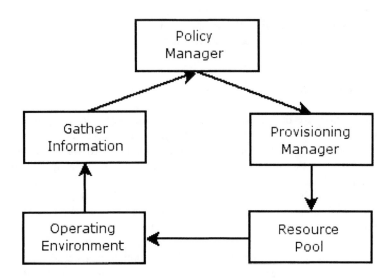

Figure 5.4 Interaction between policy manager and provisioning manager.

Here are some guidelines when choosing a policy manager:

- *Integration capabilities*–It can integrate easily with tools such as a provisioning manager and metrics acquisition tool.
- *Sensing and predicting capabilities*–It has algorithms that can predict breaches in service-level objectives.

A tool that integrates both a provisioning manager and a policy manager is the IBM Tivoli Intelligent ThinkDynamic Orchestrator. Refer to Chapter 4 for similar products from vendors like Sun and HP. For more information on planning and implementing automated provisioning, refer to [2].

5.2.6.1 Planning

Planning for policy-based operations begins by defining the scope, condition, priority, and outcome [3] an operation applies to.

- *Scope*–Defines what the policy applies to. Examples: deposit transactions in a banking application, backing up application data or file transfers of PDF documents.

- *Condition*–Defines when a policy is to be applied. Examples: when customer is a platinum member, when customer is a gold member.
- *Priority*–Defines the business value in terms of priority or monetary value. Examples: Priority 1 (highest), Priority 10 (lowest), $45 for each 24 hours of interrupted service.
- *Outcome*–Defines the expected outcome of the policy. Examples: maintain 2-second response time, operation finished in 3 hours, maintain a 128-Kbps upload rate.

By identifying the scope, deciding which areas of the data center policy-based automation will be applied becomes easier. The main objective of the planning stage is to ensure that when implemented, the policy-based automation tool guarantees that the right data center resources will be delivered to the right applications at the right times.

5.2.6.2 Implementation

The implementation process starts by ensuring that existing performance and system monitoring tools already in place are integrated with the policy-based automation system. This may mean writing scripts to format messages or information that the policy system will be able to interpret. Once this integration is complete, establish and set the desired outcome, which will trigger alerts when the outcome is not being satisfied. These alerts are acted on by system administrators who manually trigger automation workflow, by the provisioning system itself, or by a combination of manual and automated operations.

Test the policies set in place to see if they will perform the workflows when alerts are triggered in a test environment. When satisfied, promote the system to a production environment.

5.3 OTHER CONSIDERATIONS FOR AUTOMATION

Besides choosing the right tools to use when planning for automation, other areas need careful consideration. They are as follows:

- *Identify immediate areas for automation*–A breakdown of a typical total cost of ownership (TCO) for a data center will show that labor costs take the biggest share of the IT budget. Examining the labor cost in more detail will help prioritize which labor-intensive activities within the data center can be reduced through automation. Other metrics, besides labor cost, that can be used to prioritize automation activities are metrics used for measuring levels of service. Examples of these are application response time and system availability. Immediate improvements in levels of service can be attained when tasks oriented to improve application response time and system availability are automated.

- *Identify needed skill sets*–IT organizations will need access to personnel who have skills in system architecture and design for security, network, and operating systems. In addition, depending on the chosen automation tools, personnel may need to have skills in operating system scripting languages, Java, XML, Web application servers, directory server (LDAP), and database operation and usage.
- *Keep users informed*–While it is advisable that automation be done one step at a time to reduce interruptions to users, some interruptions may be unavoidable. In this case, make sure users are informed of ongoing automation activities. Provide users with status reports so they can give feedback on any system interruptions that may occur.

A data center needs to evolve from its basic structure to one that is automated to create an environment that is flexible and adaptive to rapid changes in business requirements. The book, *On Demand Computing: Technologies and Strategies*, [4] describes the five states of IT deployment within a company as follows:

- *Basic*–Environment where one will find extensive use of labor-intensive system management practices.
- *Managed*–Environment where systems management technology is applied to reduce manual administrative effort.
- *Predictive*–Environment where a management system monitors and correlates data to identify anomalies and recommend actions to IT personnel. IT personnel act on recommendations by manually triggering a workflow.
- *Adaptive*–Environment where the management system takes the appropriate action when anomalies are identified. These actions are based on policies and service-level objectives that may be breached if such anomalies are not acted on.
- *Autonomic*–Environment managed by business rules and policies.

The automation agenda serves as a guide for IT managers and CIOs to move their data centers from a basic state to one that is automated. Each step in the agenda can be viewed as an autonomous layer that can be added to the infrastructure without causing much disruption to other parts of the data center. One thing to remember is that automation does not happen overnight; plan and implement to evolve the data center rather than to disrupt it.

5.4 BEYOND AUTOMATION

To continue our discussion around IT infrastructures,[3] we will skip two levels of the Continuum of Utilities (the next two levels will be discussed in Chapters 6 and 11) and discuss level 5, virtual infrastructure utilities. Level 5 of the continuum describes relationships between separate data centers sharing resources with one another through the use of grid technology. Level 5 also provides insights into building the business value of utility computing.

5.4.1 Grid Economy

While data center automation ranks high on CIO's lists of things to do, other activities and research are ongoing in the field of automation beyond the data center. An example of this is called the "grid economy" published in [5]. In this section, we describe a system where resources from different data centers, cooperating within a grid, can be offered for use by other data centers within the grid. While the information presented may overlap some of the information already discussed in [5], this section introduces other aspects that can help bring more automation in the proposed grid economy.

Within a grid or a utility computing environment, there exist pools of free resources[4]. Examples of resources that can be free or idle at any point are CPU, servers, and disk storage. We define the owners of the resources as "providers." Also, within the grid environment, there are companies or organizations that require use of resources to run their infrastructure. We define these companies and organizations as "consumers." Consumers agree to pay the provider for the use of resources within the provider's free pool. The consumer signs a contract to pay X dollars to guarantee the use of a specific resource for a specified amount of time. Ideally, providers want to make sure that resources in the free pool do not sit idle for long periods. For the grid economy to succeed, providers need a way to create demand and know how to create "value" for the free resources.

5.4.2 Creating Demand

Creating demand for free resources may be facilitated through a system that allows consumers to bid on free resources from resource providers. This will allow free resources to be used at a lower price point instead of sitting idle. An agent-based resource entitlement arbitration system (AAREAS) is proposed for the system.

---

[3]And for a lack of a better place to put this next short section.
[4]Data centers that offer resources on demand will have a free pool of resources based on business needs. The free pool will vary according to initial and future business demands. Resources in the free pool wait to be deployed when needed.

The AAREAS allows resource providers to register their free resources and allows consumers to place bids on them.[5] Free resources are registered into a catalogue that is detailed enough for consumers to make bids. For example, the catalogue will contain such items as a CPU resource with a particular operating system (example AIX). Another example is a server with middleware installed and already configured on the server. In addition, the catalogue will also list the specific times when the resource is or will be available. For example, if the resource is in use today but will be free in two weeks time and will not be used for another two weeks after that, then the catalogue will have availability dates for the time period starting in two weeks and lasting two weeks. This enables consumers to get resources at lower rates and at the same time allows providers to create demand for their resources.

Resource providers can allow their free resources to be used for a limited time at an accepted bid price for weeks, days, or even hours. The provider can specify the availability of the resource and other specifications or restrictions as the case may be. The goal for the provider is to have its free resources utilized as much as possible.

As part of the system, the consumer will have a consumer trending agent (CTA) that can automatically place bids on resources based on recent historical usage data on resource consumption. The CTA automates the searching and bidding on resources. The consumer may program the CTA to start the bid at a specific price point and increase to a maximum bid price if necessary.

The CTA can communicate with the AAREAS to scan its database and look for a resource that matches specific criteria for resource needs. For example, the CTA may suggest that a resource is needed for an hour the next day at a specific time. If a resource is found to match the need, then a bid is placed on that resource; if it is accepted, the consumer gets a nontransferable contract to use the resource as per the specifications agreed on. When outbid by another CTA, the arbitrating system can notify CTAs that have bid on the resource that they have been outbid to give them a chance to place another bid.

The AAREAS can be designed to be implemented individually in different geographic locations. Different AAREAS discover other AAREAS, so they can communicate and cooperate which each other to find the best fit for a specific resource need that a registered consumer is bidding for.

On the producer's side, a producer trending agent (PTA) works on behalf of the producer. It can be programmed to know what free resources can be placed into the AAREAS. It can also be programmed to follow trends of free pool consumption so that it can predict what free pools will be available for future availability. This allows forecasting of free pools that can be made available and

---

[5] Contracts between the producers and consumers will be binding and nontransferable so that a consumer who wins a bid for the resource will not be able to resell the resource at a higher price. In other words, any resource that a consumer wins in a bid can be used to fulfill the consumer's own needs only.

placed on the AAREAS in the future. Figure 5.5 shows the architecture of the AAREAS.

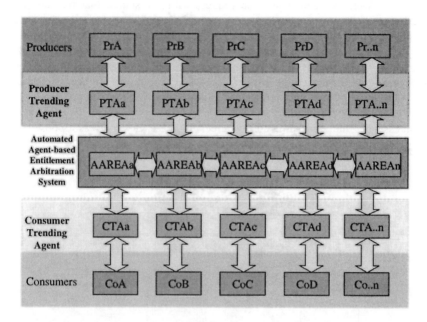

Figure 5.5 The agent-based resource entitlement arbitration system conceptual architecture.

The novelty of this approach is that resources from the provider are made available for satisfying future resource needs of consumers. This establishes a pipeline of utilization requirements, thus successfully creating demand for resources that otherwise would end up in the free pool. In terms of automation, the system provides both producer and consumer agents that aid in searching and establishing contracts with potential providers.

5.4.3 Creating Value

To create more value for certain resources that are frequently in demand, providers may choose to limit the auction to certain bidders by putting a reserve price on the resource. This allows the producer to be more in control of the value of the resource. Another way for producers to limit bidding is by sending a select group of bidders an invitation to bid on certain resources. Examples of bidders may be a select group of customers and partners or groups internal to the organization, like development or sales. The idea here is to create a tier-based system where resources that are more in demand are tiered to have higher reserve prices than those that have less demand.

Each tier will have a lowering trend of reserve pricing until a "no-reserved" price auction is reached. Tiers limit bidders to those who can afford the reserve price.[6] The AAREAS can match the request with a resource that matches the request criteria. As an incentive for bidding on tiers, producers have the option to grant the winning bidder use of other resources in the future. These additional incentives are dynamically listed and are based on future availability of free resources. The incentives may be resources that have odd configurations or leftover resources or something similar. The point is to create an incentive-based tiering system that limits the number of bidders competing for free resources that would otherwise be sitting idle.

In essence, the underutilized resources increase in value as opposed to sitting idle. Figure 5.6 is a representation of the tier-based system.

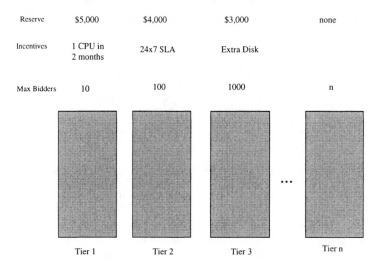

Reserve	$5,000	$4,000	$3,000	none
Incentives	1 CPU in 2 months	24x7 SLA	Extra Disk	
Max Bidders	10	100	1000	n
	Tier 1	Tier 2	Tier 3	Tier n

Figure 5.6 Conceptual view of a tier-based incentive arbitration scheme.

In the figure, the reserve price, additional incentives, and maximum bidders are specified. As shown, as the reserve price decreases, the number of bidders increases. This system limits the number of bidders while maintaining a minimum price for bidding on a certain resource.

---

[6] Consumers who are most in need of the resource and want to use the resource at a slightly lower price point.

5.4.4 Implementation

The AAREAS can be implemented as an auction-based entitlement system. The auction system is responsible for matching the bids of consumers to free resources from providers. It is also responsible for notifying consumers of bid status (outbid or winning). Interface with the AAREAS can be implemented through Web services technology. The exposed interface will be used by the CTAs and the PTAs to communicate with the AAREAS. Different AAREAS communicate and cooperate with each other, using Web Services calls, to find the best match for outstanding bid requests. Digital certificates can be used as a means of authentication as well as nonrepudiation of bids placed. Figure 5.7 shows a conceptual view of the system.

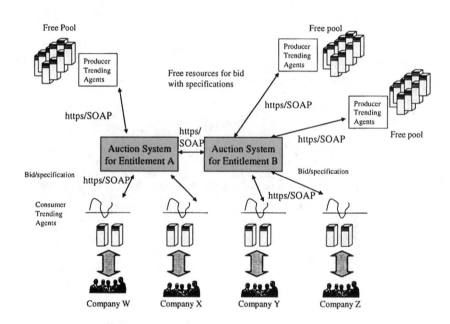

Figure 5.7 Implementation view of the arbitration system.

Just presented was a look of the future of inter-data-center management and collaboration within a grid environment, building on current grid research and adding another element, such as trending technology, to predict future resource needs and usage. Today, while grid usage is still confined to scientific research, efforts are being made to help business organizations realize the value of the grid in business and commercial applications [6].

5.5 SUMMARY

Companies changing their business model from one that is siloed[7] to one that is on demand [7] will require a more agile and flexible IT infrastructure. To create agility and flexibility within the IT infrastructure, companies will need to evolve their data centers from their basic form to one that is fully automated. CIOs need to start with an automation agenda that carefully outlines the steps in transforming the data center. The automation agenda should include virtualization, automated provisioning, and policy-based management as the building blocks for creating an automated data center. Today, with recent advances in hardware and software technologies, CIOs have a wide range of products available to help them accomplish this task.

From a utility computing standpoint, automation brings the data center one step closer to operating as a utility infrastructure provider. Business and customer demand will continue to dictate technological innovations to achieve this objective in the future. Next, we cover level 3 of the Continuum of Utilities, shared application utilities, and explore changes that need to happen to transform traditional licensed software into software offered as a service.

References

[1]   Jones, D., and A. Desai, *The Reference Guide to Data Center Automation*, Realtimepublishers.com, 2006.

[2]   Manoel, E., et al., *Provisioning On Demand*, IBM Corporation, Redbook SG24-8888-00.

[3]   Kaminsky, D., "An Introduction to Policy for Autonomic Computing," IBM Developerworks, March 2005, available at www-128.ibm.com/developerworks/autonomic/library/ac-policy.html.

[4]   Fellenstein, C., *On Demand Computing: Technologies and Strategies*, Austin, TX, IBM Press, 2003.

[5]   Buyya, R., et al., The Grid Economy, *Proceedings of the IEEE*, Vol. 93, No. 3, March 2005.

[6]   Parsons, M., "The Next Generation Grid", *CTWatchQuarterly*, Vol. 1, No. 4, November 2005, available at www.ctwatch.org/quarterly/articles/2005/11/the-next-generation-grid/1/.

[7]   Peiravi, P., Service Oriented Utility Computing, Next Generation Enterprise IT Infrastructure," *Enterprise Networks and Servers*, June 2006, available at www.enterprisenetworksandservers.com/monthly/art.php?2340.

---

[7] A business model where segments of the business are largely self-contained and vertically integrated within the organization. This results in communication barriers between segments as well as process and expense duplication across the enterprise.

Chapter 6

Software Utility Application Architecture

With software applications evolving to meet the needs of highly dynamic and agile businesses, application designs are changing radically to match this more demand-centric view, which in turn is leading to the delivery of software as a service [1]. Software as a Service (SaaS) is a term used by industry analysts covering the utility computing application space. Although SaaS is now used ubiquitously within the software industry to describe a software application that is delivered in a pay-as-you-go fashion, the term brought about feelings of cynicism when it was first introduced. Remember the application service provider (ASP) era of the late 1990s?[1] Critics were doubtful that SaaS would be any different.

Today, software companies offering SaaS are proving that they are not the same as their ASP predecessors. Instead of a reincarnation of the ASPs, critics are realizing, SaaS is a viable alternative solution to the aging business problem of upwardly spiraling application and maintenance costs. The SaaS market today is growing at a brisk rate. This is due to small software companies developing their software from the ground up with the intention of delivering their application on the Internet on a pay-as-you-go basis. Today's SaaS providers fill the need of small and medium-sized,[2] cost-conscious businesses that cannot afford to pay exorbitant licensing fees to large corporations for the use of their enterprise applications. And as these small and medium-sized businesses grow, their needs evolve as well. Evolving customer needs are forcing current SaaS providers to realign the existing SaaS architecture to meet client demands. This chapter examines[3] level 3 of the continuum of utilities—utility applications—and how the present SaaS architecture can potentially evolve and help traditional independent software vendors (ISVs) transform their applications to software utility applications (SUAs).

---

[1] Most ASP businesses went bankrupt when the dot-com bubble burst in the early 2000s citing a bad business model.
[2] Large-sized businesses are also starting to discover the value of SaaS alternatives.
[3] While the primary audience for this chapter is independent software vendors, it can also serve as a guide for companies that develop their own in-house applications.

6.1 CHARACTERISTICS OF AN SaaS

From a functional point of view, traditional enterprise applications are no different from software as a service applications. Both types of applications have the same basic purpose: to provide the right business logic needed by enterprise organizations to help them run their business.

6.1.1 Enterprise Applications

A traditional enterprise application is a complex collection of business rules translated into computer programs that work together to serve either an organization within the corporation or the corporation as whole. The collection of programs produces or uses data that is stored in a database backend that can remain persistent in the database until it is needed. Users of enterprise applications use these required applications to gain access to stored data concurrently and to access various types of input and output devices, each of which can serve a different purpose, depending on the organization using the application.

Within a corporation, several other enterprise applications may exist. As the organizations within the company become more integrated with each other, the need for these different enterprise applications to access each other's data becomes more important. Thus, the requirement for enterprise applications to integrate with other parts of the organization becomes a necessity. Table 6.1 shows a more detailed description of the characteristics of a traditional enterprise application.

Table 6.1 Detailed Characteristics of a Traditional Enterprise Application

Component	Enterprise Application Characteristic
Data and databases	Data in enterprise application databases is complex and persistent and remains persistent between multiple runs of the application.
	Data in enterprise application databases may need to persist for many years and often outlasts the hardware or enterprise application for which it was originally created.
	Database structures in enterprise application databases may change over time to accommodate new business, government, industry, and economic environment requirements.
	Data in enterprise application databases needs to be protected from failed transactions; error-recovery tools, such as transaction middleware, are used to prevent failed or incomplete transactions from being committed into the database.
Users	Enterprise applications have many people accessing data concurrently.
Input requirements	Enterprise applications require lots of input screens and forms that are used to input data into the database. Each form has its own purpose serving different parts of an enterprise organization, like accounting, shipping, or development.

Table 6.1 Detailed Characteristics of a Traditional Enterprise Application (Continued)

Component	Enterprise Application Characteristic
Integration requirements	Enterprise applications have high requirements for integration with other enterprise applications.
Size	Enterprise applications may come in different sizes—large or small—but they all have one purpose: to help an enterprise in its business processes.
Quality of service	Enterprise applications have the following: • High availability and integrity; • High levels of data protection from failure conditions; • High mean time between failure; • High level of security.
Types	Some enterprise applications are more workflow than business logic oriented. Examples of these types are inventory and supply-chain management applications. Some enterprise applications have more business logic than workflow. Examples of these types are banking or finance applications. Some enterprise applications start out small and then grow. Examples of these are expense- and time-tracking applications that later grow to have more bells and whistles.

Enterprise applications may include, but are not limited to, applications for customer relationship management (CRM), enterprise resource planning (ERP), and salesforce automation (SFA). The architecture of an enterprise application will depend on how an organization or company uses it in their day-to-day business. Some will be architected to handle more user interactions, while some will be configured to do more backend processing.

6.1.2 Software as a Service

From an operational point of view, however, some major differences exist. The differences come in the form of a different delivery, maintenance, and initial setup and configuration model.

6.1.2.1 Delivery Model

SaaS applications are enterprise applications architected with the intention of being delivered as an outsourced application outside the boundaries of the client's premises. SaaS is based on the application outsourcing business model offered at a lower price point compared to traditional enterprise applications. For SaaS providers to offer lower price rates, these providers allow companies the use of their applications while only charging on a termed-license basis. *Termed-license basis* means that consumers are granted the use of the application as long as they pay a minimal per-user subscription fee. The subscription fee can be based on a short-term annuity or a pay-as-you-use model.

6.1.2.2 Maintenance Model

The SaaS model comes with the understanding that the SaaS provider assumes all support and maintenance costs of the SaaS application. This translates into additional savings for the customer. This includes the maintenance of the application in terms of applying fixes and maintaining the servers the application runs on. While this may seem to put an extra burden of cost on the SaaS provider, SaaS applications can be architected in such a way as to provide the economies of scale needed to help the SaaS provider reduce the cost of maintenance. This type of architecture is called multitenancy. Multitenancy will be described in more detail in Section 6.2, but, in brief, it is an architecture that allows different companies or organizations to share an instance of the application, thereby reducing support and maintenance work and minimizing cost, which can contribute to the provider's bottom line.

6.1.2.3 Initial Setup and Configuration Model

Compared to a traditional enterprise application which can take anywhere from 6 to 12 months to deploy, an SaaS application can be deployed in less than a week. Since SaaS applications employ a multitenant architecture, setting up an organization to use the same instance of the application will only require a minimum amount of time and effort. Tasks include adding an initial group of users, creating a separate database for the organization, and provisioning for any other resources the organization needs to utilize the SaaS application fully. In most cases, during setup the SaaS provider can even give administrative privileges to the customer's assigned administrator. This administrator will have enough privileges to do simple administrative tasks, like adding and deleting users, assigning user-level privileges, and configuring system-type resources that will be needed by users. By assigning these administrative tasks to the customer's administrator, the SaaS provider reduces the amount of work it needs to do for the customer. Table 6.2 summarizes the differences between traditional enterprise and SaaS applications.

All of the SaaS characteristics in Table 6.2 are driven by the SaaS provider's business model–to provide an outsourced enterprise application at a lower price point to serve as an alternative to traditional licensed applications. This business model will work for the SaaS provider only if it can take advantage of economies of scale and keep its own cost of managing and supporting the application to a minimum.

Table 6.2 SaaS Characteristics That Are Not Present in Traditional Enterprise Applications

SaaS Characteristic	Traditional Enterprise Application
Multitenant, multiuser	Multiuser only
Remote management accessibility	Locally managed by customer
Installation on a managed data center	Installation at customer location
Short deployment time	Long deployment time

While today's crop of SaaS providers satisfies small to medium-sized business needs, the future of SaaS will depend on its flexibility and adaptability to changing demands. The next sections examine in more detail characteristics like multitenancy, hosting suitability, and other attributes that will produce a flexible and adaptable SaaS application.

6.2 SOFTWARE UTILITY APPLICATIONS

A research brief by Gartner [2] said that by 2008 more than 50% of the software purchased will be via service as opposed to the traditional licensed model. Over the last few years, there have been a lot of differences in opinion about SaaS applications. Today, we know SaaS applications are here to stay. As independent software vendors (ISVs) of traditional enterprise applications strive to transform their business model to accommodate an SaaS model, little has been done to study what needs to change in traditional enterprise applications to transform them into viable applications offered as services. This section presents the attributes and characteristics of an SaaS application. It will discuss attributes that can be considered essential for applications to succeed and meet future business needs.

As each detailed attribute is described to build the conceptual view of the SaaS application's technical and business architecture, it is important to remember that these attributes are additions to the enterprise attributes previously discussed. Further, whereas Section 6.1 described SaaS applications as they exist today, this section starts to fill in the gaps in the story of the evolution of SaaS applications into what will be called software utility applications (SUAs).

6.2.1 Stage One Attributes

To create an SaaS application from the ground up or transform a traditional licensed application to an application delivered as a service, the application architect needs to be aware of the attributes that make an application suitable to be delivered as a service.

The following attributes are considered stage-one attributes and are classified as "must-have" before an application, either traditionally licensed or developed from scratch, can be offered as service.

- Multitenancy/Multiinstance;
- Suitability for hosting;
- Use of a utility managed hosting center;
- Use of virtualized resources;
- Application scalability;
- Software maintenance and upgrade policy plan;
- Service level agreements (SLA).

While most of these attributes are technical and related directly to the application and its components, some attributes touch on business processes that may affect the ISV's entire business model.

6.2.1.1 Multitenancy/Multiinstance

In the context of developing or architecting for multitenancy, the enterprise application is segmented according to the following three criteria: who uses it, how it is used, and what is being used or accessed. Each of these segments represents a part of the enterprise application that will need specific attention from the application architect. By making the necessary changes with regard to the who, how, and what segments, the application can become a true multitenant application.

The "who" segment pertains to the users and administrators of the enterprise application. Both types of users need to be associated with an organization. This ensures that when a user or administrator logs in, he will only be able to affect the part of the application he is allowed to use or administer. The application architect will need to provide a means to grant a hierarchical-type user-access structure. This means that users are assigned a role not only to prevent them from accessing data they are not allowed to affect within their own company but also to prevent them from accessing data from other companies. A simple type of hierarchy is as follows:

- *End-user access*–This grants access to user files within the company the user works for. This is the lowest type of access.
- *Organization or company administrator access*–This grants administrator privilege access for administering for the client company only. This is medium-level access. This type of access is beneficial to SaaS providers since administration authority can be delegated to an administrator working for the client company.

- *Application administrator access*–This access is for the SaaS provider only. This is top-level or superuser access. This access grants the type of administrator access that can affect multiple organizations.

The concept of groups needs to be considered as well. Grouping users and company administrators into categories can ease user management. For example, users of a certain category are grouped so that a single change in the group attribute affects all users within the group. This can be useful for granting or deleting application privileges to multiple users with one administrative action.

Lastly, the application architect will need to put in place security and isolation measures, whether they are hierarchical user access or modified database tables, to make sure that customer concerns regarding the security of their data are addressed.

The "how" segment of the application pertains to the application segmentation and flow of session information between the segments. Today, enterprise applications are segmented into tiers to ease application programming and maintenance. These tiers are categorized as the presentation tier, business logic tier, and database tier. Depending on how the application is structured for scalability, each of these tiers can reside on separate machine instances within the data center, communicating through the network. If they are communicating through the network, then these applications need to communicate and transmit data on network ports using known communication protocols. It is recommended to protect these ports through tighter security by using authentication schemes that make sure only authorized messages are allowed to flow through the application.

Information flows from the presentation tier all the way to the database tier and back. This information flows within a session that is started as soon as the user logs into the application. Most Web-based applications keep track of sessions for security and for user tracking implemented as session tokens or cookies, which may persist on the client or server machine. The application should securely terminate the session by invalidating tokens or cookies so it cannot be reused inadvertently to grant access to unauthorized users. Other Web-based vulnerabilities such as those exposed by using cross-site scripting, need to be checked and rewritten to limit exposure to security breaches.

The "what" segment relates more to the data that the enterprise application creates. Data that the application creates is stored in the database backend or the database tier. Like all the components of the enterprise application, the data within the database needs to be protected. In designing the database tier, the two opposing considerations of security and design are taken into account. For example, if data from different companies is stored in one database table, backing up data for one company can be difficult without writing scripts to separate the specific company data before backing it up. The following are some more database-related topics that database architects need to be aware of:

- *Data separation*–The application or database implementation should not allow any type of user of one company to view, query, back up, or restore data belonging to another company.
- *Database queries*–A multitenant application should not permit a customer to use a database query tool to see data belonging to another customer.

Within any computing environment, there is, unfortunately the potential for malicious users. Within a multitenant environment, the risk is even greater. Multitenant enterprise applications must be made secure so that users are not allowed to issue commands to the operating system or break out to an operating system shell. Breaking out to a system shell is a known method used by users that exploit buffer-overflow programming errors. Buffer overflows are well-known sources of security problems, and providers are advised to make sure their multitenant application is secure from such buffer-overflow exploits.

Within a multitenant application, large amounts of computing activity take place simultaneously. This can contribute to the difficulty of finding out what has gone wrong if something fails. To help problem determination in certain types of user-reported problems, logging user activities in the form of audit trails is encouraged. Flagging certain types of errors or even user activities and keeping a log of them as necessary can help in determining unexplained failures or even preventing them in the first place.

In stark contrast to a licensed package application, which is usually developed for use by a single enterprise and installed locally on the customer premises, multitenancy allows a single instance of an application running from a remote location to accommodate several businesses or enterprise customers. From the point of view of the enterprise using the application, multitenancy should be transparent. A company is assured that none of its data can be accessed by another company, and all its users can work simultaneously–just as if the application were installed locally in their data center. From an SaaS provider's point of view, however, multitenancy provides a lot of benefits. Among these benefits are the following:

- Lower cost of management since multiple instances of the application are avoided;
- Lower cost of maintenance for feature upgrades and fixes since only one instance of the application needs to be upgraded;
- Lower cost of licensing fee since third-party middleware licenses can be shared;
- Lower infrastructure cost since only one instance of the application is running;
- Lower infrastructure management and maintenance cost as an integrated application instance enables easier application manageability.

Within technical systems, benefits often come with a price. In the context of an enterprise application, multitenancy requires detailed attention during design and implementation. The first and foremost concern of enterprise customers is always the safety of their data. Thus, security becomes a big issue when implementing multitenancy. Access to the database and its configuration and layout will need to be carefully planned. Chapter 8 will present more detail about designing a multitenant application from a database perspective.

6.2.1.2 Suitability for Hosting

The traditional licensed enterprise application offering is very different from the more recent application services offerings. One of the major differences of an application provided as a service is that it resides off, as opposed to on, the customer premises. SaaS providers offer application services to their clients from a remote data center. This remote data center has Internet facing capabilities that allow users to connect to and use the application over the Internet, employing the latest encryption technologies available.

In most cases, the data center is run by a third-party managed hosting service provider. Often, these managed hosting service providers only grant access to managed servers through a remote connection. Therefore, before the enterprise application can be hosted in such a facility, the application must have the characteristics that enable it to be accessed and managed from a remote location as well. While most enterprise applications today provide secure user access to the application from a Web browser, most, if not all, do not provide secure and remote administration and maintenance capabilities. The one thing application architects need to remember when designing their applications as services is that once their applications are installed inside a managed hosting center, application administrators will not be able to go physically near any of the servers running the application. For this reason, application architects need to add capabilities that allow the application to be administered remotely through a secure Internet connection.

Further, the nature of hosting on a managed hosting facility is such that hosting providers will not grant anyone superuser access to the managed servers for security reasons but instead will grant only privileges high enough to manage the enterprise application. This situation is very different compared to an enterprise application that is installed in-house at the customer facility where the application administrator may have full server administrator capabilities as well. The consequence of this restriction is that tasks that need to be done with superuser access will now have to be done through someone within the hosting facility or through the granting of temporary superuser access permissions.

The suitability and amenability of an enterprise application to being hosted requires that it satisfy characteristics enabling it to reside in a managed hosting center—that is, it must provide remote users and administrators a secure way of accessing and managing the application, respectively.

6.2.1.3 Use of a Utility Managed Hosting Center

There are two kinds of managed hosting infrastructure models that SaaS providers can choose from. The first is the traditional managed hosting model, and the second is the utility hosting model. Understanding both infrastructure models and their capabilities is essential for deciding where it's best to host the application service.

Traditional hosting infrastructures cater to SaaS owners who would rather run their application services on dedicated servers, while the utility hosting model caters to clients that prefer to run their applications in a shared utility infrastructure, where resources such as CPU, storage, and network are provided in a utilitylike manner.

The traditional hosting model requires peak capacity planning and requires the SaaS to purchase resources like servers, storage, memory, operating system licenses, and other hardware and software required to run the application. While this model gives the SaaS provider more control of resources, it has two major drawbacks: first, low demand for the application may result in underutilized servers; second, high demand for the application may exceed planned capacity.

The utility hosting model allows the SaaS provider to plan for an initial baseline usage of infrastructure resources and a following adjustment as load varies during peak or low demand. The utility hosting provider is responsible for all hardware and operating system resources required by the application service. This model offers several advantages over the traditional hosting model. In this model, the SaaS provider pays for resources only as they are utilized by the application service. Not only does the provider lower the initial cost of infrastructure, he also limits his risks of paying for the cost of managing excess capacity during low application usage seasons. More and more managed hosting providers are offering utility hosting services because they offer more flexibility to their clients, providing them with resources on demand in a pay-as-you-use fashion.

6.2.1.4 Use of Virtualized Resources

When the SaaS provider chooses to host the application service in a utility hosting model, the application must be able to run on virtualized hosting resources. Virtualization is a technology used in the utility hosting model that maximizes utilization of existing hardware resources within the hosting data center. With today's available automated provisioning and deprovisioning technologies, the utility model can respond to demand for server, storage, and network resources more quickly. To take advantage of this environment and use virtual server services, the ISV's application must not have any hardware- or platform-specific dependencies.

An example of virtual server services would be Linux on zSeries IBM servers and VMware on Intel architecture. Hardware vendors like Sun, IBM, and HP also have their own virtual technologies within their respective UNIX environments. Some types of virtualization technologies available today are

- Sun Solaris containers from Sun;
- Dynamic logical partitioning from IBM AIX;
- Micropartitioning from IBM AIX;
- Virtual partitioning (vPar) and nPartitions technology from HP-UX;
- VMWare (www.vmware.com) for Intel processors;
- Xen (www.cl.cam.ac.uk/Research/SRG/netos/xen/) on Linux;
- Microsoft Virtual Server 2005.

As the use of virtualized technology is relatively new, and implementations vary, one of the challenges for SaaS providers is to make sure that their applications are well suited to run on virtual resources by running their own performance and capacity tests before they offer their applications as services running on virtualized servers. By becoming familiar with the characteristics and configuration options of virtual servers offered through the different technologies that implement them, the SaaS provider can better understand how an application will function and perform within the virtual environment.

6.2.1.5 Application Scalability

Application architects need to make sure their application services exhibit exceptional application scalability. Scalability is an application attribute that describes the variability of user response time when a fixed amount of resources are added to support a linearly increasing set of users. In an interactive computing environment, such as when a user clicks on a button in a user interface, response time is crucial. A user who clicks a button to initiate a job and expects an acknowledgment that the job is being processed will have a different reaction compared to a user who gets a response only when the job is complete. In the latter, the responsiveness of the system processing the request becomes a crucial factor that can translate into client satisfaction with the application.

The ability to be responsive depends on the characteristics of the enterprise application. As more jobs are processed and more users log on to work, the degree of responsiveness of the application may decrease. This is where the scalability of the application becomes important. *Horizontal scalability* is the measure of how adding new resources (usually hardware) affects performance [3]. For example, doubling the number of Web servers to compensate for slow Web server response doubles response time. Horizontal scalability is the ability to add resources used by the application service to get a commensurate increase in the application service responsiveness.

Vertical scaling is also important. *Vertical scaling* is traditionally defined as scaling up within the physical server, like adding more memory or cache, to improve responsiveness. With today's multiprocessor servers, adding CPUs can also be considered vertical scaling. As new advancements in technology allow applications to integrate easily and seamlessly with each other, vertical scaling may one day be redefined as ability to scale up the application by using features provided by other applications, such as single sign-on, directory services, or digital certificate services, as a way to handle diverse business demands. The redefinition of vertical scaling will lead to the design of more flexible applications. The flexibility within the application provided by vertical scaling becomes an important feature of the application service because it allows the application not only to plug in services that it needs from external sources but to respond to customer's requirements as rapidly as possible.

6.2.1.6 Software Maintenance and Upgrade Policy Plan

The software maintenance and upgrade policy is a business characteristic of the SaaS application due to the nature of its impact on availability. It is primarily the timing and scope of the software maintenance and upgrade policy that is of concern. Unlike traditional licensed enterprise applications, where application maintenance can be scheduled and affect users of only one company, upgrading multitenant applications can affect users of several companies. The risk of applying upgrades and fixes within a shared application multiplies tenfold when applied to a multitenant application. Scheduling for application maintenance downtime also becomes more difficult since different companies have varying levels of expectations for application uptime, making it even harder to apply maintenance and upgrade patches. If at all possible, the application service needs to be designed so that maintenance and upgrades can be applied without the need to stop and restart the application, minimizing application downtime.

When creating a software maintenance and upgrade policy plan consider the following:

- Third-party software used by the application service must be maintained and upgraded. Create a plan for how to upgrade third-party software without affecting overall application availability.
- Upgrade policies and notification should clearly be stated in the SLA between the provider and the customer. The customer needs to know what to expect when upgrades occur.
- No matter how much testing can be done to ensure that maintenance fixes will not create unexpected problems for the application, something may still be overlooked. Make sure that there is a plan to back out of upgrades and fixes with the least interruption possible.
- Complaints and feedback from users using a multitenant application will arrive faster than from those who use traditional licensed applications. SaaS providers need to make sure they respond to user problem reports quickly, or they will have to contend with users not using their application and the resulting loss in revenue.

- Consider creating a notification plan that notifies users before and after applying upgrades or maintenance fixes; this way users are not left in the dark, wondering why an application may be acting up.

An inadequate or nonexistent policy plan for software maintenance and upgrades can bring widespread customer dissatisfaction, which can result in users' ceasing to use the application. In contrast to traditional licensed applications where vendors of these applications have already been paid through upfront licensing fees, SaaS providers are paid only when their application is used. The more users use the application, the better it is for the SaaS provider's bottom line—profit is directly tied to fulfilling need.

As the companies that use applications offered as services expand, they will start to ask for more enhancements of application functionality. In the near future, the ability to respond to and execute customer requests will become crucial. A well-planned software maintenance and upgrade policy can help mitigate the problems that may come up during regular upgrade and maintenance cycles.

6.2.1.7 Service Level Agreements (SLAs)

An SLA is a contractual agreement between an IT service provider and its customers that describes and promises the agreed-upon required system times for performance, availability, and response needed to support the business objectives, including industry- and government-specific objectives, for a specified duration. Sometimes the agreement specifies the conditions the SLA may or may not cover, such as failures caused by customers, downtime caused by external power failures, and conditional credit or refund amounts for missing or exceeding SLA standards. In the context of an application provided as a service, the SaaS provider needs to understand that the SLA reflects the quality of service that he is willing to provide to his customers. It is recommended that the SaaS provider make sure that the service lives up to customer expectations through the SLA. The following are the types of SLA that are included in a typical SLA document.

- *Performance SLA*–This is normally expressed in term of response time ("Bank teller transactions should not take any longer than 2 seconds") or throughput ("backup of user data and restore should average 10 MBps, 30 minutes or less for 18G of data"). Sometimes external conditions that could influence the delivery of the performance SLA are included in the performance SLA ("only applies between 12 a.m. and 5 a.m. or this type of connection is limited to the intranet connection only").
- *Availability SLA*–This is often expressed as the percentage of availability ("monthly availability of Alamo Web Server will be no less than 99.7 % per month") or as sets of conditions ("the Web hosting environment is available with less than four hours downtime per calendar month, which is an availability of 99.5%"). Downtime reasons are often listed, such as

migration and/or maintenance of operating system, applications, or hardware failures. The SLA agreement on availability will also include tracking and reporting of downtime of service components.

- Security SLA–This describes how customer data will be protected within the outsourcing environment. This may include physical access to servers, network security and firewall rules, virus and intrusion detection, and denial-of-service attacks.

- Upgrade and notification SLA–This specifies customer and provider expectations for upgrades to service components. This should describe upgrade rollbacks if something goes wrong after the upgrade. This should include expectations for customer data integrity during upgrades.

- Help desk SLA–This specifies the scope of help desk services all parties, customer and provider, are responsible for. It also specifies the support availability hours of each party and the communication medium help desk support personnel will use to reply to support tickets.

- General SLA–This specifies expectations with regard to termination of the SLA contract, ownership of intellectual properties, and indemnification of the provider from third-party claims as a result of customer activities.

- Industry-specific SLA–These are terms and conditions that relate to vertical industry-specific rules and regulations (i.e., health care, retail, auto, government). These are expressed in terms of expectations between customer and provider for all specific SLA types mentioned above. An industry-specific SLA may be driven by rules and regulations from each type of industry by government or privately held organizational affiliations. Examples of these regulations are the Health Insurance Portability and Accountability Act (HIPAA) or the Sarbanes-Oxley Act.

Stage one attributes are the most essential attributes the SaaS provider needs to consider as part of the application architecture before offering the application as a service. Attributes, such as multitenancy and scalability, are considered technical in nature because these can only be implemented by modifying and tuning the application, respectively. Other attributes, such as software maintenance and the SLA, relate more to the operational nature of the business offering. While one of the main reasons for small and medium-sized businesses to use an SaaS is lower cost, another reason is that SaaS lifts the burden of maintaining and managing the application from the end customer. As such, operational attributes are equally important because they contribute to the level of service provided to end customers.

6.2.2 Stage Two Attributes

As the client customer business grows, users of the SaaS application will demand more features and services. Stage two attributes are attributes that the SaaS provider may choose to add within 6 to 8 months of the application's general availability. The following are considered stage two attributes:

- Enterprise application integration using Web Services;
- Portal;
- Entitlements;
- Application unbundling;
- Dynamic reconfiguration awareness;
- Customer care.

These attributes will help create an application architecture that is more flexible and customer centric. These attributes will enhance the application to provide different types of application offerings through entitlements and application unbundling, allowing the SaaS provider a means to differentiate himself from other application providers.

6.2.2.1 Enterprise Application Integration (EAI) Using Web Services

Enterprise applications have the challenge of providing capabilities for integration with other enterprise applications. As enterprise end customers begin to see the value of SaaS, demand for its use will increase both for strategic and competitive reasons. Meeting customer and business partner expectations for real-time information exchange is a necessity to improve productivity, efficiency, and customer satisfaction. For this reason, the SaaS architecture will benefit by including EAI capabilities through open integration technologies. With various open standards for application integration already available, the use of open-standards based technologies, such as service-oriented architecture implemented as Web services will become the choice for integration interfaces.

There is no doubt that service-oriented architectures based on Web services will play a big role in the future, not only within the SaaS architecture but in utility computing as well. Using Web services enables greater interprogram communications than any previous distributed computing technology [e.g., common object request broker architecture (CORBA), distributed component object model (DCOM)]. From the application integration point of view, an SaaS that uses Web Services for integration will be able to integrate with other enterprise applications that have implemented Web services as their means of interprogram communications. From a utility computing standpoint, Web services will enable the proliferation of *pluggable* services for use within applications, creating more flexible and adaptable applications able to respond to any changes in business requirements.

Today, Web services can provide a viable solution for EAI between enterprise applications, and in the future, an SaaS application will use Web services to integrate and consume application capabilities provided by other enterprise applications or offer select SaaS components as Web services to other applications.

6.2.2.2 Portal

The portal is a perfect technology for disseminating timely information, as well as providing a central location for key information services [4]. Customer collaboration, personalization, customization, and experience are what portal technology is all about. In a dynamic environment, such as an application service that provides immediate customer feedback, it is important to provide a means whereby customer clients can experience value and convenience when using the SaaS application. Considered strategic at this point, careful consideration of portal technology implementation must be on the SaaS provider's agenda. Here are some benefits of portal technology:

- *Personalization and customization*–Inherently, the use of portal technology calls upon the user to personalize and customize their work environments, thus empowering them and possibly allowing them to bypass support centers as they find online the services they need.
- *Experience*–Portal technology enhances customer experience by allowing customers to be more self-reliant. It also provides for greater ease of use when using the SaaS application. New functionalities and services can be introduced and accessed through the same interface the customer is already accustomed to. For instance, users can actively define presentation and content with minimal system administration involvement.
- *Collaboration*–Whereas real-time collaboration requires the use of meetings or conference calls, use of portal technology can promote the use of asynchronous collaboration, where participants contribute to the process at different times and from different locations. This can be most useful for the SaaS provider to communicate with his customer base or have customers communicate with each other.

In practical terms, portal technology can bring immediate benefit to customers of an SaaS application by allowing the application to integrate into a community portal, where users or administrators of the applications can log on, discover relevant services to which they are entitled, access the application, or view application and service usage and billing information.

6.2.2.3 Entitlements

Entitlement, the offering of similar services at different rates in different situations, can help promote use of the services and balance out the use of the application over a 24-hour period. An example of how entitlement is already operating today can be found in airline industry pricing policy. Airlines have different pricing not just for different classes of seats (coach, business, and first class) but also different ways of pricing for vacationers and business travelers. Pricing for vacationers and business travelers is done through advanced ticket sales–tickets are cheaper when bought two weeks or more before the actual flight and gradually increase in price as the time of the flight gets nearer, catering to the requirements of business travelers.

In an SaaS offering, different entitlement models, such as the airline industry entitlement model, can be implemented. For example, customers can be classified as gold, silver, and bronze customers. Having a profile in one of these classifications may entitle the user to different variations of incentives, enticing the user to use application functions more frequently. Like the airline industry which offers the use of their executive lounge for gold members, the SaaS provider may offer higher-priority queuing of customer-support-reported problems to customers with gold member profiles.

Another variation of an airline incentive still connected with pricing is offering lower pricing for red eye flights. The SaaS provider, with the use of an access control list, can set up incentives for using the service at night or during off-peak usage hours. By doing so, the provider can smooth out the use of his service, ultimately avoiding spiking demands (which can result in the SaaS provider's paying burst-rate charges to the infrastructure provider).

So, how does the SaaS provider implement user entitlement? Entitlement is all about authorization. It is about giving access to certain services or incentives based on user profiles. If the provider configures bronze users as users that can only access the system after noon, then it is up to an authorization engine to enforce the entitlement rules. An authorization engine with the support of perhaps the metering component makes up the entitlement component of the application service. An entitlement framework can be included in the software application services framework, which can be provided as a service. Such a framework is discussed in the Chapter 7.

6.2.2.4 Application Unbundling

In a traditional enterprise application setup, users of enterprise applications may only use 20% to 30% of functionality at any one time. This often creates the perception that customers are not getting enough value from their enterprise applications and results in small and medium-sized businesses' turning to SaaS applications. SaaS applications offer just the right amount of functionality at the right price. Customer clients are not forced to buy the unnecessary functionalities that come with traditional licensed enterprise applications.

Today's SaaS offerings cater to that segment of customers in the small- to medium-sized businesses that need only the most basic application functionalities. In the future, these same businesses will grow and require more features and functions from the application. While adding new features and functionalities and offering them at reasonable rates are in the SaaS's best interest, the dilemma will be that, at some point additional price increases brought about by additional functionalities will result in an SaaS application service that only caters to larger-sized businesses. The danger here is that the SaaS application might then become an application service that only caters to larger businesses and forgets its small- and medium-sized customers.

Application unbundling will help SaaS providers provide just the right application functionalities to their small, medium, and large enterprise customers. Application unbundling can eliminate the one-size-fits-all subscription product and create a more granular offering based on functionalities. A more competitive price structure can be realized by using application unbundling that can be customized to different organizational needs, providing value and differentiation from other applications offered as services.

Application unbundling can be implemented by using existing identity and access management software, as well as software that offers single sign-on capabilities. Careful planning and data gathering and analysis need to take place before implementing this attribute. The provider needs to make sure that features to be unbundled or bundled together are features that customers will pay for and that are perceived as giving the customers more value compared to traditional licensed applications or other applications offered as a service.

6.2.2.5 Dynamic Reconfiguration Awareness

With the advent of virtualization technologies within the hardware, operating systems have been adapted to accommodate such technologies. Dynamic reconfiguration of hardware to accommodate changes in server utilization is slowly becoming the norm. Ideally, such changes within the environment, such as CPU or memory reconfiguration, should not affect running applications but there may be instances where applications may need to adjust to changing resources underneath.

When a software application is first brought up, it may query the underlying hardware resources available for its use. The application configures itself to use the maximum available hardware that it sees. However, during low usage of the application, the hosting environment may decide to reallocate underutilized resources to another application while the first application is running, resulting in unexpected behavior. Applications such as these that configure themselves to use existing hardware when they start up need to be made aware of potential hardware reallocation policies set forth within the hosting environment. As virtualization and automated reconfiguration of hardware resources becomes more standard, the opportunity to tune and optimize applications to run better on virtualized resources will become a necessity.

6.2.2.6 Customer Care

From the provider's point of view, it is cheaper and more profitable to keep a customer loyal than it is to attract new customers to the business. From the customers' point of view, it is cheaper and more profitable to find the least expensive, best-fit solution, not necessarily to stay loyal. And in a dynamic market advertising itself on the Internet, cheaper and better services are just a mouse click away for the customer. Keeping the customer happy is now one more vital way the provider can add to its bottom line.

The customer care with which the product functionality is delivered is as important as the product functionality itself. A facility that provides a customer care facility that allows customers to report, view, search, and track reported problems is necessary in a dynamic utility service environment. Enabling customer self-service support and providing timely responses make the customers aware that their businesses and interests are valued and always given the highest priority.

Just like the portal attribute that can provide collaboration between users within the same organization, the customer care attribute can provide streamlined communications between the customer and the call center representatives. The customer care facility can also provide application training materials and specialized how-to guides that can help the customer learn to use less-used functions within the SaaS application.

Stage two attributes bring forth suggested considerations that an SaaS provider can undertake as the offering gains acceptance. Each of these attributes contributes to the overall design of the SaaS in a way that if implemented can truly differentiate the SaaS application from other applications.

6.2.3 Stage Three Attributes

Stage three attributes are attributes that the SaaS provider needs to consider between 12 and 18 months of his initial service offering. The following are considered stage three attributes:

- Metering;
- Billing;
- Licensing agreements;
- Packaging for autoprovisioning;
- Designing for unattended installations.

Only once these are implemented within the application service can it be considered a true utility application.

6.2.3.1 Metering

Implementing metering within an application requires modifications to the application to measure application functionality usage. One open standard that exists today, which can be implemented to meter application usage, is the Open Group's application response measurement (ARM). ARM is a standard for measuring the availability and performance of application transactions between client-to-server or server-to-server transactions.

ARM consists of a set of application programming interfaces that the application calls. Applications that use ARM define transactions that correspond to application operations initiated by a user that can call other transactions within or outside the application. The application calls ARM interfaces that start or stop application metering. Depending on vendor implementation to support the ARM standard, the ARM interfaces act as agents that feed the data into a repository, which can later be analyzed or fed into a billing system.

Figure 6.1 shows how applications can call ARM application interfaces, which feed a data-collection system where data can later be analyzed or fed to a billing service.

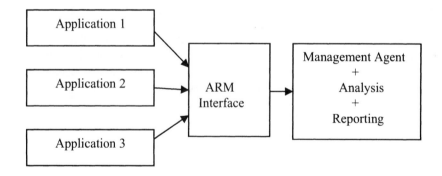

Figure 6.1 Application to ARM implementation system interaction.

Metering can monitor functional as well as transactional usage that can be used to analyze which functions are being used more than others. This data can then be utilized to offer special training sessions for customers to learn how to use these functions effectively and help them be more productive. This enables customer and company representatives to create a feedback loop to better understand customer wants and needs.

6.2.3.2 Billing

Whether done in-house or outsourced, billing is one aspect that needs to be considered when one is offering an application as a service. Billing is currently grouped with the stage three attributes because it usually works side-by-side with a metering solution. Whether customers will be billed on a monthly or a pay-as-you-go basis, several billing tasks exist that can prove challenging for the SaaS provider. Some of these challenges include, but are not limited to, rating usage, creating invoices, charging credit cards, importing metering data, and creating one-time price promotions. Billing will be discussed in more detail in Chapter 7.

Both metering and billing attributes may be the most complicated attributes to implement because these attributes touch on both the technical side of adding hooks into the application and the business side where the SaaS provider needs to decide what type of usage to meter and bill for: for instance, is it per transaction or per function used? This type of criteria can only be decided by gathering prior usage data and customer feedback. To gather usage data, metering must be implemented within the SaaS.

6.2.3.3 License Agreements

According to an IDC[4] report, customers are showing discontent with current software licensing practices. A survey by IDC showed that less than 30% of software customers believe that vendors' licensing practices are fair and that almost 70% of those surveyed believed that future licensing changes will be beneficial to them [5]. SaaS providers are encouraged to ask their middleware vendors about alternative licensing options for variable use of the middleware. As this may remain a grey area for years to come, middleware vendors will need to be made aware that traditional licensing offerings need to change to meet today's more on-demand environment.

6.2.3.4 Packaging for Autoprovisioning

Autoprovisioning is a function provided by the managed hosting provider. The autoprovisioning functionality transcends all layers of the infrastructure; that is to say, it transcends hardware, operating system, middleware, and applications. The task for the hosting provider is to autoprovision these layers to create a *server group*, a collection of resources packaged in such a way that when it is provisioned, it forms either a complete working system or a system designed to add resources to an existing system. In essence, different packages, mixed and matched, can create different combinations of server groups.

During the initial hosting setup for the SaaS, a server group is configured for the SaaS to run on. The server group is configured for the baseline (minimum)

---

[4] International Data Corporation, www.idc.com.

requirements of the application service for its initial setup on the hosting center. The baseline requirements are formulated by the utility provider with the help of performance information characteristics of the SaaS provided by the SaaS owner. Once the server group is configured, it is deployed, resulting in a complete and running SaaS application. At this point, the SaaS can begin normal operations. From this point on, it will be up to the hosting provider to meet the SaaS requirements for resources when the need arises.

Depending on what the application service may need and how the servers are set up to provide for these needs, several things can happen during provisioning of new resources. For example, some servers are configured such that a CPU can be added without having to install another instance of the operating system. Another example is that the hosting provider might configure a second server group containing a Web server to pass traffic to the SaaS if the SaaS needs an additional Web server to be able to handle more Web traffic. These variations in configuration setup need to be planned upfront to make it transparent to the SaaS once all anticipated configuration requirements for the SaaS are processed into the hosting provider's autoprovisioning system.

By using a hosting provider that offers dynamic provisioning and deprovisioning capabilities for the application, the SaaS provider can create an infrastructure environment that is more aligned with its business requirements. Take, for example, an SaaS application that serves the retail industry and is subject to rapid variable and seasonal resource requirements. The ability to autoprovision resources would be of great benefit to the SaaS provider's business as the market fluctuated, especially if the hosting provider could handle changes in demand as quickly (e.g., in a matter of hours).

Another example of an SaaS that will need dynamic configuration capabilities is a Web-conferencing service. A Web-conferencing service that caters to on-demand meetings or online conferencing requires resources to be provisioned and deprovisioned as meetings or conferences start and end, respectively. Users and resources of these conferences need to be added dynamically on a temporary basis. A resource may be as simple as setting up a new URL for customers to access, or it may be as complicated as setting up resources like file systems that are needed for temporary working directories of files and other sharable artifacts during meetings.

SaaS applications need to be designed such that they allow themselves to be autoprovisioned according to anticipated variations in workload. In addition the SaaS provider needs to work with a hosting provider that offers dynamic provisioning capabilities. Together the SaaS and hosting provider will need to formulate server groups that can be configured automatically when the demand arises.

6.2.3.5 Designing for Unattended Installation

Depending on the managed hosting environment that the SaaS will be deployed in, both packaging for autoprovisioning and designing for unattended installation may require the collaboration of the managed hosting provider and the SaaS provider. Managed hosting providers that offer automated provisioning of applications will need a way to plug the SaaS application into their existing provisioning systems. This will require the SaaS application be as automated in its configuration process as possible.

While unattended installation is built into the design of many licensed applications, the SaaS application will be designed so that different tiers can be installed and configured separately, as well as automatically. Server groups, as was mentioned in Section 6.2.3.4, will need a way to configure the application, or parts of the application, when autoprovisioning of additional resources is needed. And scripts used to install the application will need to be plugged into the automated provisioning system of the hosting provider.

Another consideration for unattended installation is the postinstallation configuration. Postinstallation activities may consist of creating database schemas and populating the tables, configuring user profiles, or tailoring for specific application parameters. Postinstallation configuration should be designed to configure the SaaS application with as little manual postconfiguration intervention as possible.

In a utility managed hosting environment, hardware resources can be provisioned and deprovisioned as needed. As such, automated deinstallation of applications or application components may also be required to save existing configurations or customer profiles for later reuse.

6.2.4 Other Attributes

Other attributes that are geared toward initiatives in promoting the service exist. Most, if not all, of them are already implemented by vendors who provide software as services and are successful at it. The following are some of these attributes:

- *Trial subscriptions*–Salesforce.com, Oracle, and Journyx.com are examples of companies that offer free trial subscriptions of some of their offerings. These companies believe that by letting customers learn the value of the services they provide, customers will be more inclined to sign up for the services.
- *Ordering (via sales force, via Web site)*–The Internet has allowed consumers to take control of processes through self-service mechanisms. Consumers and companies can order the services if self-service mechanisms are put in place. Successful vendors who are offering software as services today use this technique as a low-cost, low-maintenance marketing channel.

- *Offer catalog (UDDI, Web applications)*–In the future when enterprise applications become componentized, a catalog where consumers can discover and subscribe to services will become important. It will be more than just a UDDI catalog because it will be a directory of business services and functionalities as well.

In a nutshell, all the attributes just discussed make up the architecture of a software utility application. From an SaaS provider's point of view, the attributes can be implemented in a staged fashion. For each stage of implementation, a time frame is associated with the attributes as a suggestion as to when to start implementing the attributes depending on the SaaS provider's business objectives.

6.3 COST VERSUS VALUE

Figure 6.2 shows that the addition of attributes to increase the usability and technical features of the SaaS application incurs exponentially increasing cost. As the usability or performance of the SaaS application increases, the perceived value to the customer also increases. There is a point, however, where the value to the customer reaches a threshold and plateaus (maximum value).

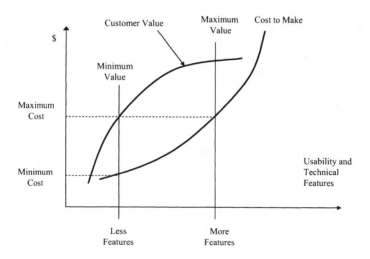

Figure 6.2 Relationship between the cost to make a product and the perceived customer value of the product.

Customers will have a price point that they will not go beyond, even if the product offers features that cost the provider money to include as part of the product. The rule of thumb is that strategic attributes become more important as the customer base using the SaaS application becomes larger. With each attribute providing value to the operation or the usability of the SaaS application, the provider is advised to carefully balance out the cost of the attribute against the projected revenue of the business. No matter how good the usability is or how excellent the performance is, customers will only pay so much for an application's use.

6.4 SUMMARY

From an application architect's point of view, SaaS architecture is vastly different from the architecture of a traditional licensed application. While an instance of a traditional licensed application is more likely to provide business logic to one enterprise customer, SaaS applications provide similar business logic to multiple enterprise customers, using a single instance of the application. Driven by a business model that requires them to use economies of scale to their advantage, SaaS providers design their applications to be multitenanted at the same time, assuring their clients that their data will be separated and protected from other companies sharing the SaaS application.

As SaaS providers build their applications with the goal of transforming them into a utility applications by adding one attribute at a time, the cost of adding these attributes will start to add up. Fortunately for the SaaS provider, there are ways to share the cost of some of these attributes. Some attributes, like billing and metering, can be bought as a service from other providers making the SaaS provider a consumer of other SaaS applications. The next chapter introduces the concept of an SaaS application framework and explores how an SaaS application can plug into an application services framework for features such as single sign-on, billing, and metering.

References

[1] Bennett, K., et al., "Service-Based Software: The Future for Flexible Software, Software Engineering Conference," 2000. APSEC 2000. *Proceedings. Seventh Asia-Pacific*, December 5-8, 2000, pp. 214–221.

[2] Correira, J., R. Fulton, and F. Biscotti, "Software as a Service Will Be Business Model of Choice in 2008," Gartner Research Brief, October 19, 2004.

[3] Fowler, M., *Patterns of Enterprise Application Architecture*, Boston, MA, Addison Wesley, 2003.

[4] Davydov, M., *Corporate Portals and e-Business Integration*, New York, NY, McGraw-Hill Professional, 2001.

[5] Konary, A., *Software Pricing and Licensing: Inside the Perfect Storm*, Framingham, MA, IDC, March 2004.

Chapter 7

Software Application Services Framework

In the previous chapter, attributes were grouped in terms of their immediate and strategic importance. These same attributes can be further grouped by their technical and operational nature to add, respectively, to application functionality and ease of use. Because the implementation of various attributes can require large amounts of development time, effort, and money, the plan to include these attributes within the SaaS application is best done at the start of the cycle during planning phases, so that their introduction is most profitably staged. When examining the characteristics of the attributes, it becomes apparent that some can only be implemented by modifying the application, while others can be implemented by sourcing functionalities from other service providers.

Indeed, SaaS applications do not have to be designed as stand-alone applications. They can be designed to use outsourced services for functionality that otherwise would have been costly to develop in-house. Two primary examples of functionalities that an SaaS application can outsource as services are billing and metering. From a conceptual point of view, functionalities such as these can be provided within a framework of common services. In this chapter, we will refer to the provision of functionalities in this manner as the software application services framework (sasf).

Before we begin our discussion of the software application services framework, it might be helpful to discuss the concept of a framework in general. For the purposes of this discussion, a *framework* is an all-encompassing specification for the collective set of products, components, and procedures necessary to create and deploy an enterprisewide technology solution [1]. A framework is also a set of cooperating classes that make up reusable design for a specific class of software [2]. In both definitions, the recurring theme is this–it is a collective set of reusable objects, products, components, or widgets that, when used, contribute to the totality and enhancement of a product. Hence, a software application services framework is a set of services for applications that are grouped together and, when used, contribute to the totality and enhancement of the SaaS they service. Since they are SaaS related, these services communicate through well-known industry-standard interfaces and use Web services as their means of communications.

7.1 COMMON ENABLERS

The service applications grouped together to make up the sasf are termed *common enablers*. Each of the common enablers within the sasf contributes to the wholeness of the SaaS application. By definition, the common enablers are services that the SaaS application can utilize for business or strategic functionalities, allowing the SaaS application provider the ability to concentrate more on the core business offerings.

Of the common enablers most often grouped into an sasf, services for billing and metering usually rank highest. Closely behind them come the common enablers of identity management, single sign-on, and application provisioning. Each of these common enablers adds value to the overall architecture of an SaaS application and will now be discussed more in depth.

7.1.1 Metering

While metering of an application is often synonymous with billing for application usage, there are other reasons to meter SaaS applications. One use of metering is for data mining. Depending on what metered data is collected, varying types of data can be gathered and analyzed to create profiles for the use of the different parts of the application. Profiled data can give the SaaS provider insights into a customer's application usage, and this insight can then be used to improve the quality of service of the application.

Another use for metering is application monitoring. By monitoring the application, the SaaS provider can be assured that the application is providing the right level of service to its customers. Performance problems, such as application bottlenecks or lack of system resources, can be identified early so that preventative measures can be taken. Utilization and transactional data can be collected and analyzed in real time which can show if the application is functioning at optimum or suboptimum levels. Table 7.1 compares the different uses of metering and their different characteristics.

Table 7.1 Differences Between Data Collection Usages

	Monitoring	Data Mining	Metering for Billing
Purpose	Observing or comparing against set thresholds. Used for SLA, debugging and maintenance.	Observing application usage. Used in business analysis that can result in competitive advantage.	Keeping track or count usage of functions or features.

Table 7.1 Differences Between Data Collection Usages (Continued)

	Monitoring	*Data Mining*	*Metering for Billing*
Method of interpreting data	Data may be averaged out for trending purposes. One time measurement to compare to certain thresholds. Trace data that allows interpretation of data flow.	Collect as much customer data points as possible. Business analytic algorithms used against data to produce competitive pricing analysis, demand curves, sales forecasts, and market segmentations as examples. Collected data may come from different sources and be combined to produce business analysis.	Rating schemes applied against metered data that will result in customer billable usage. Method of interpreting is not a function of metering component; it is usually performed by a different component, such as a billing engine.
Frequency of collecting data	Collection of data may be in set intervals (e.g., every 3 or 5 minutes). Or collection may depend on hooks placed along set code path. In this case, collection of data is done every time that code path is taken.	The more data collected, the better. So, the more frequently it is collected, the better.	Decide metrics to charge or bill customer every time a particular functionality or feature is used. Collection of data depends on user use of functionality and feature.
Real-time requirements	High: Data used is collected and compared to threshold that can sound an alarm.	Medium to low: Data collected may be needed to react to fast-moving market conditions, or data may be needed to do historical analysis or market segmentation.	Low: Data is not used until next billing cycle– every 2 weeks or every month.
Storage length	Short: Data collected, used and discarded when purpose of collection is done.	Very long: Requires 10 or even 20 years for historical purposes.	Medium: Once metered data is used for billing purposes, data may remain only as needed, sometimes for a year or less.
Usage	Data collected tied to a shared resource.	Data will apply to a user account, a group of users, or a market segment.	Metered data is tied to a user account.

Metering can be implemented by the SaaS provider independently, or it can be subscribed to from a metering provider. In the subscribed form of metering, the SaaS provider still needs to modify his application to add metering hooks specified by the metering application. When data is collected, it is stored in a database maintained by the metering provider. The service may also include data aggregation. This data is then used for billing, monitoring, or data mining. Figure

7.1 shows the SaaS application using a metering service provided by a service provider within a utility hosting center using the service for different purposes.

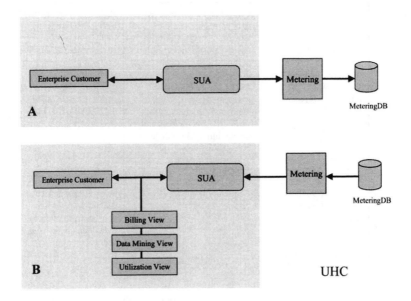

Figure 7.1 Metering can be used for billing purposes, data mining, and resource-utilization control.

The true value of metering comes in the form of providing exact metrics to measure return on investment accurately for an enterprise application. From an enterprise company's point of view, knowing exactly how it uses and pays for the application makes comparing similar services to the ones it already has easier.

7.1.2 Billing

The simplest strategy for billing in a shared application environment is to charge each subscriber a set monthly fee. This is simple and easy to administer. In most cases, the basis of the monthly fee is derived through some empirical means multiplied by some coefficient factor to make sure the SaaS provider profits from the whole operation.

While this billing strategy works in the short term, it leaves a lot to be desired for the long term. For instance, some subscribers may use more resources than others, even though they pay the same monthly rate. This can lead some subscribers to inadvertently abuse the application to the detriment of other subscribers.

There are different types of billing models that the SaaS provider can choose from. Each has its advantages and disadvantages. The following are the types of billing models.

Per-user billing model—This model charges a user on a monthly basis. The monthly fee entitles the user to unlimited use of the SaaS application. Monthly charges may vary, depending on the services and functionalities subscribed to by the user.

Advantages:
- From a user's perspective, the bill is easy to understand.
- From an owner's perspective, billing is straightforward.

Disadvantage:
- Entitlement to use the application is not based on usage of the application or resources, which can lead to some users' using more resources than most average users.

A monthly billing model may consist of a monthly base charge to access minimum set functionalities and further monthly fees for additional functionalities subscribed to.

Concurrent user billing model—This model charges a group of entitled users to access the SaaS application. An example of this would be an on-demand Web-conferencing service, where concurrent users use resources of an Internet-based system simultaneously. The price may be based on number of users and scaled up as more users access the application. This offers the use of a resource in a more controlled fashion. Pricing may also be based on a more granular level–as in pricing the use of the application by time (4 hours of use).

Advantages:
- It is easy to bill.
- It is easy for customer to understand.
- It provides a better incentive for use by users (group discounts).

Disadvantage:
- More complex user administration algorithms are required to administer different types of entitlements to diverse groups of users.

The concurrent-user billing model gives rise to a type of billing structure where functionalities of the SaaS application are grouped into functionalities that large, medium, or small companies will use. For example, a large company may require 35 functionalities from the application, while a small company may only need 10. The SaaS provider can offer different application functionalities grouped according to the size of the business needing to use such functionalities and bill accordingly.

Usage billing–An entitled user is only charged for what he or she uses. Usage pricing that is based on a user rate provides both entitled users and SaaS providers with a win-win situation.

Advantages:
- Entitled users are only charged for what they use.
- Measuring data enables data mining capabilities, prevention of abuse, and the monitoring of usage for performance metrics.

Disadvantages:
- It requires complex metering capabilities within the application.
- It discourages more use of the application.

Hybrid billing model–This combines per-user, concurrent-user, and usage billing models. Software utility application services may use different models to encourage use of the service and at the same time discourage abuse.

Advantages:
- It allows greater pricing flexibility.
- It may encourage more use of the application.
- It gives entitled users more control of pricing-structure choices.

Disadvantages:
- It can be complicated to administer.
- It may discourage use of application due to cost variability.

Billing for application or service usage is the recommended way of operating a software as a service application. This, together with the metering attribute, enables the application owner to bill accordingly. Even if the application owner does not choose to bill for application usage, it is still beneficial to use a billing service because it offers more specialized expertise in the billing arena than the application owner has in-house (i.e., outsources noncore competencies).

Billing is and will be a big issue for present and future SaaS providers, as it requires knowledge of and experience in billing practices that cannot be learned overnight. Today billing-solution providers like Portal Infranet, Boardtown Corporation Platypus Billing System, and TeleKnowledge Group, Ltd., have responded to the need of application service providers for the service. For SaaS to be complete, billing services will have to be one of its core components.

7.1.3 Application Provisioning and Management Services

Within the software application services framework is a provisioning component responsible for the provisioning of users and their corresponding application resources. In an SaaS environment, an application availing itself of the application provisioning services provided by the sasf turns the responsibility of user and application provisioning over to the framework. By adhering to well-defined standards, the application can allow any provisioning service to interface with it.

In late 2001, the Organization for the Advancement of Structured Information Standards (OASIS) Provisioning Services Technical Committee (PSTC) was formed to define an XML-based framework for exchanging user, resource, and service provisioning information. Since then, several activities, including the release of a committee draft of Version 1.0 of the standard, have taken place with regard to the creation of the provisioning standard. This standard is now known as the service provisioning markup language (SPML) and can be used as the standard for interfacing an application to the sasf.

The PSTC defines provisioning as "the automation of all the steps required to manage (set up, amend, and revoke) user or system access entitlements or data relative to electronically published services." The model adopted by the standard is one of a client passing control information to a server that acts on the provisioning request. Based on Web services invocation, the client issues a service request call targeting a service point, which then acts on the request and sends back a response to the client.

In our case, the SaaS application is the eventual recipient of the service request, and the sasf acts as the client. The advantage to having this kind of setup is that the SaaS provider can delegate user and application provisioning to an administrative person representing the organization subscribing to the SaaS. The application provisioning service will allow the SaaS provider to delegate this authority to different administrative personnel from different organizations with the guarantee that these administrative personnel will only be allowed to manage users within their own organizations.

The sasf provides two kinds of provisioning services:

- *User provisioning*–User provisioning features operations like add, delete, and modify user. These are typical application provisioning functions whose control will be given over to the application framework. The application framework will be responsible for giving hierarchical-type access to authorized system administrators for a given application.
- *Application provisioning*–Application provisioning is the component of an application that provisions user resources after a user is added. For example, a user might need temporary space while working on a Web form. Provisioning this resource would be part of the application provisioning.

Although the standards proposed by the PSTC provide for a standard interface between the framework and the application itself, it leaves open what features the framework can actually have in terms of customer end-usage scenarios. From the enterprise point of view, the user provisioning component should be able to do the following:

- Delegate a hierarchy of user administrators to administer the application.
- Subscribe an organization to use the application.
- Create secure administration domains so that no unauthorized personnel can access other organizational domains they should not have access to.
- Store password and profile information for users.
- Grant and restrict subscribers to their respective entitlements.
- Enforce user password policies.
- Authenticate and authorize subscribers on a single sign-on basis.
- Grant or restrict access to subscribers depending on time of day, priority, or business function.
- Grant or restrict access to different modules of the application.
- Log information for user administration needs.

Providing an application provisioning and management system will not only alleviate user and application administrative responsibilities of the SaaS provider, but it will also manage multiple SaaS applications for the SaaS customer.

7.1.4 Service Level Agreement Services

SaaS applications will no doubt raise enterprise dependence on the Internet to higher levels. By using SaaS applications, enterprise organizations are committing themselves to the quality-of-service guarantee, including availability, reliability, and response time, that come with outsourced application services provided over the Internet. Today, an SaaS provider who has SLAs with its client customers, in turn, may also have their own SLAs with other providers. This has resulted in SLAs becoming more complex and wider in scope.

An SLA is a unique, single-service agreement between a client and a service provider. Mostly, it is implemented as a manual procedure that would require customization unique to both party's requirements. Now, let's assume that an SaaS provider wants to provide SLAs for different clients. The provider will need to create SLA templates that can be customizable, create a method that will monitor many SLAs, and generate violation report for the subscribers. To service and manage all his clients' needs, the SaaS provider will have to create a complex system that has well-defined service-level definition, automatic processing of service-level thresholds, and an interoperable report mechanism.

In the conceptual view of our sasf, we offer a SLA service as a Web service that any application or service can subscribe to for delegation of SLA processing.

Figure 7.2 shows an SaaS application using an SLA service within the sasf. Here, the service level agreement service (SLAS) is advertised for a Web service, and the SLA service provider is a guarantor for the software service level agreement.

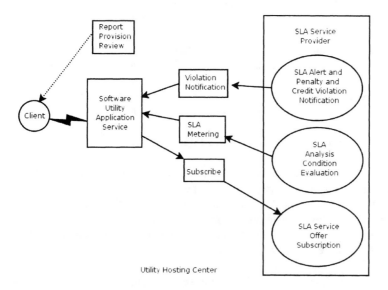

Figure 7.2 An SLA service provider can provide customized SLA service to subscribers of a software utility application.

The SLA service is made up of components, such as the analysis and condition evaluation and the measurement and management components. The measurement service receives data from different monitoring agents that monitor the SaaS performance, availability, and other metrics agreed to by the SaaS provider and the client. The analysis and condition evaluation service evaluates the data received from the measuring service and analyzes it according to agreed-on terms in the SLA. And last, but not least, the management component implements the alert, penalty, and credit violation management of the SLA.

7.1.4.1 Related standard

The Web Service Level Agreement project (WSLA, www.research.ibm.com/wsla) provides a framework for specifying and monitoring SLAs for Web services. WSLA is a critical component in a Web service environment where the customers rely on services that may be subscribed to dynamically and on demand (customers order services over the Web without a customized SLA between customers and providers as needed). The WSLA framework consists of a flexible and extensible language based on XML schema and a run-time architecture comprising several SLA monitoring services. WSLA defines various types of SLAs, especially SLA parameters and how they are measured, and relates them to managed resource instrumentations. WSLA also defines services to monitor Web services to enforce the agreements within the SLA. In addition, WSLA is a distributed monitoring framework that can be deployed in a single site or across multiple sites. This translates an SLA into configuration information for the individual service provider components and third-party services to perform the measurement and supervision activities. Some examples of SLA monitoring services using IBM Emerging Technology Toolkit (ETTK, www.alphaworks.ibm.com/tech/ettk) are user profile, metering, and accounting, contract, and notification services.

7.1.5 Identity and Access Management / Single Sign-On

An identity, in the context of computer systems, is an identifier presented to computer systems for the purpose of giving a person access according to his or her access rights to the system. A person can have several different identities for different systems or even different identities for the same system [3]. Several business drivers exist for implementing identity management within an SaaS environment. They are as follows:

- *Security*–Centralizes authority, preventing unauthorized access to information and services a business does not want anyone to have access to.
- *Efficiency*–Lowers cost, improves productivity, improves business and value chain efficiency, improves customer service, and accelerates time to market. Improves quality of service for customers and enables customer satisfaction.
- *Consistent treatment to the individual*–Gives a consistent look and feel to everyone accessing resources.
- *Conformance to regulation*–Can enable an organization to meet regulatory requirement. An example is the U.S. Health Information Portability and Accountability Act (HIPAA), which requires certain authorized individuals to have access to patient records, while maintaining strict constraints on confidentiality.

Access management is the ability to manage security and access to applications based on user roles or business rules. Having one central repository where these roles and rules are kept, and where changes are made to access rights for potentially numerous services, can alleviate complexity of managing employees, partners, and suppliers in a dynamic environment. Imagine having to create 100 users of certain roles and access for several different applications, each application of which has its own way of granting access to these users, only to delete them the next day because they were only temporary users. Compare this to having one place to create the roles, which are then propagated through the access management application. The following are business drivers for access management:

- Prevention of unauthorized access by using a single security-policy server to enforce security across multiple file types, application providers, devices, and protocols;
- Web single sign-on for maintaining password and user integrity;
- Robust auditing and information-gathering tools for discovering problems or potential problems.

Sometimes an application may offer different services and access to it may require subscribers to log in more than once. Single sign-on capability alleviates multiple sign-on requirements. Employing access and identity management allows the implementation of a single sign-on solution within the sasf.

When the use of software utility applications from external, or even internal, utility providers become widespread, companies will start to ask for single sign-on access for all its multiple utility applications that its users have access to. Using the identity and access management feature of an sasf gives them this ability. The following are the benefits to using an identity and access management application:

- It provides a unified authentication and authorization to secure a single enterprise or a federated environment.
- It lowers application development, deployment, and management costs by delivering unified identity and security management.
- Central management of user accounts makes it easy to terminate (clean up) user access to all systems that the user is registered to.
- It dramatically improves customer ease of use and turn around time for fulfillment.
- Audit management in a central location makes it easier for auditors to audit security and access protocols and processes. An audit trail can be established.
- It distributes workload to enterprise customer staff by offering hierarchical access to manage their own users.
- It makes service enablement based on entitlements easier. Entitlement is discussed as an attribute of an SUA in earlier sections.

Specific vertical industry benefits include the following:

- *Health regulation compliance (HIPAA compliance)*—Limiting access to individual health care information to a minimum. Access is granted only to perform job functions that are related to treatment, payment, and other necessary operations.

- *Retail*–Handling peak seasons like Christmas, when they do their largest short-term hiring. Access to systems by temporary or seasonal workers can be managed with ease. Adding and deleting can be done in one central location. There are no more missed accounts when cleaning up after the seasonal need.
- *Education*–Managing students, teachers, and school district staff who may need access to different resources within the educational IT infrastructure.

The entitlement attribute discussed in the previous chapter plays a big role in the need for security features, such as identity and access management and single sign-on. While most enterprise applications already have their own methods of protecting access to the application, the majority of them may not offer a comprehensive set of security and access management features suitable for offering the service within an SaaS environment. Implementing such security features in the application is not trivial and is also costly. But when used in a shared environment, like a software application services framework, a product that offers identity and access management and single sign-on capabilities can be used and shared by several SaaS applications, spreading a cost that would have otherwise been shouldered by an individual SaaS provider.

7.1.6 Other Services of the Software Application Services Framework

While not ranked as high as previously mentioned enablers, other enablers add value by offering a common service that SaaS can take advantage of. Here are some of them:

- *Directory services*–Directory services may be offered as a separate service for SaaSs that wish to keep directory-type data of users and user profiles. Instead of having to maintain their own directory servers, SaaS applications can avail themselves of directory services offered by the directory services provider.
- *Mail*–Providing a mail service to the SaaS application to use for e-mail notifications about the application is essential to better quality of service.
- *User/enterprise qualification*—Credit check, valid legal entity checking, and qualification are services within an sasf that can be beneficial to an SaaS application. With self-service enrollments that encourage users and enterprises to serve themselves, automated qualification checks provided as a service can eliminate delays in granting users and enterprises access to services as quickly as possible. Business relationships should still be established between consumers and providers of services, but eliminating any manual process with the right automated workflow will not only speed time to market, but it will also save on cost by eliminating inefficiencies along the way.

Next we discuss how an sasf becomes more than just a concept and turns into reality.

7.2 FROM CONCEPTUAL VIEW TO REALITY

Several things need to come together for the conceptual software application services framework to become a reality. First, present and future SaaS providers need to know that companies like IBM,[1] Jamcracker,[2] Grand Central Communications,[3] USinternetworking,[4] and OpSource[5] offer SaaS enablement services and are forming SaaS ecosystems that bring together providers in one environment where organizations can buy application software services for salesforce automation, human resource management, customer relationship management, and much more. These companies not only enable traditional software applications to become SaaS applications, they help independent software vendors extend their markets, eventually increasing revenues.

Second, a framework such as the sasf needs to be created with an established set of standard interfaces so that SaaS applications will be able to use the services offered within the framework with ease. Enterprise applications plugging into the framework will be able to add these interfaces into their applications easily using well-known standard specifications.[6] For more Web services standards used in utility computing environments, please refer to Chapter 2. By enabling applications to interface with the framework through well-known standards, these applications are not locked into one vendor-specific framework.

Third, enterprise application programmers, developers, architects, and development managers need to have the buy-in to use the sasf. The not-invented-here (NIH–i.e., we did not invent it here, so we are not using it) syndrome, where developing in-house solutions is more favored than buying software applications developed elsewhere, needs to be overcome. Adding fuel to the NIH syndrome is the idea that using the sasf is akin to software reuse. In the early years of software application development, software reuse had one big obstacle to overcome: the notion that software reuse was detrimental to the creative-thinking process. Today, however, software reuse has less push back due to the growing complexities and manageability of software applications. The biggest issue in getting buy-in that needs to be addressed is cultural. By using services offered within the sasf, software applications will be giving up some control over how these services are managed and administered. The issues of control, the NIH syndrome, and

---

[1] www.ibm.com.
[2] www.jamcracker.com.
[3] www.grandcentral.com.
[4] www.usi.net.
[5] www.opsource.net.
[6] Made available through standards organizations like OASIS.

software reuse push back will all need to be hashed out before there can be buy-in for the sasf.

Finally, providing the framework for SaaS applications will need to be offered as a type of service itself. The framework provider will be responsible for creating a secure environment where SaaS providers can establish a presence. This framework will need to run in a utility data center where hardware resources are available on demand to meet the dynamically changing business needs of clients. Figure 7.3 shows the conceptual view of a software application services framework with the most common services components. The boxes in the middle of the figure represent SaaS applications that can be enterprise applications, componentized business functionalities enabled as Web services, SaaS applications with unbundled functionalities, and even plain old hosted applications.

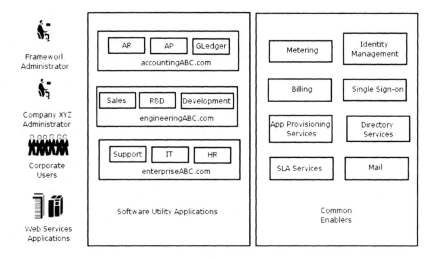

Figure 7.3 A conceptual software utility application framework used by software utility application services from different domains.

The left of Figure 7.3 shows the type of user access the framework allows—framework administrator, company XYZ administrator, corporate users, and Web services. Security for Web services is handled by a Web Services gateway, while security for users is handled by access and identity management components. A catalog of services is maintained within the framework for easy search and registration for users and company alike.

7.2.1 How Does sasf Fit into a Utility Infrastructure?

From a data center point of view, the sasf is a software application that will need servers, storage, and other resources to run on. The sasf provider will manage, maintain, and create SLAs for other service providers that will use some of the sasf-provided services. The sasf will incorporate Web services management capabilities, which will form the basis for managing Web services within the framework. Figure 7.4 shows how the sasf fits within a utility data center.

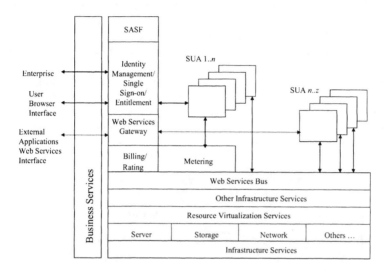

Figure 7.4 How the sasf fits into the utility environment.

In Figure 7.4 several SaaS (or SUA) applications use services offered by the sasf, such as metering, billing, and identity management. The figure also shows another group of SaaS applications offering Web services to other applications using the Web services gateway, which provides protection from malicious Internet attacks in the form of denial of service and unauthorized access. The sasf functions like any other software application. It uses all layers of the utility computing environment starting with the infrastructure services.

7.3 BUSINESS BENEFITS OF HAVING AN sasf

The research firm IDC estimates that spending on SaaS will reach $10.7 billion in 2009 [4]. As demand for applications offered as services grows and demand for licensed applications falters, ISVs that sell traditional licensed software will be forced to evolve their business models to include providing their applications as services. As this trend continues, customers will become more accustomed to using applications provided over the Internet, and inevitably they will demand features such as single sign-on and unified billing statements for all their applications. To be able to satisfy customers' requirements and keep them loyal,

SaaS providers will need to provide these features through an application framework.

Figure 7.5 shows the cost to develop an SaaS application with and without using the sasf. The solid lines represent the old cost to develop the SaaS and customer value (otherwise known as the customer's willingness to pay for more features included within the SaaS). The solid line that represents the old cost to develop the SaaS shows the increasing development cost as more features and enhancements are added to the SaaS. As the cost of development increases, the price point at which the SaaS is offered also increases as shown by the solid line that represents the customer's value. As the figure shows, while adding more features to the SaaS affects the customer's value for performance in a positive way, customer's value has its limits. How then can future customer requirements be implemented while keeping development cost down, thus maintaining an offering price point that customers are still willing to pay for?

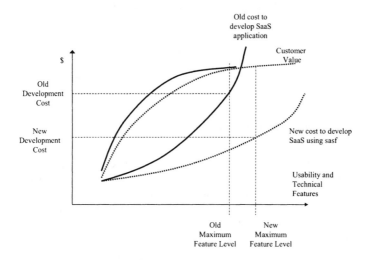

Figure 7.5 The use of the sasf increases the ability to add additional features to the SaaS without increasing development costs.

The curved dotted line in Figure 7.5 represents the new cost to develop the SaaS using the sasf. The figure shows that using the sasf to implement features such as metering, billing, single sign-on, and application provisioning reduces the cost of developing the SaaS application. With the development cost reduced, we can maintain the price point at which customers are willing to pay while enabling the addition of more features.

Section 7.2 discussed several things that need to happen before the sasf becomes a reality. To that list we add one more item—the SaaS provider needs to be willing to use application framework features as services as provided by an application framework provider. In this manner, development cost to add new SaaS features for customers is reduced in the same way as SaaS customers reduce their cost by subscribing to SaaS applications.

7.4 APPLICATION MANAGEMENT CASE STUDY

Enterprise application management ranks high in the wants and needs of private enterprises. In many of today's enterprise environments, users will typically have a user login and password for each system they have been granted access to. A typical user in today's enterprise will have a minimum of three accounts to access three separate systems within the enterprise. Separate systems usually mean that there are separate administrators that manage the system as well as different processes that need to be followed in a stepwise fashion for access to be granted. For a new user to get access to those systems means going through several people, as well as processes, before getting access to three separate systems. Figure 7.6 shows a typical workflow when a new user needs to enroll in different systems before he or she can start doing any productive work.

The figure shows a new user sending in a request to his manager for access to several systems within the company. The manager sends e-mail to four separate administrators to give his employee access. Once in the system, the administrators send an e-mail confirmation back stating the user has been added to the system. Only then will the user be able to access those systems. In this case, several steps were needed to process the request to get access to the systems.

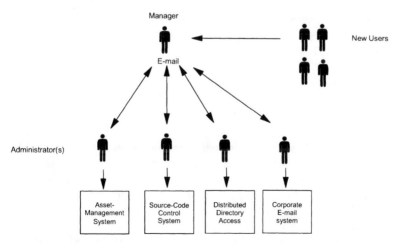

Figure 7.6 A typical workflow when a new user needs to enroll in different systems before he or she can start doing any productive work.

With the use of an application management framework, the process of granting access to the new users can be streamlined and automated. An example is the delegation of authority to grant access to a single point of contact, in this case, the manager of the employee. In addition, the application management framework can grant access to disparate systems from a single point of entry, eliminating the need to have multiple user entries and passwords for each system. With single point of access, users are authenticated and granted access from a single system that can grant them access according to roles, groups, or entitlements.

Figure 7.7 shows how automated application provisioning and single sign-on can replace administrators for the different systems. Workflow is also streamlined by giving the managers authority to grant access to different systems. In this simple case study, application management can be achieved with the use of an application management framework.

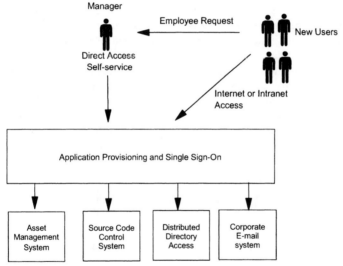

Figure 7.7 Automated application provisioning and single sign-on can replace administrators for the different systems.

Just like the application management framework that can be useful to streamline workflow and manage employee accounts through a single sign-on portal, the software application services framework can be used to manage disparate software application services that are used by the enterprise organization. By using an sasf, different SaaS applications can be accessed through the sasf, providing similar benefits as the application management framework. Figure 7.8 shows a different view of the framework. Instead of managing systems developed in-house, the framework is now used to gain access through a single point of access for SaaS applications from different SaaS providers.

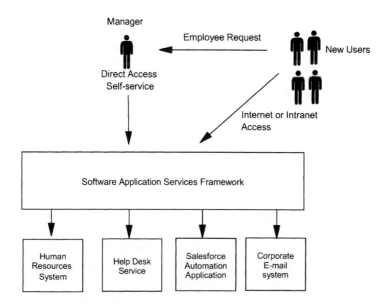

Figure 7.8 A sasf used as a portal to access several SaaS applications from different service providers.

As was mentioned earlier, companies like IBM, Jamcracker, and OpSource are building ecosystems that make available applications provided as a service. It will not be long before these same companies begin to provide a software application services framework that can be used to access services from the ecosystem from a single access point.[7]

7.5 SUMMARY

The enterprise software application industry is in the midst of an evolution–software is moving from being sold as a licensed application to being offered as a service. Current and future SaaS providers are taking careful steps to develop their software applications to meet the needs of their customers. As SaaS applications gain market share in the enterprise application space, SaaS providers are aware that adding more features to their SaaS applications may mean adjusting the price point at which the SaaS application is currently offered.

To curtail development expense, SaaS providers will need to find ways to add features like single sign-on, billing, metering, and automated SLA monitoring functionalities, and to do so without incurring large development costs. An

---

[7] As of this writing, Jamcracker already provides such services through their Jamcracker Service Delivery Network. See www.jamcracker.com.

application services framework offered as a service is one such solution. Today companies like IBM, Jamcracker, and OpSource are establishing SaaS ecosystems where customers can subscribe to software as a service applications. It is inevitable that these ecosystems will be accessed through a portal that presents a single look and feel to customers accessing several applications within the ecosystem. In the Chapter 8, we show an example of how multitenant applications can be implemented from the database layer.

References

[1]   Davydov, M., *Corporate Portals and e-Business Integration*, New York, McGraw-Hill Companies, 2001.

[2]   Gamma, E. et al., *Design Patterns: Elements of Reusable Object-Oriented Software,* Boston, MA, Addison-Wesley Professional, 1995.

[3]   "Business Scenario: Identity Management," The Open Group; July 2002.

[4]   "Worldwide and U.S. Software as a Service, 2005-2009 Forecast and Analysis: Adoption for the Alternative Delivery Model Continues," IDC #33120, March 2005.

Chapter 8

Designing Multitenant Applications from a Database Perspective

SaaS applications were originally designed for use by small- to medium-sized businesses (SMBs). The introduction of SaaS applications gave the SMBs an alternative to traditional enterprise licensed applications. The SaaS applications provided the SMBs with just the right functionalities. More importantly, the market price point of the software as a service offering was considered to be the quintessential success factor in the small and medium business market space. The price point of an offering determined the depth and breath of market propagation of the offering in the SMB space. This market tier is traditionally very sensitive to price points, since SMBs' revenues do not support expensive per-license enterprise software models.

For early SaaS providers, it was vital in this space to map the price of offerings with the budgets of SMB customers without compromising on the features and the quality of the offering. SaaS providers worked diligently to successfully tailor their offerings to their customers' budget constraints. Today, we see that this method has proven to be a key factor enabling the market momentum of SaaS to continue at a tremendous rate.

From a technical perspective, the challenge was to make an offering that was an end-to-end hosting solution, while maintaining the right balance among price point, granularity of the offering, capacity of the system, and cost of implementing the offering. This was where the multitenant architecture came into play. The architecture of the application and its initial deployment footprint were vital in determining the choices offered to the market success of the program itself. This chapter describes some of the recommended architectural choices available in a multitenant application so that the price, granularity, capacity, and cost can be optimized.

Multitenancy stems from the paradigm of utilizing the same resource/service for servicing multiple entities. This leads to higher utilization of the resource, thus broadening the serviceability at the same capital cost with a reduced price point by amortizing the costs over a larger base of customers over time.

From an application architecture perspective, the relevance of multitenancy comes into focus at two different levels.

- Micro level–At this level, multitenancy can be applied to the resource components and the service components of the system. The resource components of the system constitute the database, the application, and the infrastructure, whereas the service components of the system constitute the provisioning of resources/services, like the provisioning of hardware, network, and service enablement features, like single sign-on, billing, and rating.
- Macro level–At this level, multitenancy can be applied to the system as a monolithic environment.

This chapter focuses more on the micro level and specifically talks about the database resource. Some sections also give specific product examples taken from real customer design implementations and experience.

8.1 IMPLEMENTING DATABASE SYSTEMS FOR MULTITENANT ARCHITECTURE

The database is the most important resource in an enterprise application. The success of many organizations depends upon information stored in database management systems. The database can contain sensitive data that can make an organization more competitive in the marketplace. Given this importance, it is essential that proper care and management of the database be given top priority within a hosting infrastructure.

When implementing a multitenant software application, the utility application provider can configure the database backend for the application in two ways:

- As individual databases/instances;
- As shared databases/instances.

Both implementations will have different impacts on the manageability from a hosting perspective, which we take into consideration using the IBM DB2 product in the next sections. The following lists the impact of implementing individual databases/instances:

- Backup and recovery is on a per-customer basis without any customized scripts.
- The downtime during recovery is localized at the customer rather than affecting the whole system.

- Maintenance cost is reduced since no custom SQL scripts are required to back up and restore a database. Standard DB2 commands are used to achieve this service.
- Isolation of data is at the customer schema level rather than the record level. It provides a level of comfort that the customer records are not overlapped with his competitors' records in a single table.
- Provides greater flexibility while running queries at each individual customer level.
- Integration of external systems at the database tier for individual customers becomes much less complex and more efficient. This will enable more premium services to be offered for each individual customer for integration.
- Customized individual reports, if sold as a premium service, can be developed with less complex queries and more localized context to the report.

The following lists the impact of *not* implementing individual databases/ instances:

- Custom SQL scripts have to be maintained to back up and recover customer data, thus increasing the cost and risk to offer a backup service offering. No standard DB2 commands can be issued to back up or recover a customer. System administrators will have to learn SQL to back up and recover databases. They will have to maintain SQL scripts, which will increase the demand for highly skilled system administrators.
- During recovery, all the customers will be rolled back to the same point in time. This will penalize customers who do not have corrupt data at that time.
- Isolation of data is not at the schema level. Individual customer records will be in the same table as their competitors', giving a false sense of insecurity and reducing the appeal of boarding in the environment.
- There will be a sizable amount of performance impact on the database queries because the query now has to execute on a large number of records compared to a small set of records.
- If there is any memory corruption, database corruption, or malicious activity, it cannot be localized to a single customer. It will affect the whole database. We will have to restore the whole database, which will increase the time to recovery. This will affect the downtime of the system.
- If the database is one big database, extraction of information for reporting will be very complicated since the queries have to do multiple joins over many tables and bigger sets of data.

8.2 DATABASE ARCHITECTURE SCENARIOS

A database design can be implemented in different ways. How the database is implemented determines the cost of managing the database at a later stage. The next sections present the different design scenarios and their corresponding advantages and disadvantages.

8.2.1 Scenario 1A: One Instance, One Database for Multiple Customers

For this scenario, we are using two tablespaces per customer. For example, "Customer 1" has tablespaces Customer1_1 and Customer1_2. Each customer should have its own set of tablespaces in order to allow for some separation of data and also to allow backups at the tablespace level. A more detailed analysis can be performed later to estimate a better number of tablespaces per customer. The database is shown in Figure 8.1.

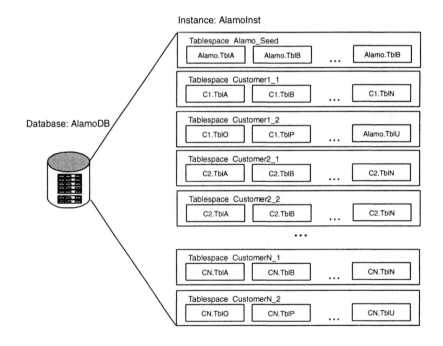

Figure 8.1 Configuration of one instance, one database for multiple customers.

Description:
One instance: "AlamoInst"
One database: "AlamoDB"

Note: There is a limit of 4,096 tablespaces in a database. If only one tablespace is used per customer, then a maximum of 4,094 customers can be supported per database. Two tablespaces are already used for the DB2 catalog and tempspace.

Some points to consider about this implementation include the following:

- Use system managed storage (SMS) versus database managed storage (DMS) tablespaces if indexes/large objects need to have their own tablespaces.
- Relationship among tablespaces referential integrity.
- There is a limit of 4,096 tablespaces per database. One tablespace is required for the DB2 Catalog, and one temporal tablespace per page size is needed. Thus, assuming only 4K page tables are used, then only one 4K temporal tablespace is needed. Therefore, 4,094 tablespaces (4,096 – 2) are required.
- A different schema name needs to be used per table if the same table name is used. For example, tableA for customer 1 is referred to as c1.tableA, while tableA for customer 2 is referred to as c2.tableA.

Note that in DB2, a "schema" is simply a logical grouping of objects; it is not the definition of the database structure. The maximum number of customers that can be supported per database can be calculated as follows:

Maximum number
of customers   =   (4,096 – 2)/number of tablespaces per customer

For the example used in Figure 8.1, (4,096 – 2)/2 = 2,047 customers.

Advantage of this configuration:

- Minimal changes are required for the application architecture, as it assumes using one database in the first place.

Disadvantage of this configuration:

- A critical disadvantage is in the area of recovery. By having the data of all customers in one single database, the design is prone to affect all customers should this database become unusable or corrupt.

Because tablespace backups can be performed, and each customer uses separate tablespaces, customers who inadvertently corrupt their own data may not affect other customers. There are other considerations to be taken into account, however. For example, tablespaces need to be recovered to a minimum point in time to make sure it is consistent with the DB2 catalog. In cases where data is shared among customers (partnership relationship), one tablespace from one customer may have a relationship with a tablespace of another customer, thus recovery may become tricky. From an administrative point of view, tablespace recovery may become an administrative nightmare with the potential to affect many customers.

If for some reason the only way to recover from a problem is to restore from a full backup, then all customers will be restored to the same point in time when this backup was taken. If backups are taken every night, there is a chance all customers will lose one day of information.

8.2.2 Scenario 1B: One Instance, One Database for Multiple Customers, Using Several Databases

This is similar to scenario 1A; however, to limit the impact of recoverability mentioned in scenario 1A, the number of customers can be split into several databases, where each database contains the data of several customers. As an example, a limit of 200 customers can be set. In our example, we have two databases, though there can be up to 256. Figure 8.2 shows the configuration.

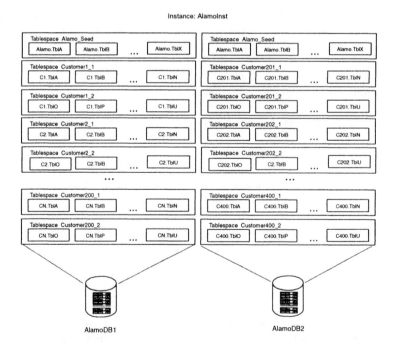

Figure 8.2 Configuration of one instance, one database for multiple customers, using several databases.

Description:
One instance: "AlamoInst"
Two databases: "AlamoDB1" and "AlamoDB2"

Given that one instance can have at most 256 databases active, the maximum number of customers supported under this scenario can be calculated as follows:

Maximum number
of customers   =   256 * number of customers per database

For this example, we are assuming 200 customers per database are supported; thus, a total of 51,200 (256 * 200) customers can be supported.

Advantage of this configuration:

- With this configuration, you limit the impact of customers affected should a database crash. For example, in the figure, if database "SiebelDB2" crashes, this will not affect the customers in database "SiebelDB1."

Disadvantages of this configuration:

- Application needs to be modified to allow for connecting to several databases.
- Seed data may have to be duplicated in each database (optionally, it can be stored only on one database).
- Relational connect (federation) may have to be used if a query needs to access tables from different databases.
- There is still the problem of affecting many customers should a database crash, though the impact has been limited.

8.2.3 Scenario 2A: One Instance, Multiple Databases–One Database per Customer[1]

In this scenario we try to maximize customers' data independence by assigning one database per customer. Figure 8.3 shows the configuration.

---

[1]   There is a limitation of 256 *active* databases in one instance. Thus, the maximum number of customers that can be supported simultaneously would be 255, assuming one database were used as a "seed" database.

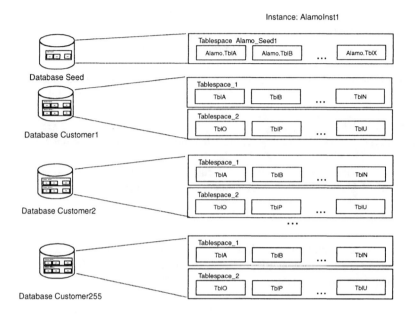

Figure 8.3 Configuration of one instance, multiple databases, using one database per customer.

Description:
One instance: "AlamoInst"
255 databases: "Customer1," "Customer2"... "Customer255"

Given that one instance can have at most 256 databases active, the maximum number of customers supported under this scenario can be calculated as follows:

Maximum number
of customers   = $256 - 1 = 255$

This assumes that the seed data will be kept in one separate database.

Advantages of this configuration:

- This configuration allows for the most flexibility and independence in the area of recoverability.
- Databases can be monitored separately from a DB2 perspective.
- Though most database configuration parameters will likely be set with the same values for all databases/customers, you have the flexibility to change values for different databases.

- The exact same data definition language (DDL) can be used for each database; that is, there is no need to use a different schema name for each table. For example, tableA in database Customer1 can have a full name of "db2admin.tableA", and tableA in database Customer2 can have the exact same full name. Since databases are independent units, there will be no conflict.

Disadvantages of this configuration:

- The application needs to be modified to allow for connecting to several databases.
- All application tables may have to be duplicated in each database.
- Relational connect (federation) may have to be used if a query needs to access tables from different databases.
- Performing administration on many databases could be considered a disadvantage (e.g., backing up 1,000 databases versus 1 database), though scripts or the task center can be used to minimize such work.
- Connection pooling needs to be set against each different database.
- If only 1 instance is used, up to 255 databases/customers can be supported at the same time.

8.2.4 Scenario 2B: One Instance, Multiple Databases–One Database per Customer Needing More Instances to Support More Than 256 Customers

This scenario is similar to scenario 2A; however, by using more than one instance you are able to support more than 255 customers. Figure 8.4 shows the configuration.

Description:
Two instances: "AlamoInst1," "AlamoInst2"
256 databases: "Seed," "Customer1," "Customer2"... "Customer511"

The number of customers that can be supported under this scenario is limited only by the hardware used. Assuming an application's seed data is kept in a separate database per instance, the following formula can be used to obtain the maximum number of customers that can be supported:

Maximum number
of customers   =   (256 − 1) * number of instances

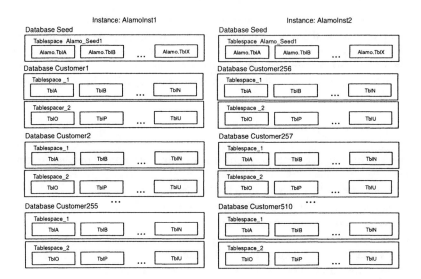

Figure 8.4 Configuration of one instance, multiple databases, using one database per customer needing to have more instances to support more than 256 customers.

Since we have two instances in this example, we could support 510 customers concurrently.

Advantages of this configuration:

- This configuration allows the most flexibility and independence in the area of recoverability.
- Databases and instances can be monitored separately from a DB2 perspective.
- Though most database configuration parameters will likely be set with the same values for all instances and databases/customers, you have the flexibility to change values for different databases and instances.
- An unlimited number of customers can be supported.

Disadvantages of this configuration:

- The application needs to be modified to allow for connecting to several databases and in several instances. All connectivity configurations are done at the DB2 client and should not be an issue.
- Seed data may have to be duplicated in each instance.
- Application tables may have to be duplicated in each database.

- Relational connect (federation) may have to be used if a query needs to access tables from different databases and in different instances.
- Performing administration on many databases could be considered a disadvantage (e.g., backing up 1,000 databases versus 1 database), though scripts or the task center can be used to minimize such work.
- Connection pooling needs to be set against each different database and in different instances.

8.2.5 Scenario 3: Multiple Instances, Multiple Databases–One Instance per Database per Customer[2]

This scenario allows for the most flexibility from a DB2 perspective as it allows you to configure the database and database manager independently of each database and customer.   In this scenario, each customer will have its own database, and each database will reside in its own instance. The scenario is shown in Figure 8.5.

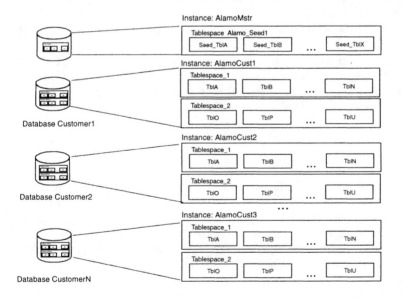

Figure 8.5 Configuration of multiple instances, multiple databases, using one instance per database per customer.

---

[2] There is no limit to the number of instances.

Description:
Four instances: "AlamoMstr," "AlamoCus1," "AlamoCus2," "AlamoCusN"
Four databases: "Seed," "Customer1," "Customer2," "CustomerN"

The number of customers that can be supported under this scenario is limited only by the hardware used. Assuming an application's seed data is kept in a separate database in its own instance, the following formula can be used to obtain the maximum number of customers that can be supported:

Maximum number
of customers   =   Number of instances – 1

Since we have four instances in the example, we could support three customers concurrently.

Advantages of this configuration:

- This configuration also allows the most flexibility and independence in the area of recoverability.
- Databases and instances can be monitored separately from a DB2 perspective.
- Though most database configuration parameters will likely be set with the same values for all instances and databases/customers, you have the flexibility to change values for different databases and instances.
- An unlimited number of customers can be supported.

Disadvantages of this configuration:

- The application needs to be modified to allow for connecting to several databases and in several instances. All connectivity configurations are done at the DB2 client and should not be an issue.
- Tables may have to be duplicated in each database.
- Relational connect (federation) may have to be used if a query needs to access tables from different databases and in different instances.
- Performing administration on many databases could be considered a disadvantage (e.g., backing up 1,000 databases versus 1 database), though scripts or the task center can be used to minimize such work. This work may require more time if more instances are used.
- Connection pooling needs to be set against each different database and in different instances.
- Though minimal (a few megabytes), there is some extra overhead for having several instances active at the same time.

8.2.6 Scenario 4: Using DB2 for OS/390 and z/OS Version 7

All preceding scenarios targeted DB2 UDB V8 for UNIX, Linux, and Windows. This scenario describes how DB2 for OS/390 and z/OS Version 7 could be considered as an option.

The maximum number of customers that can be supported under this scenario is 65,217, which is the maximum number of databases that can be created in a subsystem. Assuming the application's seed data is kept in a separate database, then the following formula can be used to obtain the maximum number of customers that can be supported:

Maximum number
of customers   =   65,217 – databases used for system purposes

Figure 8.6 shows this example.

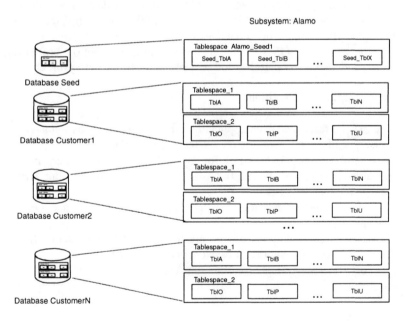

Figure 8.6 A database configuration using DB2 for OS/390 and z/OS Version 7.

Description:
One subsystem: "Alamo"
Four databases: "Seed," "Customer1," "Customer2," "CustomerN"

In the example scenario, we have four databases that can support three customers concurrently. In order to understand the advantages of DB2 for OS/390 and z/OS Version 7 in more detail, refer to [1].

Advantages of this configuration:

- This configuration also allows the most flexibility and independence in the area of recoverability. Each customer using this application will still be assigned its own database, and backups can be performed per database (image copies of the tablespaces belonging to a database).
- You connect only to the subsystem, and this allows you access to all databases inside this subsystem. You do not connect to individual databases. DB2 Connect software will be required at the application server.
- Databases in DB2 for z/OS and OS/390 are not "independent units" as defined in DB2 Windows/UNIX/Linux. With DB2 for z/OS and OS/390, you can write one query accessing tables in different databases without a need for relational connect. "Seed" data can reside in its own database and can be shared among the other databases.
- DB2 for z/OS and OS/390 are great for online transaction processing (OLTP) and also for availability and scalability (with Parallel Sysplex).

Disadvantages of this configuration:

- There may be resistance from application providers as they may not have the necessary skills and be working on a Windows/Intel platform.
- Issues resolved with DB2 UDB for UNIX/Linux/Windows may not be applicable to DB2 for OS/390 (e.g., dictionary sorting order); but further investigation may be needed.
- The managed hosting provider may not have DB2 for z/OS and OS/390 skills either.
- A limit of 65,217 databases can be created in a DB2 subsystem. If this amount is not enough, another subsystem needs to be set up.
- Extra cost may result if DB2 for OS/390 is used.

8.3 SUMMARY

Each scenario in the preceding sections presented its own advantages and disadvantages. As mentioned early in this chapter, the database represents the customer's prized possession. The need to take care of it from a hosting perspective is imperative at the highest level. Some customers may not worry too much about how their data is stored (i.e., with other customer data or separately), but others do.

The other consideration is that the cost of managing a database for multiple customers becomes more complex if the wrong design decisions are made in the design of the multitenanted application. Here are recommendations for implementing the database resource in a multitenant application:

- First choice, from a pure technical DB2 perspective, would be scenario 4 (DB2 for OS/390 and z/OS Version 7). The design allows for maximum flexibility and the backing of a tried and tested environment, the mainframe.
- Second choice would be scenario 2B, one instance, multiple databases. The reason for this selection is that of flexibility and independence in terms of recoverability. From a database perspective, recovery is a crucial consideration.

The worst design considerations are scenarios 1A and 1B. They do not provide any level of comfort in the areas of maximum data recoverability, least amount of administrative intervention, and least impact on other customers.

Reference

[1]   Chong, R., "An Introduction to DB2 for OS/390 and z/OS System Structures for DB2 Distributed Users," available at   www-128.ibm.com/developerworks/db2/library/techarticle/0207chong/ 0207chong.html.

Chapter 9

Other Design Considerations

In this chapter we turn our attention to other design considerations for SaaS applications and utility computing. Among the topics of discussion for this chapter are a Web services metering design and a monitoring library for SaaS applications based on an open standards solution, an update and notification strategy that can be used within a software application services framework (sasf), and a utility computing tool based on model-driven architecture (MDA). The intention for discussing these designs and implementations is to show systems designers and implementers how today's technologies like service-oriented architecture (SOA) implemented as Web services (WS), portal technology, and MDA can be used to create technologies that help promote the inevitable shift toward utility computing.

9.1 DESIGN OF A WEB SERVICES METERING INTERFACE

Most SaaS applications today use a billing model that charges users on a monthly basis. In most cases, this means users are given unlimited use of the SaaS for as long as they pay the monthly charge. Unless the SaaS provider intends to provide unlimited hardware resources to satisfy all usage demand for the SaaS, this type of billing model may, in the near future, be enhanced to one that is more granular, like those enabled through the use of a metering service. In this respect, SaaS providers will have the choice of offering their applications as monthly paid services or as metered services.

Chapter 7 discussed a software application services framework from which SaaS applications were envisioned to get common services; one of these was a metering service. To enable an SaaS application to interface with the metering service within an sasf, we need to design an interface that is reliable and robust. For the purpose of this section, we assume a metering service that is already available within the sasf, like the one described in [1].

A software utility application framework that offers a metering service and exposes itself through WS technology needs a Web services client or agent that can handle delayed responses from metering the WS endpoint. Network latency and delays, system sluggishness, third-party application bugs, and database downtimes are factors that a Web services client need to overcome intelligently to prevent unnecessary delays when sending metered data to the metering service.

This design shows two Web services client methods that handle client-application metered data. The first method handles the sending of streams-based[1] data from client to server and the second handles a non streams-based requirement. The design is not only transparent to the server, but it handles error conditions on both client and server endpoints and overcomes the synchronous nature of Web services.

9.1.1 Metering Interface

In an ideal WS environment, where network latency and delays or application bugs are nonexistent, data sent by a WS client is always guaranteed to reach its intended WS server endpoint. Unfortunately, there is no guarantee that such an ideal Web services environment will ever exist; therefore, provisions need to be made to overcome problems such as network latency and delays or application bugs. To put the problem into better perspective, an SaaS application (acting as a WS client) that intends to use a remote metering service (WS server) cannot afford to lose metering data that will be used eventually to bill its customers. The SaaS application requires a mechanism that can reliably send raw metering data to a remote metering service in a reliable and auditable manner.

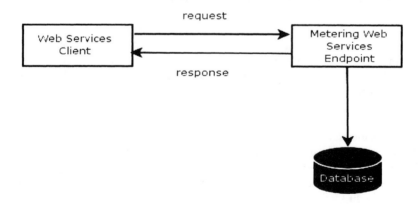

Figure 9.1 A simplistic view of a client and server metering interaction.

The proposed metering interface design alleviates the use of computer resources on the client side by managing threads through synchronization objects. The design also allows both the client and server to effectively synchronize data

---

[1] Stream-based data means data that must be sent in some orderly fashion.

they have sent and received, respectively, satisfying an orderly type of data transmission requirement.

Figure 9.1 shows how an application uses a metering service exposed as a Web service.

9.1.1.1 Streams-Based Requirement

In the scenario shown in Figure 9.1, there are two requirements that the client is required to meet. First, the client needs to send data in an orderly fashion. Second, the client needs to wait for an acknowledgment back from the server to make sure the server received the data safely. As the server receives data from the client, it keeps count of the total number of metering records sent by the client. The metering service sends an acknowledgment back to the client that contains the total number of metering records received. The acknowledgment sent by the server is then examined by the client and used to verify that the server received previously sent data. After verifying that the last data sent was received safely, the client sends the next batch of data to the server. This type of communication is known as a synchronous type of communication between client and server.

Table 9.1 shows an example of data flow between a WS client and server. The transmission begins at L1, where the client sends the first batch of 10 records to the server. The total hash count sent from the client is zero at this point to notify the server of the start of a new transmission. The server receives the data, records the transmitted record count, and resets its hash counter to zero. Before sending the acknowledgment back to the client, the server updates its hash count with the number of records received from the client and sends this number back as the received hash count in the reply, L2. When the client receives the server's reply, L2, it knows that the server received the records safely as indicated by the received hash count. The client updates its own hash count with the hash count received from the server and sends the next batch of 10 records to the server, L3, together with the new client hash count, 10. When the server receives the transmitted data, it matches the received client hash count with the current hash count it has for this client. If they match, then the server knows the data received is the next batch of data from the client. The server updates its hash count by adding the number of records received to the currently recorded hash count for the client. The server then sends a reply back to the client with the updated hash count, L4. The client receives the acknowledgment and updates its hash count. The communication between the client and server goes on until all data from the client has been received by the server safely. As one will note, the transmission goes on in an orderly and synchronous manner.

Table 9.1 Transaction Flow of Metering Service Shows the Number of the Packet Count Transmitted with Each Packet

	Transmitted Total Audit Hash	Transmitted Record Count	Client Action	Received Packet Hash	Received Total Audit Hash
L1	0	10	Send	10	0
L2	10		Receive		10
L3	10	10	Send	10	10
L4	20		Receive		20
L5	20	10	Send	10	20
L6	30		Receive		30
L7	30	10	Send	10	30
L8	40		Receive		40

The scenario just described presents a major problem for the client: it has to wait for the server to respond before it can proceed to its next task. Even if the client is designed to spawn separate threads to send data to the server, the server might crash, or network problems can arise, leaving all threads waiting for a response. For this type of orderly and synchronous communication requirement, the method proposed to handle such requirements is shown in Figure 9.2.

The design has two components: the queuing component and the data-sending component. The queuing component is used when data to be sent to the metering service cannot be sent immediately. This component is made up of a data file that acts as a buffer, where data that cannot be sent is written to. The sending component sends metering data as data is collected. When a thread cannot send the data because another thread is already waiting for a reply from the metering service, instead of waiting, the second thread writes the unsent data to the data file of the queuing component.

The algorithm works by using synchronizing objects (So1 and So2). When a thread, T1, is created to handle the sending of data to the metering service, it tries to lock So2. If T1 succeeds in taking the lock, it then sends the data and waits for a reply. The lock is held until the thread receives a reply from the metering service. If another thread, T2, is created to send the next batch of data, it will try to lock So2 and fail because So2 is currently held by T1. When thread T2 fails it proceeds to lock So1, which is the synchronizing object for the persistent data queue. The persistent data queue is where all data that cannot be sent immediately is concatenated for transmission later. After saving the data to the persistent data queue, T2 unlocks So1 and exits. Subsequent threads do the same thing if So2 is locked. This allows thread resources to be released when they are not needed.

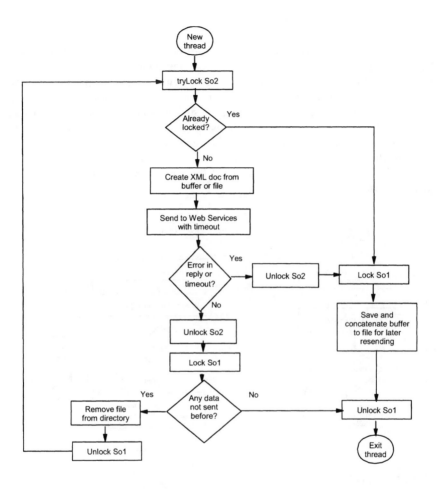

Figure 9.2 Queuing and sending components for a metering client.

When T1 gets a good acknowledgment from the metering service, it wakes up and unlocks So2. It proceeds to lock So1 to look for any unsent data; if any data is found in the queue, T1 removes the data from the queue, unlocks So1, and tries to lock So2, which starts the sending process all over again.

If thread T1 happens to receive an error response from the server, it unlocks So2 and locks So1. Once So1 is locked, T1 writes the unsent data into the persistent data queue. After writing the unsent data to the queue, T1 unlocks So1 and exits. If T1 never receives a reply, the design implements a timeout mechanism so that the thread is not left to wait forever. This is treated as an error response and proceeds as if an error reply had been received from the metering service.

9.1.1.2 Nonstreams-Based Requirement

For a nonstreams-based requirement, the algorithm is similar to the streams-based design except it does not require synchronizing object, So2. The design is presented in Figure 9.3. As in the previous design, a thread is spawned to send metered data to the metering service. The thread waits for a response or times out if no response is received. If an error occurs, such as a bad response or a timeout, the thread locks So1 to synchronize the writing of records in the persistent data queue. After writing the unsent data, the thread exits.

If the thread succeeds in sending metered data, it checks to see if there is any unsent data in the persistent data queue. If there is, it removes the data from the queue and tries to send it.

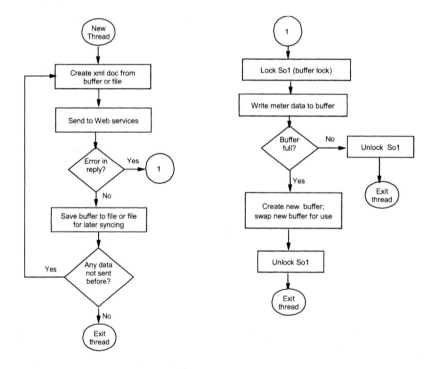

Figure 9.3 A proposed design for a nonstreams-based requirement.

In addition to designing an interface to send data to a metering service, one needs to take into account auditability. As any lost data may mean loss of revenue for the SaaS provider, sent data needs to have an audit trail, either at the sending or receiving end, to make sure data sent is not lost or corrupted on the way to the metering service. From the client side, an audit trail can be implemented by recording sent data to persistent storage. This data can then be compared to data received at the metering service. For more information about the design of a metering service that incorporates an audit trail, refer to [1].

9.2 APPLICATION MONITORING IMPLEMENTATION

Within the boundaries of the corporate firewall, a typical distributed enterprise application environment may exist. To monitor the state of the enterprise application, system administrators use software that keep an eye on the overall environment and monitor the state of hardware resources. Administrators are alerted when hardware errors are detected so that potential problems may be averted. By keeping the hardware environment in shape, combined with the enterprise application's own logs, system administrators can be assured that the application is functioning properly.

With new standards and technologies that allow the creation of distributed applications that reach beyond the boundaries of the corporate firewall, however, the typical monitoring scenario just described will not be adequate to monitor the enterprise application.

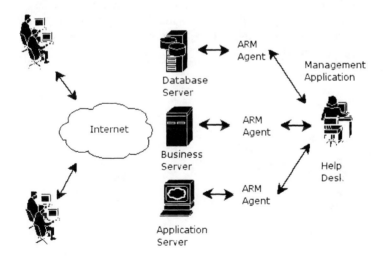

Figure 9.4 ARM configuration scenario.

Chapter 7 discussed several uses of application metering: for the purpose of billing and for monitoring application functionalities and service levels. An open standard that can be used to implement application metering and monitoring is the

Application Response Measurement (ARM)[2] standard from the Open Group.[3] ARM provides a set of application programming interfaces (APIs) that enterprise or SaaS applications can use[4] to monitor application usage and transactions. Figure 9.4 shows applications using ARM to monitor and gather information about transactions for a typical enterprise setup consisting of an application server, a business server, and a database server. Each component has been instrumented with ARM APIs that communicate with an ARM agent. The ARM agent is responsible for sending information it collects to a central management application. The central management application then correlates information from each agent and presents it as a whole to the analyst.

The following sections describe how an application can use ARM to monitor transactions for the purpose of problem determination or monitoring levels of service.

9.2.1 Determining Problems Using ARM

For the purpose of our discussion, we define a transaction as any unit of work that is necessary to fulfill an intended purpose. An example of a transaction might be a user clicking a button on a Web page to display the names, addresses, and phone numbers of people in the local community. In this case, the data to be displayed may reside in a database, and the Web application is programmed to query the database, wait for a response, and then display the data to the user. Figure 9.5 shows a Web setup where a user interacts with an application server to display data coming from a remote database server.

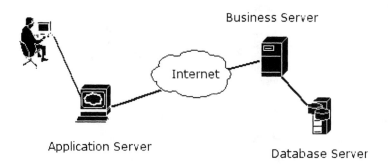

Figure 9.5 Typical setup for Web transactions.

In the typical scenario of the Web-based transaction, failure to display data on the user's terminal in a timely fashion may prompt the user to call the help desk to

---

[2] As of this writing, the current release and version is ARM 4.0 Version 2.
[3] www.opengroup.org/management/arm/.
[4] An application is instrumented with ARM APIs that can report the status or start and end of transactions.

investigate the problem. The help desk then notifies a system administrator, who starts a series of inquiries into the state of each component that makes up the whole environment. Is the local network down? Is the database server not responding? Is the Internet connection down? This process continues until the problem is found.

In an ARM environment, however, the same problem can be found without having to query each component that makes up the whole environment. Figure 9.6 shows the same Web environment where each component is "ARMed," allowing each to report the status of a transaction to a central management application that collects ARM information. At the help desk, the management station is monitored or queried to find exactly where the problem is occurring.

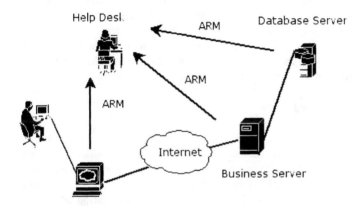

Figure 9.6 Web environment using ARM.

Between the start and end of a transaction, the application may call several ARM APIs that allow the collection of information for the transaction. The ARM standard describes this information as properties of a transaction. These properties provide a way to identify each transaction uniquely so it can be measured and monitored accurately. ARM associates each transaction as having the following properties:

- *Identity properties*–Identify the transaction or application. Examples include "Alamo CRM application," and "Query customer transaction."
- *Context properties*–Include additional properties that may be unique for each instance of a transaction or application. These may be user names, group names, or URIs.[5] Examples are "User–George Gardner" and "Group–Accounting."

---

[5] Uniform resource identifier.

- *Relationship properties*–Provide a way to show how transactions are related to each other in a distributed environment. In a client-server environment, a server may act as a client to another server, while acting as a server to a user (client). ARM provides a way to distinguish between these roles to map out the flow of the transaction accurately. In our example, the user is a client of the application server, and the application server is a client of the business server.
- *Measurement properties*–Can be used to detect bottlenecks, measure response times, and understand overall transaction performance. Examples are response time, status, and time of day.

For each transaction, information such as the identity, context, relationship, and measurement properties is collected in each leg of the transaction. All of this information is gathered by ARM agents, which forward it to a central management station. The central management station presents the collected data in a format that displays a complete picture of the transaction, allowing help desk personnel to diagnose problems faster.

9.2.2 Monitoring Service Levels

As ARM agents can collect data at each leg of a transaction, it is easy to see how one can use this data to monitor service levels for any given application. Figure 9.7 shows the transaction flow from the user to the database server. In each leg of the transaction (T1-T2, T2-T3, T3-T4), ARM measurements are taken in terms of start and end time of each leg. Each leg of the end-to-end transaction adds time to the total elapsed time of the whole transaction, which comes close to the perceived user response time. This elapsed time may vary, depending on other factors, such as network traffic and load on each server (application, business, and database).

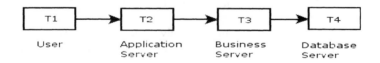

Figure 9.7 User-to-database server transaction flow.

In an interactive environment, such as a user clicking on a button and waiting for data to be displayed on the screen, response time needs to be at or above acceptable levels. If the response takes too long, the user starts to wonder if something is wrong, prompting the user to log a support call.

In an environment where each component of the application is ARMed, each leg of the transaction can be looked at to see where a bottleneck is occurring. For example, if the whole transaction takes 1.7 seconds to complete, each leg of the transaction will have contributed to this total, as shown in Figure 9.8.

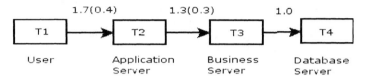

Figure 9.8 Response time of each leg of the transaction.

From T1 to T4, the total elapsed time to complete a transaction is 1.7 seconds. The number in parentheses represents the elapsed time it took for T2 to send a response back to T1 when T2 received the response from T3. If the total T1 to T4 response time were to jump to 5 seconds, we could easily determine which leg of the transaction contributed to making the total elapsed time larger. More information about ARM can be found at [2].

9.2.3 ARM 4.0

The ARM standard provides a set of APIs that software vendors can use to instrument their applications. Language bindings for C and Java applications are provided, and a software development kit (SDK) is available for download[6] from the Open Group ARM Web site.

9.2.3.1 C Binding Example

The following is a simple program that shows how an application developer instruments the application with ARM APIs to measure transaction response time. In this example, the call to arm_start_transaction signals the ARM library to start timing the transaction response time. Upon return from the actual transaction operation, the arm_stop_transaction is called to signify the end of the transaction operation to the ARM library.

```
#include <stdio,h>
#include  "arm4.h"

static arm_id_t        appl_id;
static arm_id_t        trans_id;
static arm_app_start_handle_t appl_handle;
static arm_tran_start_handle_t trans_handle;

int start_transaction_1()
{
```

---

[6] www.opengroup.org/management/arm/page.tpl?CALLER=admin.tpl&ggid=704.

```
        /* Register transaction class with ARM agent. */
        arm_register_transaction(&app_id,"Trans_1",
           ARM_ID_NONE, ARM_FLAG_NONE, ARM_BUF4_NONE,
          &trans_id);

        /* Now start the transaction measurement. */
        arm_start_transaction(appl_handle, &trans_id,
           ARM_CORR_NONE, ARM_FLAG_NONE, ARM_BUF4_NONE,
           &trans_handle, ARM_CORR_NONE);

        /* do actual transaction */
        printf("Are we in sync?\n");

        /* Stop the measurement and commit the transaction to ARM.*/
        arm_stop_transaction(trans_handle, ARM_STATUS_GOOD,
           ARM_FLAG_NONE, ARM_BUF4_NONE);

        return 0;
}

main()
{
        int rc = 0;

        /* Register application class with ARM agent. */
        arm_register_application("SimplePorgram", ARM_ID_NONE,
           ARM_FLAG_NONE, ARM_BUF4_NONE,&appl_id);

        /* Start the application instance for the ARM agent */
        arm_start_application(&appl_id, "Examples",
                ARM_STRING_NONE, ARM_FLAG_NONE,ARM_BUF4_NONE,
           &appl_handle);

        rc = start_transaction();

        /* Stop the measurement and commit the transaction to ARM.*/
        arm_stop_transaction(trans_handle, ARM_STATUS_GOOD,
           ARM_FLAG_NONE, ARM_BUF4_NONE);

        /* Destroy all registered metadata. */
        arm_destroy_application(&appl_id, ARM_FLAG_NONE,
           ARM_BUF4_NONE);

        return rc;
}
```

In real enterprise applications, the application starts once, and the transaction piece executes as many times as needed. The arm_register_transaction call establishes the identity of the transaction by generating a unique transaction ID that can be used to generate a report about the transaction.

ARM also provides binding for the Java language. Both C and Java binding reference documentations are available for download from [3].

9.2.3.2 Application Response Measurement (API)

Table 9.2 presents some of the ARM 4.0 APIs and descriptions used in the previous section.

Table 9.2 ARM 4.0 APIs

API version 4.0	Description
arm_register_application	Called during application initialization, registers the application identity. The application identity provides the fundamental instrumented application scope and basis for subsequent ARM 4.0 calls.
arm_start_application	This routine establishes the started application instance in preparation for making ARM 4.0 transaction calls. This interface is called during application initialization, after the application with ARM is registered.
arm_register_transaction	This routine registers a transaction identity. A transaction identity provides a category of transactions, commonly referred to as a transaction type, which will execute under the registered application for subsequent ARM 4.0 calls for transaction monitoring and measurement.
arm_start_transaction	Called during transaction processing, this routine establishes the started transaction instance. A started transaction instance provides the foundation for transaction monitoring and measurement.
arm_block_transaction	Called during transaction processing, this routine indicates that the started transaction instance has become blocked behind an event.
arm_unblock_transaction	Called during transaction processing, this routine indicates that the blocking event has been relieved for the started transaction instance.
arm_bind_transaction	Called during transaction processing, this routine indicates that the current thread is performing on behalf of a started transaction instance. Binding enables the system to measure the processor utilization of a transaction because it establishes an exclusive processing relationship between the thread and the transaction.
arm_unbind_transaction	Called during transaction processing, this routine indicates that the current thread is no longer performing on behalf of a started transaction instance.
arm_stop_transaction	This routine ends the started transaction instance recognized by the ARM implementation. A call to this interface is the expected way for an instrumented application to end a started transaction instance.

Table 9.2 ARM 4.0 APIs (Continued)

API version 4.0	Description
arm_stop_application	This routine ends the started application instance recognized by the ARM implementation. A call to this interface is the expected way for an instrumented application to end a started application instance.
arm_destroy_application	This routine deregisters the registered application. A call to this interface is the expected way for an instrumented application to deregister an application.

The ARM APIs are designed to be used only when needed. In other words, ARM measurements for applications and transactions can be turned on and off as appropriate. Applications and transactions are registered once to give them unique identifiers. The unique identifier is then used in subsequent ARM measurement calls. The ARM APIs also provide calls to work with blocked transactions and multithreaded applications. For more information about the APIs refer to [4].

9.3 A DESIGN FOR AN UPDATE AND NOTIFICATION POLICY

Compared to an on-premises[7] enterprise application designed to be accessed only by users of a single company, an SaaS application is designed to provide access to users of more than one company. During maintenance or upgrade cycles, system administrators of both on-premises and SaaS applications must have a plan to schedule downtime and be ready to restore the system to its original state in case something goes wrong after maintenance or upgrade. With only one specific customer to provide service to, system administrators of on-premises applications have an easier time coordinating maintenance and upgrade tasks compared to their SaaS counterparts. For the SaaS system administrator, scheduling the tasks becomes more difficult because more customers from different companies can have a wider range of needs for application availability.

The following is a design for an update and notification policy that can be implemented by the SaaS provider to help alleviate the tasks of scheduling maintenance and upgrades. The update and notification policy design promotes a self-service front end that enhances quality of service as well as customer experience. The description provides a method for implementing a software update and notification policy for SaaS applications within a utility infrastructure.

---

[7] Installed and managed locally within the organization.

9.3.1 Design Details

Before delving further into the design, some specific roles need to be defined for each of the parties involved–enterprise, ISV, and hosting provider. Table 9.3 shows the roles and describes the responsibilities each of these entities play.

Table 9.3 Roles Defined for Each Entity Involved Within the Proposed Policy

Enterprise	*Independent Software Vendor*	*Hosting Provider*
(Subscriber Company)	(SaaS Provider)	(Utility Hosting Provider)
Enterprise end user–subscribes to SaaS application	SaaS end user–enterprise company subscribing to SaaS	Hosting provider end user–SaaS provider uses hosting resources
Enterprise administrator–delegated by SaaS provider to provision and entitle enterprise users subscribed to SaaS	SaaS administrator–maintains and upgrades the SaaS application, sets up subscription policies	Hosting administrator–provides hosting infrastructure and backup/restore services

The design considers the two main steps in the maintenance process–the update process and the notification process. Both processes apply not only to the SaaS application but to middleware and the operating system that the SaaS uses.

9.3.1.1 Update Process

The update process potentially involves updating user documentations and upgrading program modules. User documentations and informational text are updated in a cumulative fashion. The process stores these texts in a persistent, easily accessible storage so that they can be searched and sorted programmatically.

Upgrades to program modules can be classified into bug fixes and feature upgrades. Both may require the SaaS application, middleware, or operating system to be brought down and back up before they take effect. Although it is advisable that the upgrade not cause interruption to service, in some cases it may be inevitable.

9.3.1.2 Notification Process

The notification process is designed to inform system administrators and users about pending and recent changes to the SaaS application, middleware, or operating system. This can be anything from documentation updates to addition of new features. The notification process is designed to provide two types of information that reach two different groups of people. The first type of information is directed at enterprise administrators. This type of information will contain detailed information about bug fixes, enhancements, and new features that are about to be applied or have been applied to the SaaS environment. The second type of information is directed toward enterprise users. This information is less detailed than that presented to the system administrators and only contains information about new SaaS features and upgrades.

Both types of information displayed to system administrators and enterprise users can be customized through user profiles. The profile settings can filter the type of information relevant to their functions.

9.3.2 Inherent Design Characteristics

Inherent to the design are characteristics that add to user and system administrator productivity and SaaS provider profitability. Informing enterprise users of new features as they become available can improve productivity by enabling users to use new features as soon as they become available. Upgrade information provided to enterprise administrators gives them the necessary knowledge to investigate reported problems affecting the upgraded system. Enterprise administrators that respond to reported problems by enterprise users will be able to relate the reported anomaly to recent upgrades, giving the users more confidence to report the problem to the SaaS administrator in a timely fashion.

For the SaaS provider, having the avenue to inform his customers of new features as they become available increases the chances of their being utilized without delays. In terms of his business, immediate use of new features translates into more utilization of the application which generates more revenue[8] for the SaaS provider.

9.3.3 Detailed Description of the Design

Ideally, enterprise users will be able to access SaaS applications from PDAs and browsers, as shown Figure 9.9. Potentially, each user can subscribe to different SaaS applications from several SaaS providers at the same time. In the figure, SaaS provider 1 offers applications 11, 12, and 13; SaaS provider 2 offers applications 21, 22, and 23; SaaS provider 3 offers applications 31, 32, and 33; and so on. User A is shown to be subscribed to applications 11, 21, and 41 from providers 1, 2, and 4, respectively.

In an SaaS ecosystem like that shown in Figure 9.9, a user logs in through a single sign-on component to access SaaS applications he or she is entitled to. The ecosystem is set up such that the origins of the SaaS applications are transparent to the user—as if the applications were offered by only a single provider.

---

[8] This may only hold true if the SaaS application implements a metered billing model.

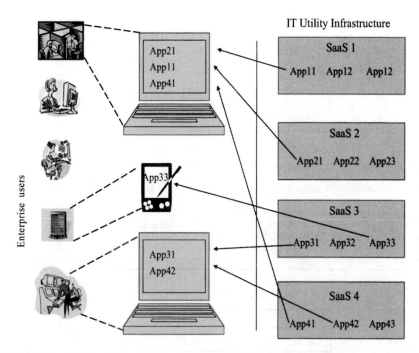

Figure 9.9 Notification policy can alert application users from different access instruments. Each SaaS (e.g., SaaS1 , SaaS2) may be owned by different independent software vendors (ISVs).

In this environment, SaaS providers are still responsible for maintaining and managing their SaaS applications. Each SaaS provider will need a way to notify users about recent upgrades and changes to the application.

9.3.3.1 Software and Documentation Updates

It was mentioned earlier that updates to user documentation and program modules can take place. Every time the SaaS application is updated, informational text about the update is cumulatively gathered and stored in persistent storage. This informational text can then be retrieved programmatically and displayed by users of the application. The upgrade process steps are shown in Figure 9.10.

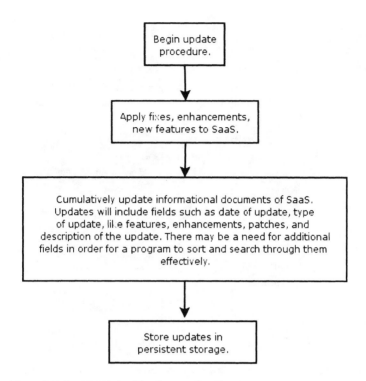

Figure 9.10 A proposed algorithm for upgrade policy.

Cumulative updating of informational text is associated with searchable fields, such as date, type of update, and description of enhancements and patches. These fields make it easier to search and display information relating to recent updates.

9.3.3.2 Notification Policy

Several key areas are addressed by the notification policy. From an administrator's perspective, the policy notifies the enterprise administrator of patches and enhancements that can affect his users. From a user's perspective, the policy notifies enterprise users only about features that they care about. For the SaaS provider, the policy gives him the avenue to notify his users and delegated administrators with timely information. Timely information enables users to utilize new features as soon as they are available and gives administrators knowledge they need to support users of the application.

Administrator and user notification information comes from text that is updated as discussed in the previous section. The notification component is programmed to search for updated information and displays it as needed.

Users and administrators can click on an "http link" on their main login page to display information. Notification may also come in the form of the first screen after login so that users and administrators are informed immediately. The characteristics on how users and administrators display their information can be set through individual profiles. Figure 9.11 shows the notification process.

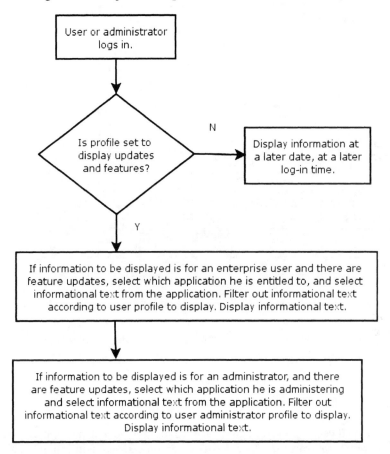

Figure 9.11 The algorithm when user or administrator logs in to system with update and notification policy implemented within the system.

Informational text for users and administrators will vary. While administrators may be interested in all updates regarding the application, users might only be interested in application features that have recently become available. Administrator pages include informational text on both the SaaS features that have updates and any fixes that were applied during the most recent update. Figure 9.12 shows what might be displayed on an administrator's notification page.

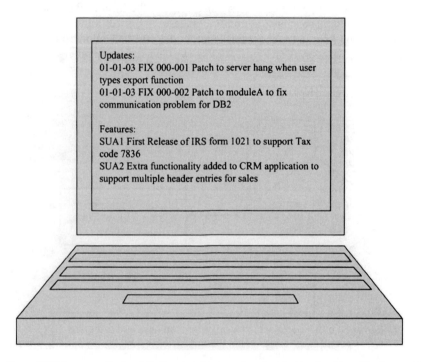

Figure 9.12 The screen displayed for the administrators when they first log in with notification turned on.

User screens might only display information about the SaaS. Thus, on the user's screen, only the last two lines of the administrator's screen may be displayed.

9.3.3.3 Profile for On-Demand Notification

Another embodiment of the design is the ability for an enterprise user and administrator to set specific characteristics for on-demand notification. This profile sets the filters as follows:

- Nonintrusive time of day notification–Unlike other notification avenues, like e-mail, paging alert, or telephone call, time-of-day notification set to one's choosing are more convenient and customer friendly.
- Number of lines to display—This provides a way to accommodate handheld devices that can only display limited lines of text at a time.

- Name of applications to display information for–Setting an option to display only applications pertinent to a customer's line of work reduces the amount of nonspecific data a customer is exposed to.
- Text filters that filters for words within the description of the updated information text–This is another way to limit information displayed on the screen.

Figure 9.13 shows an example of a profile screen.

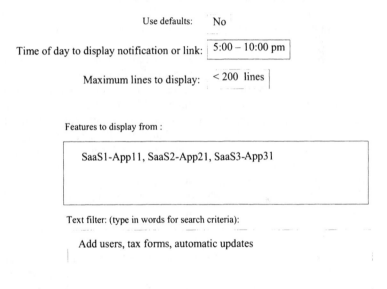

On-Demand Notification Profile

Use defaults: No

Time of day to display notification or link: 5:00 – 10:00 pm

Maximum lines to display: < 200 lines

Features to display from :

SaaS1-App11, SaaS2-App21, SaaS3-App31

Text filter: (type in words for search criteria):

Add users, tax forms, automatic updates

Figure 9.13 A conceptual configuration screen for filtering options.

While the focus of the design is to notify users and administrators of SaaS updates, the system can also be used to notify users and administrators about updates to middleware, the operating system, or any other component that may affect the application.

The design of an update and notification policy stems from the need of users and administrators for up-to-date information. The design encourages users to help themselves with information that can improve their productivity and provide administrators with information that alerts them to changes in the application and environment the SaaS is operating on. It can be implemented with portal technology and adopted for use by SaaS providers within an SaaS ecosystem.

9.4 A TOOL DESIGN FOR UTILITY COMPUTING

Tools were designed and created to make complex tasks easier to manage and complete. Thanks to the modern-day word processor a 300-page book can now be spell-checked in a matter of minutes.   A programmer using an integrated development environment (IDE) can write, compile, and deploy Java programs on an Internet server in a matter of hours. Addresses and contact numbers for business establishments can easily[9] by found by Googling them on the Web. With tools like the word processor, IDE, and Google, tasks that used to take days, hours, and minutes to complete are reduced to hours, minutes, and seconds, respectively.

Tools for developing software applications have been in existence since the invention of the first computer. Although crude, these tools, which included linkers and loaders, were able to produce program codes that ran specific tasks. In the 1970s, tools for the UNIX environment, like the text editor *vi* and the document search tool *grep*, became widely used within universities. In the 1990s IDE tools from vendors like Microsoft, Borland, and IBM came out to support development of more complex applications with graphical user interface (GUI) and networking capabilities.

A little later, after IDEs came into existence, computer-aided software engineering (CASE) tools that integrated with existing IDEs were being developed. The CASE tool concept came from the need to manage the software development life cycle. For large software development projects, the CASE tool was the right tool to handle tasks such as project management, business analysis, software analysis, and source-code storage and control in a single environment.

In early 2000, Web services standards based on service-oriented architecture (SOA) were beginning to take shape. Today's SOA is based on open standards technologies like the extensible markup language (XML). An XML-based file that describes service interfaces available for use is called a Web services definition language (WSDL) file. With a WSDL file, software functionalities can be made available in a more flexible manner.[10] Today, SOA based on Web services technology has introduced a new software application paradigm–one that allows software developers to publish (describe) their software application functionalities as well as to discover (directory/broker) and subscribe to (invoke/bind) other software functionalities as services. With the introduction of this new paradigm, IDEs have once again evolved to support a new technology.

---

[9] Provided these business establishments have a web presence.
[10] Compared to other forms of interface definition files used by older SOA-based technologies like common object request broker architecture (CORBA).

Figure 9.14 shows the progression of toolsets that have come about to meet the needs of developers and integrators as new advances in technology have been introduced.

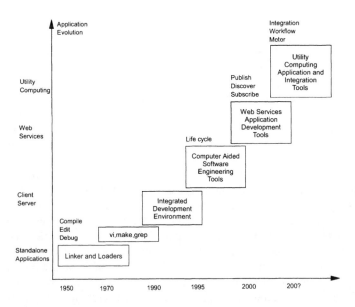

Figure 9.14 The advancement in toolsets was built on top of previous toolsets.

Each new toolset that superseded the last was implemented such that it provided the functionalities of the older toolset. This was done for backward compatibility as well as to provide a richer set of new functionalities. As the figure shows, advancements in toolset design were based on advancements in new technology. As new technologies became widespread, tools that supported these technologies also came into existence. As we consider the emergence of utility-based computing technology today, we anticipate that new tools that support utility-based offerings will become a reality.

9.4.1 A Utility Computing Development Environment Tool

In the context of this book, we define utility computing as a paradigm for delivering IT functionalities to end customers like that by which electric or water utilities deliver their products. IT functionalities can take the form of hardware resources, software applications, and business functionalities. Technologies like virtualization and the Internet are enabling hardware resources to be available when needed. The maturation of Web services technology is making way for software applications to integrate seamlessly with business functionalities, creating a monolithic application made up of application software developed from different parts of the globe. Just as electric and water utilities make electricity and water available through their respective infrastructures, modern technology is making it possible for IT functionalities to be made available over the Internet as utilities.

Today, software applications in the form of Web services functionalities are playing a big role in the enablement of externalized services that other software applications can use. These Web services are published through a UDDI (see Chapter 2) directory service. Once published, these services may then be discovered and eventually subscribed to by an application developed to discover and use such services. Today, the use of UDDI is in its infancy. Only a handful of vendors establish new vendor-to-vendor relationships discovered through the UDDI services. In the future, as the use of UDDI becomes more widespread, more vendors will be able to advertise their services as well as categorize them by their patterns for reuse.

Categorizing Web services by their patterns for reuse allows other software applications to find an exact match for the service they need, making it easier to discover Web services among the hundreds or even thousands that may be advertised within a UDDI repository. In May 2004, the OMG adopted the reusable asset specification (RAS) as a new standard that defines XML schemas that package reusable software assets for exchange among applications via Web services and other protocols. Standards such as the RAS will enable programmers to package their application software as reusable assets and describe them in such a way that architects and programmers can get a better description of these assets for their own projects.

From a utility computing perspective, RAS can be extended to package IT functionalities such as hardware resources, software applications, and business functionalities in such a way that they are described according to their functionality, availability, and capabilities. The XML Schemas that are used to describe these IT functionalities are then placed in a UDDI-type service, where a tool can then find them in an automated fashion. This tool will be the next topic of our discussion.

9.4.1.1 An MDA-based[11] Approach

Today's CASE tools are being superseded by MDA-based tools. Like their CASE predecessors, MDA-based tools are mostly stand-alone and self-contained. They provide a model-driven approach to creating software applications through visual modeling techniques, allowing a designer to depict the design in a highly abstract level before it is translated into a platform-specific software application. The proposed design of the utility computing tool of the future is based on today's MDA paradigm with some additional support for discovering external services.

---

[11] Model-driven architecture provides an open, vendor-neutral approach to the challenge of business and technology change. MDA is the idea of creating new vendor-neutral IT functionality from business objectives as proposed by the Object Management Group (OMG), see www.omg.org/mda.

The proposed tool incorporates a discovery functionality to locate IT functionalities packaged according to the RAS. This will enable designers to discover utility functionalities during the design phase and then generate code that will use these utilities in the application.

The tool combines automated discovery and matching of utility computing services that are advertised as external functions from anywhere in the world. The proposed tool can be used to input specification parameters that any user, be it an architect, application developer, CIO, or business analyst, can input and then let the tool discover services according to the desired parameters. Figure 9.15 shows the conceptual view of the utility computing tool.

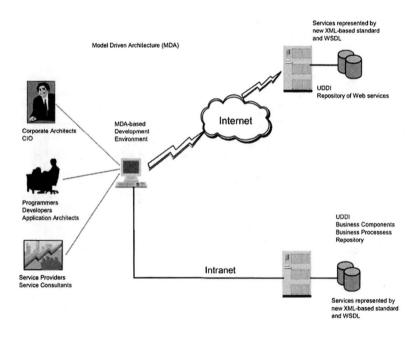

Figure 9.15 A conceptual implementation of a utility computing tool.

CIOs, application architects, and services providers will use this tool to search repositories of services whether they be on the Internet or within their own intranets.

- CIOs and corporate architects will use this tool to discover, at design time, business components that are available within their organizations. They will use the tool to establish high-level relationships with external providers of business functionalities allowing estimation of the cost of such services (pay as you go).

- Application architects and programmers will use this tool to discover Web services components that are available for reuse. They will establish high-level relationships, allowing for functional and system testing before a more permanent relationship is established.
- Service providers will use this tool to discover services to build a portfolio to offer their clients, establishing client-vendor relationships that otherwise would have been a manual process without the automatic discovery of services.

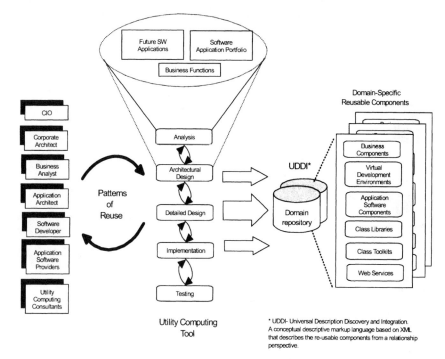

Figure 9.16 Utility computing tool concept of the future. Adapted with permission from Software Reuse, A Holistic Approach, Even-Andre Karlsson, John Wiley and Sons Limited, 1995, p288

Although the discussion of the design has centered on the RAS, we need not limit the criteria for searching and classifying only to RAS. Additional parameters, such as domain,[12] programming language, availability, cost, platform, geographic location, company experience, industry experience, customers, and years in business may be used to extend the description of services. These additional criteria can be used to automate and even rate the selection of available advertised services.

---

[12] Example of domain-specific criteria include business process components, Web services, application software components, virtual development environments, and others that may be defined in the future.

Figure 9.16 shows the conceptual design of the utility computing tool of the future. The tool is built on top of today's MDA tools with added functionality for new technology, such as utility computing. The figure is a modified version of a diagram from [5]. It shows how an MDA-based tool of today searches a local, Internet, or intranet repository to look for records that match criteria fed as input from users[13] of the tool. MDA-based tools, with its inherent support for the platform independent model (PIM), are perfect tools to build on because utility computing requires a similar inherent characteristic in the form of virtualized environments.

The utility computing tool of the future will not be a stand-alone tool but a tool that goes out to the Internet to search for services that will fit the business model being designed, the software application being developed, or the configuration requirements to build a portfolio of services from other services. As the shift toward reuse and shared resources becomes more prevalent, a tool that increases the likelihood of finding the right resources and services will be forthcoming.

9.5 SUMMARY

A listing[14] of over 450 companies offering SaaS solutions is evidence of the growth of SaaS applications in the last few years. SaaS applications, which were once mostly offered by small startup companies for small and medium-sized business, have also caught the attention of large software vendors. Large traditional software vendors like Oracle and SAP are now offering versions of their applications in the form of SaaS offerings. With a more mature Internet that offers faster and more reliable connections worldwide, SaaS applications can now be offered and accessed from any country in the world. As SaaS providers face more competition, they will have to find ways to keep their customer base loyal. New models for billing and technologies that help monitor levels of service are just a few ways that SaaS providers can help stay one step ahead of their competition.

Discovering reusable software, IT infrastructure services, and business components is the new feature for a redesigned MDA-based tool. Referring to the history of the software industry, software reuse was once thought of, among other things, as stifling to creativity. But with software technology becoming more complex and as faster time to market becomes more of a necessity, reuse of software has become more acceptable. From an infrastructure perspective, ever since the Internet bubble burst, data center and server consolidation has been at the top of every IT manager's priority list. Cost-cutting initiatives, such as virtualizing IT resources, that can result in increased utilization continue to drive

---

[13] Such as CIOs, corporate architects, application architects, software developers, ASPs, and consultants.
[14] See SaaS Showplace at www.SaaS-showplace.com/pages/1/index.htm.

for new data center investments. A tool such as one described in the last section can be used to discover reusable software, as well as "ready to be utilized" infrastructure resources and business components services.

References

[1]   Albaugh, V., and H. Madduri, "The Utility Metering Service of the Universal Management Infrastructure," *IBM System Journal*, Vol. 43, No. 1 2004, available at www.research.ibm.com/journal/sj/431/albaugh.pdf.

[2]   Johnson, M., "Monitoring and Diagnosing Applications with ARM 4.0," available at www.opengroup.org/tech/management/arm/uploads/40/6357/ARM_4.0_paper.pdf.

[3]   Application Response Monitoring, Issue 4.0, Version 2, C or Java Binding, available at www.opengroup.org/management/arm/.

[4]   Open Group ARM download site at www.opengroup.org/management/arm/.

[5]   Karlsson, Even-Andre, *Software Reuse, A Holistic Approach*, New York, John Wiley and Sons, 1995, p. 288.

Chapter 10

Transforming to Software as a Service

While it is true that the concept of software applications offered as utilities in the form of SaaS applications is not new, it is also far from being well defined. An SaaS application is viewed in so many different ways depending on how one defines software applications offered as a service. With more businesses turning to SaaS applications for their enterprise needs, more traditional independent software vendors (ISVs) are looking into adding SaaS offerings to their product portfolios. This chapter is all about transforming software applications into an SaaS and will be of value to ISVs currently offering licensed software and wanting to create a new offering for their customers in line with today's utility computing paradigm.

ISVs thinking of offering software as services today are struggling to define the changes needed to their businesses as well as their applications. For some ISVs who already host their applications within a managed hosting facility for their customers, the progression to software as a service may be simpler. But for those ISVs who are still in the licensed business mindset, the prospect of offering their software as a service may be daunting. With customer demand growing in the software as a service area, ISVs at this point have little or no choice but to investigate their options in this up and coming market opportunity.

Transforming traditional licensed applications into software application services entails the transformation of both the ISV's business model and the technical architecture of its application. Careful deliberation of both business and technical attributes need to be done in unison. We show an example of the application transformation program[1] (ATP) that can mitigate risks involved when venturing out into a utility paradigm and that encompasses both business and technical aspects of the transformation.

---

[1] The structure and the framework of the program deliver an end-to-end process that is streamlined for transforming traditional software applications into hosted applications or software as a service applications.

10.1 APPLICATION TRANSFORMATION PROGRAM

The worldwide project management method (WWPMM) defines a *program* as a group of related projects and other activities managed in a coordinated way to achieve a common long-term objective. In the context of transforming traditional applications to software as a service applications, we define an application transformation program for software applications as a program that follows a sequence of steps organized to streamline an end-to-end application transformation that concludes with the hosting of the application within a managed hosting or utility hosting infrastructure. It is important to understand that software applications offered as services will need to be accessible through the Internet and hosted in a centrally managed hosting location. A program that offers an end-to-end transformation is one that helps ISVs transform not only the technical aspects of their applications but their business processes as well.

Before businesses adopt any new technology, they need to investigate the benefits and the risks associated with the technology to see if it can help their businesses grow. These companies will look for business partners who have a proven track record implementing the new technology. ISVs will be looking for a well-defined methodology that works and takes away unnecessary steps to achieve its goal–that is, to learn about the new technology, see if their business is a match for the new technology, and finally implement the technology. This is the essence of the ATP program.

The ATP is an end-to-end structure or framework that has the processes and procedures to streamline the steps needed for traditional licensed applications to be transformed into software as a service applications. It covers the business and technical aspects of the transformation. It supports the transformation at all levels of business and all layers of the application architecture, including the infrastructure it will run on.

The typical profile of an ISV that goes through this program is one looking for a partner to share the associated risks, such as vendor relationship and viability [1], which have been associated with outsourcing parts of the IT infrastructure. Following a program like the ATP assures an ISV that it does not go through the same path as the one taken by application service providers in the dot-com era. A program like the ATP steers the ISV away from taking unnecessary risks and educates the ISV in transforming its application through best practices and experiences from leading industry consultants of utility computing. The major steps in the ATP program are as follows:

- *Assessment*–Assessment of ISV application for hosting in a managed hosting center and identification requirements for application transformation;
- *Transformation*–The step in the program that helps ISVs transform their application into an SaaS application;
- *Deployment*–Deployment of a transformed application into a managed hosting environment;

- *Evolution*–Provides a continuing service to evolve the application using the latest technologies available.

Figure 10.1 shows the high level step-by-step process of the ATP.

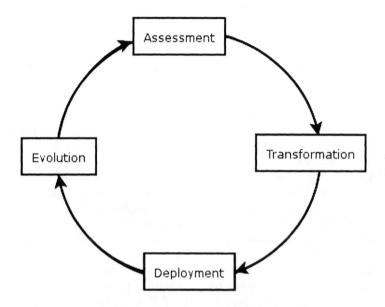

Figure 10.1 Activities within the application transformation program.

The next sections elaborate on the steps within the program and explain them through a case study. The case study presented involves an independent software vendor whose revenue from sales of its licensed software application has declined over several consecutive quarters and that expects the trend to continue in the near future.

10.1.1 Assessment

Assessment is the activity in the program where the ISV receives detailed education in the technologies, tools, and services needed to become an SaaS. The ISV receives education in the benefits of hosting in a managed hosting facility. A high-level assessment of the application architecture and its hosting characteristics is performed.

The high-level assessment produces a report that is presented to the ISV. The assessment report provides the ISV with recommended hosting configuration solutions and recommended actions to take to transform its application into an SaaS. These recommended actions will include both business and technical requirements.

At the end of the assessment phase, the ISV takes with it all necessary information to decide whether to continue with the program or not. The high-level assessment of the hosting configuration tells the ISV what its configuration will look like in the managed hosting center. The high-level application assessment tells the ISV what application characteristics have been identified as potential work items for transformation. The assessment activity delivers the following work products:

- *Data center hosting presentations*–Presentations that introduce the ISV to the managed hosting environment, focusing more on the business aspects of the model than the technical aspects. Business aspects include what it means to host an application in a remote data center.
- *Introduction to variable pricing models*–Discussion of different pricing models that can be formed through partnerships between the ISV and the hosting provider.
- *Software application service case studies*–Different case studies that present successful implementations of software application services. These also present lessons learned from these case studies so that the ISV avoids mistakes made through previous implementations.
- *Qualification questionnaire*–A questionnaire gauging the ISV's readiness to transform to a service-oriented business.
- *SaaS technical education*–This is a technical education that delivers detailed information on SaaS application services architecture.
- *Business model/metric guidance*–The ISV is given guidance on business models and metric options for its application. Correct metering of application usage is critical to the success of the business. The business objectives must be in line with measurement metrics that will eventually be used to bill end customers. The ISV can use this as a starting point for further study of its business practices. With this guide, the ISV can go back to both business and technical organizations in the company and discuss strategies for business as well as technical implications and implementations.
- *Assessment (hosting architecture and SaaS attributes)*–An assessment is made by technical consultants to assess hosting configurations. Depending on customer-provided information, like a capacity planning guide, it is possible to run the numbers through a modeling tool that can predict initial and future hosting configuration requirements for the customer. The ISV's application is assessed for hosting amenability as well as the architecture that will make it an SaaS.
- *Assessment recommendations*–The recommendations are contained in the assessment report given to the ISV before leaving the assessment phase. Each section is discussed with the ISV to make sure it understands how the recommendations came about. The assessment report contains the following sections:

o *Hosting platform*–Recommended hardware configuration for the managed hosting center. This can include recommendations for virtual CPUs or logical partitions in a particular server platform, storage capacity, network bandwidth, and memory requirements.

o *Product technology*–Recommendations for application modification. It includes recommendations for technology implementation based on maturity stages of the business. The SaaS attributes discussed in Chapter 6 are implemented in stages as recommended based on the expected growth of the client business.

o *SaaS roadmap*–A guide that can encompass a recommended path for ISV's future growth in the SaaS business space.

10.1.1.1 Case Study

The ISV, Alamo SCM, Inc., is a fictional company. It is medium-sized company that offers a suite of supply chain management software applications. Its main source of revenue for the past 10 years has been the sales and maintenance of its application sold as a licensed product for medium and large companies. It enjoyed double-digit growth year over year in its first four years of operation, riding the wave of the dot-com mania. In the last several years, however, Alamo has seen licensed revenue drop, first noticing it flattening out. Potential customers who traditionally bought new licensed applications suddenly were harder to find due to tightening budgets brought about by an uncertain economic environment and budgetary constraints. Now Alamo is also seeing some of its once-loyal customers trying out new services from smaller, more agile competitors who are offering their services at lower initial costs and for monthly subscription fees. Making the news worse, Alamo predicts that the trend will continue in the future.

Alamo is a perfect candidate for the ATP. It is looking for a reliable partner to help provide it with expertise in application transformation as well as hosting experience. The ATP provides Alamo with the education it needs to get started with the goal of creating new markets for itself (i.e., offering hosted applications or hosted services, which the ISV operates as an SaaS application provider) and keeping its existing customer base loyal.

During assessment activity, Alamo is introduced to different managed hosting technologies and offerings, the nuances of operating an SaaS model, and new requirements when selling and marketing hosted applications. Along the way, Alamo is educated on the ATP process—what the ATP is all about (i.e., steps, procedures, processes, deliverables) and how the relationship can become a partnership that will result in a win-win situation between the ISV and other parties involved.

The data center education is geared toward a technical audience. The audience will be the CTO, chief application architect if different from the CTO, and a few of their lead application programmers. These sessions are intended to educate the ISV on managed hosting and different technologies that are all applicable to them. The education also touches on life in a hosted environment. Since Alamo has never had any experience with hosting, these sessions provide them invaluable information on what hosting is all about. By learning what happens within a hosting environment, the architects of Alamo's application will have a better understanding of what changes they need to make to their application to live in a hosted environment (i.e., security, remote administration access, remote customer access and so on).

If the managed hosting center uses utility computing technology, the sessions will include education on the utility hosting center. The utility hosting center is an infrastructure that offers true utility infrastructure computing. The utility hosting provider offers pay-as-you-go infrastructure. This means that instead of purchasing servers, the ISV purchases CPU cycles. Depending on the ISV, this may or may not make any difference. It will only make a difference to someone with a preconceived notion of what a traditional data center looks like. Alamo is more interested in how to make sure it orders the right amount of CPU for its customers. Questions like these and others that pertain to hosting operations are all explained in detail to make Alamo as comfortable as possible, once it decides to transform its application into an SaaS.

After the education presentations, the assessment starts to focus on Alamo's application. The main audience for this session is Alamo's chief architect or the lead application programmer. Alamo will be asked specific questions ranging from typical customer configurations (number of servers, module placements on servers, required storage, versions of operating systems, and so on) to remote accessibility by customers and system administrators, security policies, and scalability. This part of the assessment deals mainly with the hosting characteristics of the application. This assessment is designed to answer one question—is the application suitable for hosting.

The application architecture assessment is the part of the assessment phase that looks at the application's readiness to become an SaaS application. Depending on Alamo's software application architecture, SaaS attributes described in Chapter 6 can be implemented in stages. During the application architecture assessment, ATP technical consultants can walk Alamo through each of the attributes and ask more specific questions about the application architecture to make further assessments as to whether the application is ready for a particular attribute.

While the assessment touches solely on technical aspects of the application, Alamo is also reminded that changes it decides to implement in its application may affect some of its business processes. Adding an application service provided over the Internet to its current business model changes not only its business model, but sales and marketing channels, support structures, and even customer relationships.

It takes about a week to complete the assessment report. If, during the creation of the assessment report, the technical consultant has questions about Alamo's application, the proper person at Alamo is contacted through e-mail communications and, if necessary, a direct telephone call. The assessment report will contain Alamo's typical customer installation and current product description. It will contain hosting recommendations and hosting configurations. The assessment will contain recommendations for application changes in terms of software utility attributes. With regard to application transformation work, an estimate is given as to how much effort the ISV needs to put in to make changes to the application. The ISV has the option to do this itself or ask for outside help regarding technical and business process assistance.

In a nutshell, the assessment report is a work product that Alamo can use as a starting point when discussing with all stakeholders within its organization what commitments they will have to make to create an application offered as a service. At this point, Alamo has not committed to doing anything. With the help of the assessment report, Alamo will be able to decide which decision to make next.

10.1.2 Transformation

The transformation phase begins with a recap of the assessment report handed to the ISV at the end of the assessment. The assessment report provides a starting point for technical discussions about SaaS attributes such as hostability, multitenancy strategies, metering algorithms, and service programming interfaces needed to interface the application with the software application services framework of the hosting environment.

During transformation, the ISV begins to understand the architectural changes needed by the application. Business processes pertaining to operating an SaaS application also become clearer. The ISV is introduced to the tools and assistance available to the ISV. The kind of assistance available can include, but is not limited to, business, architectural, hosting, performance, and development consulting. The transformation phase has the following work products and activities:

- *Transformation workshop*–This educates the ISV about technical and business requirements needed to transform into an SaaS.
- *Recommendations for application modifications*–An application modification recommendation report is given to the ISV to consider. It contains a staged-implementation approach of architectural changes for the application.
- *Application transformation*–The ISV can engage application architects to help transform the application into an SaaS application. This may include

architectural help in transforming to a multitenant application or adding metering and billing services.

- *Test and verification*–Once application and business transformation are complete, a test and verification of the application is performed to make sure the application performs and functions as expected.

10.1.2.1 Case Study (Continued)

The transformation phase begins with a workshop that presents Alamo with more education on technologies needed to transform its application into a hosted software application service. The workshop presents Alamo with high-level technical comparisons between licensed product offerings and compares them with products delivered as a service over the Internet.

Alamo will receive education on the hosting center and its utility computing offerings. It will get information on the different standard services it can avail of including ordering their initial base configuration to initially run their application. It is also presented with services that are offered within the infrastructure, such as metering and billing services. These services are already provided within the infrastructure in anticipation of ISVs who want to implement metering and billing for their applications. Alamo is also educated on the tools available to enable them to use these services quickly.

The workshop concludes with Alamo getting all the right guidance to implement and transform its application and business model into a software application service. Alamo has the option of doing all of the application and business transformation itself with very minimal guidance, or Alamo can engage external technical and business consulting services.

In Alamo's situation, the top priority is transforming the application so that it can be remotely administered and securely accessed by its users through the Internet. At this point, Alamo has decided to transform its application into an SaaS in stages. Stage one is to make sure the application contains all the necessary features and security so it can be "hosted." Alamo's initial offering will not be a metered type of usage; instead, users will be billed a set price per month. Alamo chose to do the first stage of technical transformation itself, since it had already started doing some of this work prior to entering into the ATP. Future stages planned include the addition of metering, billing, and automated SLA services provided by third-party vendors specifically service SaaS applications.

Once all application transformation work is completed, the application is tested and verified in an environment that can simulate customer enrollment and access through the Internet. Some ethical security hacking is done to ensure that security glitches are uncovered and fixed before the application goes "live." After all test scenarios are passed, the transformation phase ends.

10.1.3 Deployment

After transformation, which can last as long as 6 months, the ISV, together with the transformed application reenters the ATP mainstream in the deployment phase. The fully transformed application is assessed once more, this time by hosting architects to make sure the application is amenable to the hosting environment. The hosting architects gather information for hosting and boarding requirements. Information gathered during the assessment phase is used and is reverified in case new requirements have changed previous information. Configuration, hosting requirements, and preenrollment to any utility services within the hosting environment are all done during this phase.

The ISV and hosting provider establish a service level agreement that includes but is not limited to provisioning decisions, expected uptimes, expected turnaround times for provisioning and deprovisioning resources, and backup and restore time frames.

Before installing the application, delivery architects in the hosting centers configure and provision the servers according to information gathered in the latest assessment. The following procedures are entered into the workflow for execution:

- Installation operating systems and middleware stack requirements;
- Configuration of disk storage requirements;
- Configuration of network connections and load-balancing requirements;
- Verification of CPU baseline measurements.

Once the servers are configured, the application is installed and configured. The ISV does a final test run on the application before it opens for business. The deployment phase includes the following activities:

- *Boarding of application onto the hosting center*–The application is installed and loaded on the hosting center.
- *Execution of joint marketing plan*–Once the application is ready to take in its first customer, the ISV, in partnership with the hosting partner, executes a joint marketing plan.

10.1.3.1 Case Study (Continued)

Alamo enters the deployment phase and is engaged by hosting architects at the hosting center. Alamo goes through an assessment similar to the ATP assessment phase but more focused on application configuration details. In this assessment, Alamo is given the opportunity to revise the initial requirements for hosting it had provided during the assessment phase. During the assessment phase, Alamo had projected an initial customer base of 4 organizations with 250 users; now it is projecting 10 organizations with an average of 150 users each.

Among Alamo's enablement activities with the hosting architects are planning for load-balancing configurations, Internet connections, and security guidelines and establishing service level agreements with the hosting provider. Once all planning activities are completed, a report is produced that documents the deployment activities.

In the deployment phase of the end-to-end ATP engagement, the Alamo SCM application finally goes online. The Alamo SCM application is installed on a server group that includes a particular server platform, a supported version of the operating system, middleware, and other server platform utilities for server monitoring. After the application is installed, Alamo technicians test the application remotely and fix any problems found before going online. Once the application is tested, the first Alamo SCM customer can use the Alamo SCM suite of applications offered as a service.

10.1.4 Evolution

The evolution phase of the program is part of life-cycle support of the ATP. As new technologies present themselves, it is important that these technologies are explored in terms of capabilities that may enhance the SaaS application. The evolution stage is a commitment by the hosting provider to the ISV that it will provide the ISV with information to help evolve the SaaS application using the latest utility computing technologies. The evolution phase includes the following activity:

- Assistance with implementing new technologies for utility computing.

10.1.4.1 Case Study (Continued)

After eight months of operation, Alamo SCM is doing great. ATP has opened up new business opportunities for Alamo and Alamo has successfully achieved its goal of keeping its customers loyal through trial subscriptions to its application service. This allows the customers to study the benefits of application services without looking at other competitor products.

Currently, Alamo is looking into incorporating metering in its application. Alamo wants to study further the use of its application to see if adding metering functionality makes sense. Alamo knows that adding metering functionalities to its application will allow it to offer a true pay-as-you-go service. It knows that to penetrate newer markets and gain more customers with very dynamic business needs, Alamo needs to revisit its pricing strategy. Alamo needs to adopt more granular pricing models, allowing its customers more flexibility.

10.2 BUSINESS MODEL SCENARIOS

A tool for modeling business scenarios can be used to offer guidance for ISVs wanting to transform not only their applications but their businesses. A modeling tool is used to show four different pricing and deployment options the ISV can consider.

The five scenarios as depicted in Figure 10.2 start off with the *end consumer's* asking how he or she is going to run the application. The answer will be either using an on-premises or off-premises installation. The first of the two scenarios is the on-premises scenario where the ISV sells its application to the end customer. In this case, the application is installed on the customer's premises. The on-premises model offers two modes of paying for the application and the operating environment. The two on-premises models are as follows:

- End-consumer premises installed application–fixed pricing;
- End-consumer premises installed application–variable pricing.

Both scenarios have different implications for the ISV with regard to its current pricing models.

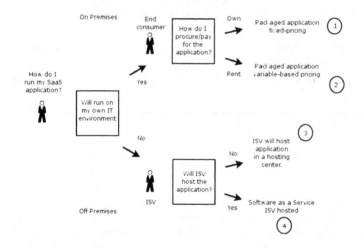

Figure 10.2 Different scenarios an ISV can choose to offer software applications.

If the end consumer chooses to run the application off-premises, then a different path is taken where two other scenarios are presented, this time involving the ISV, which is represented as the outsourcing partner, and the owner of the software application. As attention now focuses on the ISV, the modeling tool asks the ISV if the ISV will be responsible for hosting the application. Depending on the ISV's answer, the path will lead the ISV to different scenarios:

- Software as a Service–externally hosted;
- Software as a Service–ISV hosted.

The modeling tool goes through each of the two off-premises scenarios, providing high-level, indicative financial results to demonstrate the impact of adopting an SaaS model strategy. The first option, software as a service scenario, externally hosted, is the one that most ISVs going through the ATP usually take. In this case the ISV partners with the hosting provider for managed hosting services only. The ISV will remain responsible for application maintenance and offers the application as a multitenant application on a subscription basis. In this scenario, the ISV application is hosted at the hosting partner's utility hosting centers.

The second option, software as a service scenario, ISV hosted, is a model wherein the ISV does all of what is required to offer software as a service. In this scenario, the ISV does it all–offers the application in its own data center, maintains and manages the application, markets and sells the application, and provides its own path to evolving into a true utility computing model. This might be the least taken path by ISVs going through the ATP. The cost of a data center alone, which may run between $1 and $2 million, may not sound as enticing, considering that the ISV can use utility hosting centers for the same purpose. The modeling tool can be designed to have the following characteristics:

- Designed to provide high-level indicative financial results to demonstrate the impact of SaaS model adoption;
- Use publicly available financial information (i.e., 10-Ks) where available or estimates to create a baseline of financial performance;
- Model the assumed level of investment required and the opportunity created across each of the five on-demand scenarios.

The business modeling tool[2] can be offered as a comprehensive tool that covers the five different business scenarios. Among the input data considered in the tool are customer financial information, market segmentation, including geographic and industry-specific segmentations, costs such as building one's own data center, cost of transforming into a multitenant architecture, and more. After the tool is fed with all the necessary information, the ISV is shown several what-if scenarios as to the different options the ISV can take. The business modeling tool is a powerful tool that shows ISVs the different scenarios, costs, and possible outcomes of the different models.

---

[2] The business modeling data is not meant to be used as business cases for investment, but as directional results to describe the implications of a business proposition of software utility application services to revenues and costs, which can set the table for a deeper level of discussion.

10.3 FROM LICENSED SOFTWARE TO SaaS—A CASE STUDY

Journyx.com is an independent software vendor that offers Web-based time-, expense-, and project-tracking solutions. It introduced its tracking application in 1997 as a licensed software application. Today, it boasts of more than 300,000 users in over 10,000 organizations.

Journyx first offered its time-tracking application as a licensed application targeting small-to-large companies that needed to track time spent on different projects. Journyx's application was written from scratch and was designed to be Internet capable. The ability to access the application securely over the Internet and to administer it remotely were the key attributes and design objectives of the Journyx time-tracking application.

Journyx is successful in selling its application to customers who manage the application themselves. In addition to application software, Journyx provides consulting services to help its customers customize the application according to their needs. The service includes the necessary training of the company administrator who will handle the time-tracking application.

With the demand for Internet application services exploding in 1999, Journyx ventured into the world of providing its application over the Internet as a service. It was not hard for Journyx to get started on creating an application service since the application was already well suited for Internet delivery. What Journyx did not realize were the problems it would soon face providing real-time service to companies of different sizes and in different geographic locations. According to Journyx's CEO and founder, Curt Finch, the SaaS business was particularly hard to maintain and keep up. The manager in charge of making sure the application was running perfectly kept getting calls in the middle of the night from overseas customers for application support. To say the least, maintaining and managing the application was, according to Mr. Finch, a money-losing proposition for Journyx.

Journyx maintained and managed a bunch of servers in a colocation arrangement with a local Internet hosting provider. To make sure that servers were fully utilized, Journyx had arranged installed instances of the application on servers according to their customer's time zones. For instance, if there were a customer with an 8-hour time-zone difference from the east coast, Journyx would place that customer's application instance with a customer from the east coast. This would mean that the customer on the east coast would start to use the server as the other customer signed off for the night. The solution was a manual and simple implementation of infrastructure management that took into consideration utilization of servers by different organizations in different time zones.

Today, Journyx has managed to grow its SaaS business, which now makes up 20% of its total revenues. Mr. Finch acknowledges that his licensed application offering had lost some business to its SaaS offering. On the other hand, Journyx has also managed to maintain a more loyal customer base in its SaaS offering. As an SaaS provider, Journyx charges its customers a monthly fee per user with a minimum number of users and 2- or 3-year contracts with early termination penalties. This worked well for Journyx until a particular class of customers demanded a better pricing scheme that was based on the dynamic nature of their businesses.

An example of this type of customer is a staffing agency which employs four or five permanent employees but manages between 500 to 1,000 temporary workers at any one time. As Journyx's pricing scheme was based on user accounts staying active for the term of the contract (2 to 3 years), a fluctuating user base, such as that of the staffing agency, did not fit the current pricing scheme. In this case, if a company other than the staffing company had 27 users, Journyx would charge it for a minimum of 30 users; and that would be fine for the life of the contract. But if a staffing company said it had 1,000 users and then the next week its staff dropped to 500, then a long-term pricing scheme was not going to work. To solve this problem, Journyx had to devise a more granular pricing schedule. In this case Journyx created a pricing structure to accommodate a staffing business by changing its long-term contracts of 3 years to shorter-term contracts of 30 days. The change allowed for staffing agencies to use Journyx's SaaS offering in a more flexible fashion.

By restructuring its pricing policies, Journyx was able to expand its market. When asked about utility-based pricing like metering for usage, Mr. Finch was quick to admit that utility-based strategies like utility pricing is the way to go in the future. Today, Journyx maintains its SaaS environment and is keeping its options open for future enhancements as it grows its business.

10.4 SUMMARY

Transforming an enterprise application into an SaaS is by no means trivial. It will require expert help and adherence to established standards and best practices. Today, out of necessity, ISVs are looking at ways to grow their businesses and keep their customers loyal. As the case study of Journyx shows, being flexible and receptive to customer needs helps open new opportunities while keeping other customers loyal.

One only needs to enter the word "SaaS" on Google to see pages of companies offering SaaS-related transformation services. Companies like IBM,[3] OpSource,[4] and WebApps, Inc.[5] offer SaaS services that include transforming applications into SaaS. This chapter described an implementation of a process called the Application Transformation Program (ATP). The process helps ISVs transform their applications into software application services. The process covers both technical and business transformation which can give ISVs the advantage of predicting future demand and growth for their business. This process is structured, repeatable, and globally deployable.

---

[3] www.ibm.com/isv/sas.
[4] www.opsource.net/solutions/saas_enablement.shtml.
[5] www.saas.com.

Reference

[1]   Ross, J., and G. Westerman, "Preparing for Utility Computing," *IBM System Journal*, Vol. 43, No. 1, 2004, p. 7.

Chapter 11

Virtual Services for Organizations

Level 4 of the continuum of utilities refers to shared-process utilities. While this level may not have direct links to utility computing from a technical perspective, shared processes can be set up in a manner that can take advantage of services and tools based on utility computing. First, however, we need to define what shared-process utilities are all about. The concept of shared-process utilities originates from the need to streamline business processes and organizations. Business process reengineering has been the way most companies streamline their businesses.

Business process reengineering has been around since the early 1920s [1]. It is the reorganization or reengineering of business organizations from being task oriented to being process centered for the sake of maximizing value for today's demandcentric customer [2]. It was only in the 1960s, however, that business process reengineering became more of a practice within large organizations. Since then, businesses have reorganized and outsourced themselves to such a point that while they were able to achieve breakthrough improvements, they did so at the cost of creating organizations that are out of control and barely recognizable to its business leaders [2]. Toward the end of the business process reengineering movement in the mid-1990s, *business process reengineering* had become just another term for "another round of layoffs or outsourcing." Today, the same business leaders are trying to regain control of their organizations by trying to understand each business process in detail, down to each component that makes up the end-to-end process. While trying to regain control of their organizations, business leaders not only have to face old problems like global competition and demanding customers, but they also have to face new problems like Internet viruses, new government regulations, and economic uncertainty. Business leaders today need a new way of regaining control of the organization and new ways of doing business to meet ever-increasing customer expectations in the new global economy.

There is opportunity for businesses to do just that. Improvements beyond reengineering processes must evolve to reengineer business components within these processes. With the rise of open standards, the ubiquity of the Internet, and the proliferation of newer technologies like real-time business-data analytics and

209

massive computing power, organizational improvements can easily become a reality. After reengineering the business, the next logical step is to improve its performance. Just as a newly developed software application goes through performance testing and tuning, reengineered business processes will have to undergo performance transformation to improve the business.

With business process complexity on the rise, breaking the process down into its components and analyzing them one at a time gives CEOs the opportunity to assess which components are core and noncore, which are redundant, what can be standardized, and what can be virtualized. By applying a utility computing paradigm to the business process, components can be transformed into virtual components serving vertical industries that can provide higher levels of service as well as flexibility. Business transformation for performance revisits the process of business process reengineering once more, but this time it analyzes components within the process. In a large organization, several hundreds of processes may exist. Within these processes, one will find redundant components that can be standardized to serve across process boundaries. Business transformation for performance is not business process reengineering. Business transformation is what happens beyond that and how today's new utility computing advancements are applied to businesses. This chapter introduces the concept of business process componentization and a new paradigm of offering utility business services that takes advantage of utility computing technologies.

11.1 BUSINESS TRANSFORMATION FOR PERFORMANCE

In the continuum of utilities outlined in Chapter 1, each layer builds on top of the previous one. In the fourth level of the continuum, business processes are broken down within siloed[1] business organizations. To understand their business constructs, forward-looking enterprises are breaking down their business organizations into their basic business components. Within the whole enterprise, business organizations will deconstruct their processes into business functions that can be classified as producing business functionalities within the organization.

Focusing on improving performance in support of business requirements makes siloed business organizations obsolete. Deconstruction and analysis of discrete business functionalities can lead to fixing gaps or eliminating redundancies, as well as identifying core and noncore business functions. Once business deconstruction into basic components is performed and core competencies versus supporting components are classified, business can focus on producing products that are truly market driven.

---

[1] A business model where segments of the business are largely self-contained and vertically integrated within the organization, resulting in communication barriers between those segments and process and expense duplication across the enterprise. See www.ibm.com/services/ondemand/insurancepov_1.html.

Siloed business deconstruction and transformation into componentized business functions must begin with a shift in corporate mindset to–understanding current and future initiatives in the context of being flexible, responsive, resilient, and focused. Business executives need to recognize that cultural aspects, as well as technological architecture and business process redesign, must be taken into consideration not as separate entities but as entities that are all connected to each other. Thus, making a change to one may affect another. A new business component model that breaks down a business into components and creates relationships between the components (otherwise known as activities) must first be realized. The component-based business model is a business design technique that creates the construct of the business by identifying the unique and stand-alone set of business building blocks, while detaching from the boundaries and confinement created by inertia, organization, product, channel, location, and legacy data. By deconstructing business into the components of business activities, business can often find gaps and overlaps in the business components required.

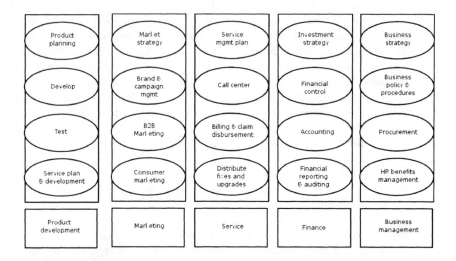

Figure 11.1 Shows how business units within an organization can be componentized into core and noncore business components.

One example of business deconstruction is shown in Figure 11.1. This figure depicts an enterprise deconstruction, where siloed business organizations within a fictional enterprise have been decomposed into components. The business silos represent product development, marketing, service, finance, and management. Services within each business silo are shown within the vertical boxes. For example, product planning, development, test, and service plan/developments all belong to the product development business silo. Market strategy, brand and campaign management, B2B marketing, and consumer marketing are different aspects of the Marketing business silo. As the silos are deconstructed, the company can determine if individual components in a silo, such as the "test" component within the product development silo, are a noncore business functionality, or they can conduct gap analysis and determine whether the silo lacks some unique procedure and execution service to function properly. Once this is determined, the company can look into filling in the gaps for this component internally or totally outsourcing the component.

Identifying which are "core" or "noncore" business components and which are inefficient are the key steps in the deconstruction process. Through componentization, unique data points of a business component can be identified and thereby help create decision points to facilitate identifying noncore and inefficient functionalities. Having identified noncore and inefficient functionalities, the company can do either of two things:

- Fix the gaps through internal activities involving the analysis of the current organization and the development of a goal-oriented operating model. For example, a large banking institution that has grown in size through mergers and acquisitions may find out that it has no consistency in its current product offerings, resulting in delay of new product releases, competition among internal organizations, and confused customers. In this scenario, the company, after analysis of the current situation, set a goal to standardize product offerings across business units. By setting a goal to have a consistent product offering, the company was able to develop a shared and collaborative process that could be used by all its business units. This new process resulted in eliminating siloed organizations and created collaboration between business units, which reduced time to market for new products. In this case the end result came in the form of shared services and processes across business units.

- Externalize functionalities as common services that can be shared by other organizations within the company. Common services that are found to be similar within different organizations or processes to create a common service shared by organizations can lead to lower transaction costs. As efficiency and cost reduction remains a major focus of organizations today, noncore functionalities will continue to be targets of cost and efficiency actions. Organizations will collaborate with external partners and networks to provide them with noncore functionalities such as human resources services, accounting services, and IT services, to name a few. Just as IT infrastructures become commoditized, business functionalities are heading in the same direction. Business functionalities will be provided by a network of specialized services providers in their respective fields (e.g., HR services, accounting services, or IT services).

Componentization is a way to simplify how executives look at their operations. On one hand, executives can identify unique and autonomous building blocks that make up the overall company. These building blocks are, in essence, the company's core competencies, which they can focus on, allowing them to differentiate themselves from their competitors. On the other hand, componentization can help identify redundant processes within different organizational structures that can be combined and externalized to reduce cost and optimize overall company performance. Figure 11.2 shows a conceptual view of componentization to identify similar activities from different processes.

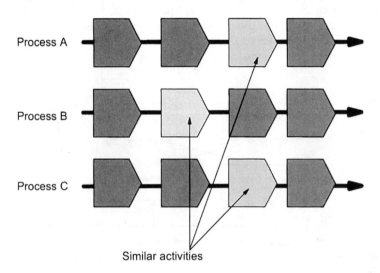

Figure 11.2 Componentization helps identify similar activities in different processes.

In this example, a company that has processes A, B, and C from different organizations is analyzed and discovered to have a similar activity within those processes. Although the processes come from different organizations, a step in each of the processes is identified to have enough commonalities that it can be used by the different organizations. Componentization can give the executive a more granular view of activities within the organization, which, with further investigation, can allow for similarities to be discovered so that activities can be combined.

Just like identifying similar activities within processes, similar functional business components can also be identified from different business units. Externalizing these business components can then become a viable option. Next, we examine the concept of externalized functions coming from a business service marketplace.

11.2 BUSINESS SERVICE MARKETPLACE FACILITY

The building blocks of an organization are the people, business processes, and technology that create components providing value to the organization. A business process may be thought of as a workflow that creates an end-to-end set of activities, resulting in the fulfillment of a business objective. In today's modern organization, it is common to find that business processes are supported by new technology. A workflow to process payment for an airline ticket purchased on the Internet may include checking airline seat availability, making the airline reservation, validating and verifying credit card information, and issuing tickets. Each activity in the workflow can be considered a service provided by the ticketing agent, the airline company, and credit card authorization agent, each backed up by their respective infrastructures to provide such business services as needed.

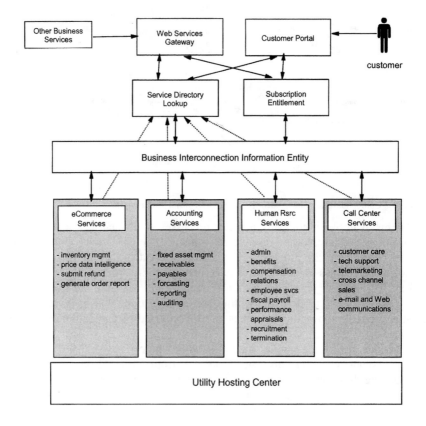

Figure 11.3 A conceptual business service marketplace where services can be subscribed to via a service portal or Web services interface.

To provide these business services requires networked capabilities among the services and the security for businesses to access them. They also need to be measurable with the option to be billable. One can envision that a conglomeration of vendors can get together and set up a service marketplace that provides business services to business entities and acts as a clearinghouse for the service function providers. A marketplace provider can set up a services framework where service function providers can "set up shop." Their users (subscribers) will be authenticated and authorized for the service functions, while transactions are recorded, metered, and billed based on usage. Figure 11.3 shows a conceptual business service marketplace, where services can be subscribed to via a service portal or Web services interface.

An on-demand service marketplace could be constructed with utility computing components that were discussed in previous chapters (i.e., software as a service application, services utility application framework, utility hosting center). A utility hosting center environment can provide virtualized infrastructure components, while the utility services application framework can offer atomic, common, basic business services like metering, billing, and identity management. Each business service must also be atomic (transaction oriented), open to subscriptions, measurable, and billable. All business application services must be interconnected (able to subscribe to each other). Functions performing business services within the infrastructure will become building platforms for setting up the business service marketplace.

The example shows how some of the common services from our fictional organization can be externalized and provided as service components. These components provide the business processes and technology that can be plugged back into the organization, allowing the business to use standardized services throughout the company.

11.2.1 Technology for a Business Service Marketplace

Once a conceptual view of the business marketplace is established and the necessary business services are categorized and defined, the next task will be creating, importing, and constructing the necessary technology to deliver the business services. The chosen technology must contain utility computing features and characteristics such as variability, resilience, and standards compliance. Resource virtualizations (e.g., CPU on demand, storage on demand) and autonomic characteristics (monitor and detect-on-demand) will be important. Figure 11.4 shows a technology implementation that can be constructed to implement the business service marketplace.

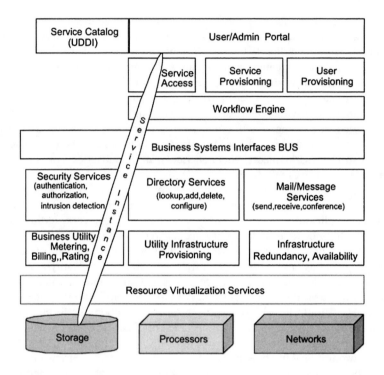

Figure 11.4 A technology implementation that can be constructed to implement the business service marketplace.

The building blocks of the infrastructure are themselves pluggable components that can be provided by other service providers.

11.2.2 Role of Business Service Marketplace Provider

Once organizational business units within the company identify components that are similar and noncore, they have the option to reorganize internally or seek external providers to help fill the gaps in their business functionalities.

Business application owners or ISVs who are looking into extending their market share or creating a new business can have their applications transformed into a discreet set of application services. Once transformed, these business applications will need a place or a service ecosystem, where their services are advertised, rated, and subscribed to. The service marketplace owner, whether it is a trade organization or a major IT corporation, will need to provide a business bazaar for business service consumers and business service providers. They will become a service clearinghouse, provider of underlying technology, security guarantor that ensures entitlements are met, qualifier of business services, and manager of the service ecosystem. Only a major entity with vision and integrity or a business neutral governing entity will be qualified for this task. One can imagine a flexible business future where the concept of a utility computing ecosystem is set up, business services are advertised, and enterprise organizations subscribe to these services as needed. Figure 11.5 shows another conceptual view of a business marketplace where business components are advertised and used by enterprise systems or components.

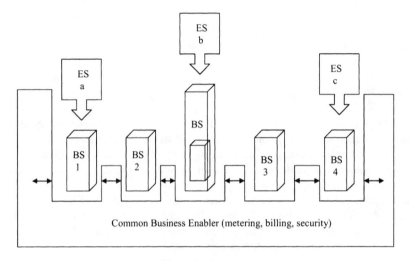

Business Service Marketplace

BS: Business service advertised
ES: Enterprise component uses business service

Figure 11.5 Another conceptual view of a business marketplace where business components are advertised and used by enterprise systems or components.

Today's emerging technology and standards, like the service-oriented architecture and Web services standards, are allowing vendors and businesses to offer and connect business functionalities respectively. Commoditization of IT is already happening. In an economic environment that is becoming more global everyday, it will not be long before we see the emergence of a business service marketplace that sells service functionalities as commodities.

11.3 VARIABLE VIRTUAL COMPANY (CASE STUDY)

The following case study is presented with permission from IBM and Lam Research. The case study focuses on a utility service from IBM called Product Lifecycle Management (PLM) for on-demand business. This service encompasses all layers of utility computing touched on in this book, namely, the infrastructure, software application, and business components.

Based in Fremont, California, Lam Research Corporation (Lam) provides semiconductor manufacturers with equipment they need to fabricate chips. The company's Etch systems are used to shape the microscopic layers into circuits; Lam's chemical mechanical planarization systems ensure surface uniformity on "wafers" as they are layered with material during their manufacture. Both processes are critical in the manufacture of today's most advanced chips. Founded in 1980, Lam maintains customer support centers throughout the United States, Asia, and Europe to meet the complex and changing needs of its global customer base.

Like the semiconductor industry it serves, the semiconductor equipment industry is marked by extreme swings in demand. As demand changes, chip manufacturers make necessary adjustments to their production schedules as well as their investments in fabrication facilities and equipment, or "fabs." These adjustments quickly percolate down the industry value chain to equipment manufacturers like Lam, which must then adjust its own production schedules to meet the rising or falling demand. For their own competitive survival, semiconductor equipment manufacturers have thus been compelled to operate in a reactive mode, with rapid adjustment a necessity.

The tight link between semiconductor manufacturers and equipment vendors is also seen in the increasing levels of consolidation in both industries. Among chipmakers, key drivers of consolidation are the industry's natural maturation, and the fact that fewer companies can afford to invest in the enormously expensive fabs needed to build today's state-of-the-art semiconductors. As the number of chip vendors has fallen, equipment vendors selling into this denser market have been forced to follow suit, generally through acquisitions designed to broaden product lines and improve cost efficiencies. As a result of this consolidation, it is expected that by 2010, 80% of industry revenues will be generated by just half a dozen equipment manufacturers. For Lam and its peers, this is expected to mean an increasingly unforgiving competitive environment with success derived from agility and effective cost control.

Extreme volatility in demand for semiconductors leads to highly cyclical demand for Lam's products among semiconductor manufacturers. Consolidation of semiconductor manufacturers and equipment vendors has led to increased competitive intensity in Lam's market and the resulting strategic importance of cost control. Lam relies heavily on ERP and manual processes to manage data for complex design functions. Lam wanted to increase its efficiency in design engineering, manufacturing, and field service team operations, while enhancing collaborative design capabilities. Rather than focusing on each of these areas separately, Lam needed a complete solution that would address these core functions in an integrated, end-to-end manner. Enter PLM, which manages the development and support of complex physical products throughout the entire product life cycle. Lam's volatile marketplace and the cyclic nature of its business posed a particular challenge to funding and transforming its engineering and design processes with a PLM solution. To operate in this environment successfully, Lam wanted to implement a variable-cost business model that would improve the Company's financial performance during downturns.

Having established the need to build variability and focus into its business model, Lam embarked on a journey toward becoming a "variable virtual company" by outsourcing its noncore functions, like facilities management and human resources services [3]. Once noncore functions were outsourced, Lam focused on PLM to integrate processes required to design, build, deploy, and maintain products and support its product-development efforts.

Lam chose to leverage IBM's PLM on-demand offering to fill its needs for a variable-cost "utility-style" service rather than embarking on a traditional investment in applications, hardware, and infrastructure. The service reduces capital investment with no direct outlay for hardware, software, or services. IBM provided all PLM services, including consulting services. The service is priced based on named users per month and bundles of software, implementation services, infrastructure hosting and management, and application management and maintenance.

By implementing a variable business model in its product life-cycle management implementation, Lam will enhance its competitive position. Among the many expected benefits are:

- Enhanced productivity across all functions in the value chain;
- Accelerated time to market for core products;
- Enhanced knowledge management;
- Enhanced customer service through use of collaborative design tools;
- Variable costs and flexibility to cope with inevitable business cycles;
- Accelerated "time to benefit."

Author's Notes:

IBM's PLM for on-demand business is a utility offering that includes application, infrastructure, and services as utilities. The service is bundled and is priced based upon named users per month using the service. As the service is new, it is expected that it will evolve into unbundled services and move toward a more microtype billing instead of the named users per month type of billing, depending on customer demand. The move toward utility services like the IBM PLM for on-demand business is upon us; expect to see more services like this for other industry sectors from other companies as demand grows. IBM's PLM for on-demand business includes the following business processes:

- Bill of material management;
- Engineering change management;
- Part number management;
- ERP interfaces;
- Life cycle and aftermarket support;
- Supplier collaboration;
- Knowledge and intellectual property management;
- Project management.

The service is bundled with the following PLM software hosted by IBM's utility hosting center located in Boulder, Colorado. As of this writing, the application software is provided by Parametric Technology Corporation and includes Version 7.0 of the Windchill suite. Applications include PDM-Link and Project-Link.

11.4 SUMMARY

This chapter presented a conceptual and perhaps futuristic glimpse of a utility services ecosystem where business components can be offered, advertised, and subscribed to–this is called a business service marketplace. In some respects, the business service marketplace concept may already look familiar. Business-to-business collaborations are in place today between private enterprises. They create their own e-commerce business rules and abide by them to avoid disputes that may arise in the course of doing business with each other. The envisioned business service marketplace improves on this concept by treating business processes as utilities. A governing body or the marketplace provider will act as the pseudomanager who keeps the ecosystem in order. Utility computing technology will be used in all layers, including infrastructure, applications, business components, and functions.

A fine example of a marketplace for business is CapOneSource, LLC (www.caponesource.com), which, according to its Web site, is a not-for-profit alliance of providers and consumers of common corporate services. Members and providers share in the vision of reducing costs and increasing productivity by aggregating demand for services through a single, highly capable supplier. Founded in July 2003 by Lam, Varian, Mattson, and Credence, the group has ballooned to 26 firms as of this writing, with plans to grow each year.

As of this writing, the alliance lists 17 providers, with plans to expand the list, providing services such as:

- *Finance and accounting*–Tax management, financial reporting, receivables, travel;

- *General services*–Benefits administration, E-learning, facilities – real estate management, office productivity, security
- *Operations*–Warehousing and logistics, direct and indirect procurement, freight
- *Information services*–Help desk, applications support, data center, networks and communications

Published reports mention savings to CapOneSource members in the 30% or more neighborhood, which is likely to make any company executive enjoy the benefits of the alliance.

Today, more than ever, CEOs need to understand their organizations as they embark on growth projects. Componentizing business functionalities to identify the building blocks that make up the company will ease identification of noncore business functionalities. These noncore functionalities can then be externalized, paving the way for these components to become more standardized. Just like software reuse, where common components are standardized to be used in different parts of the application, common business functionalities can be identified and standardized to be used within the whole organization. Componentized business functionalities will be offered and sold in the same fashion as software applications which were once developed in-house and are now commodities sold by software vendors.

References

[1]   Strassmann, P., "The Roots of Business Process Reengineering," *American Programmer*, June 1995, available at www.strassmann.com/pubs/reeng/roots.html.

[2]   Hammer, M., *Beyond Reengineering*, New York, New York, HarperBusiness, 1997.

[3]   "Lam Research: A Variable Virtual Company Focuses on the Core," available at www.ibm.com/jct03001c/software/success/cssdb.nsf/CS/GJON-5XENHE? OpenDocument&Site=default.

Chapter 12

The Future

There is much to look forward to in the future of utility computing. Companies like IBM, HP, and Sun are continuing to develop infrastructures based on architectures that provide utility-type services. These architectures include servers, storage, and networks that can be configured and used on demand. Coupled with intelligent software management applications, these hardware resources can be orchestrated to provide IT resources in a more on-demand fashion.

In the application space, small-, medium-, and large-sized companies have realized the importance of software as a service offerings. Even after the demise of most ASPs in early 2000, net-native vendors offering their software applications as services continue to make headway and to grow their customer bases. Salesforce.com, whose application offering has become the poster child for subscription-based pricing, is proving that providing software as a service is a profitable business as shown by increased customer sales[1] over the last few years.

While some consider utility computing as just another form of outsourcing, it really is not the same thing. Utility computing represents a paradigm shift that requires a different way of looking at the objectives of the business. From a technological standpoint, utility computing offers new tools and techniques that can provide more flexible and affordable solutions to the dependency on IT infrastructure that does not work. From a business perspective, the utility model allows companies to focus more on their core strengths while letting go of noncore functionalities. As a whole, we can view utility computing and the utility model as something more than outsourcing—it is a solution that not only brings about technological transformation but business transformation as well.

12.1 THE FUTURE OF THE IT INFRASTRUCTURE

CIOs have been working on maximizing utilization and lowering data center costs over the last few years. In those years, companies have become more aware of the low rate of return on investments they have made in their data centers. These

---

[1] As reported in its annual reports.

companies have invested large amounts of money on their IT infrastructure only to find out that overcapacity and low utilization rates abound. Slowly, they are consolidating their data centers, servers, and other hardware components. Virtualization technology is allowing hardware to be shared and utilized more by different organizations within the same company. Better software management applications are allowing these organizations to take more control of their IT resources and so reduce costly manual operations. The realization that IT infrastructure costs can be contained is setting in. In the future more components in the data center will be replaced by new ones that implement utility computing technologies.

It is possible to envision an IT infrastructure of the future that will provision and offer IT functionalities as needed. Today's hardware servers already implement the necessary architecture to provide hardware provisioning. Software management applications that intelligently monitor usage and control provisioning and deprovisioning resources as needed are generally available as well. Metering functionalities that keep count of hardware resource usage can be installed in the infrastructure for later billing or auditing. In time, these technologies will evolve such that they can easily be integrated, alleviating customer concerns about complexity.

Today, managed hosting providers such as IBM, Sun, HP, ATT, and EDS offer their own utility computing solutions. Adopters of these services use them as solutions that supplement their own business needs. CIOs term these tactical decisions *selective* or *smart sourcing*.[2] In a survey done by IDC on utility computing, of 34 potential utility computing customers, 64% expressed interest in leveraging some type of utility computing service [1]. In the future, managed hosting offerings based on utility-type environments will shape the acceptance of utility computing within the corporate data center. In today's economic environment, CIOs are cautious to try new technologies. It is in the utility provider's best interest to provide a clear and strategic vision that can provide a compelling, robust value proposition to gain customer trust [2].

No doubt, CIOs are well aware of failed outsourcing deals as well as successes. These failed dealings, more often than not, lead CIOs to go with in-sourcing strategies rather than outsourced offerings. This is why in the future we will see more vendors offering utility computing services that cater more to customer preferences. Figure 12.1 shows a summary of infrastructure utilities services that will be common offerings in the future.

Vendors offering utility computing products and services will cater to customer preferences for managing and retaining control of their infrastructure. These offerings may be named differently depending on the vendor and provider of utility infrastructure, but essentially these offerings fall into one of three categories–private, hybrid, and public infrastructures. The offerings are based on

---

[2] In selective or smart sourcing, companies know exactly what they need to outsource that would make more economic sense for utility providers to offer.

where the infrastructure is managed, the customer's tolerance for managing complexity, and the economic viability. The more complex the infrastructure gets, the greater the tendency to transition the infrastructure from a self-managed infrastructure to an externally managed one. The more standard and utilitylike it gets, the better the chance that the infrastructure will be outsourced.

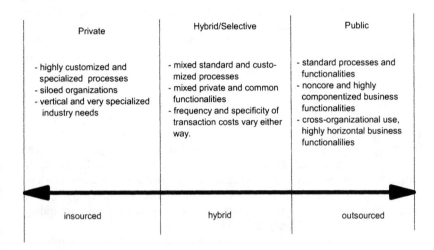

Private	Hybrid/Selective	Public
- highly customized and specialized processes - siloed organizations - vertical and very specialized industry needs	- mixed standard and customized processes - mixed private and common functionalities - frequency and specificity of transaction costs vary either way.	- standard processes and functionalities - noncore and highly componentized business functionalities - cross-organizational use, highly horizontal business functionalilies
insourced	hybrid	outsourced

Figure 12.1 Utility offerings and their characteristics.

Further in the future, grid technology that allows sharing and aggregating of hardware resources will come of age. While still widely used for technical, scientific, and high-performance work, grid technology will make headway into several industry sectors (e.g., financial, government, health care). Virtual infrastructure utilities supporting a grid economy will enable the sharing of resources across IT infrastructures.

12.2 FUTURE OF SOFTWARE UTILITY APPLICATIONS

Software as a service applications will continue to provide business value, especially for small-, medium-, and large-sized businesses. For any organization that may not be enamored with the idea of spending large amounts of money for upfront licensing fees and waiting the long deployment time for a CRM application, being able to use one for less than $70 per month without delay is reason enough to use SaaS applications. Changes in business attitudes regarding licensed software are shaping the landscape for software vendors to look into complementing their licensed offerings with application utility offerings. This is why large ISVs such as Siebel, SAP, and Peoplesoft (an Oracle company) now offer their own SaaS applications.

While there are more new ISVs offering SaaS applications today, some not so new ISVs have established profitable, licensed product offerings and are reluctant to jump onto the SaaS bandwagon. These ISVs fear they will cannibalize current product offerings if they offer a SaaS version of their product. These ISVs fear their revenue, which mostly comes from upfront licensing and yearly maintenance fees, will be lost by offering a SaaS application. Revenue generated through a SaaS offering is small and spread out over a long period when compared to upfront licensing and yearly maintenance fees that licensed offerings produce. The established ISV that already offers a licensed product offering often asks itself: With hundreds of millions of dollars worth of business at stake, will it be worth establishing a new line of business at the risk of jeopardizing the existing one?

The answer is yes. First, economic uncertainty experienced early in the new millennium[3] has enterprise companies looking for better and cheaper alternatives to current expensive and often hard-to-maintain applications. ISVs that currently sell licensed applications will want to keep their customer base loyal and not lose it to the competition. Second, since ISV profits have either stopped rising or have fallen in recent years, ISVs need to generate revenue by tapping into expanding markets within the small- and medium-sized business space.

In the future, the trend will be for current licensed applications to morph into software utility applications. We will see these applications offered first as services, then as unbundled services as they break away from the traditional bundled offerings. More applications will be offered as components that can be easily subscribed to individually or used to form a bigger application service. Customers will be able to pick and choose from different offerings, which will enable them to create their own portfolio of services fitting their exact needs.

In 2004, an article [3] said that SaaS is coming soon. At the time of this writing, SaaS has not only arrived, it is here to stay.

12.3 VERTICALIZATION AND SPECIALIZATION

Verticalization and *specialization* are words that will best describe the actions of consumers and providers of services, respectively, in the future. Verticalization, from a consumer's point of view, will mean consuming services from providers that are more attuned to the consumer's specific industry. This means that providers who pay more attention to the business requirements of their consumers will win more business from consumers in industries that are vertical in nature. Therefore, specialization, from a provider's point of view, will mean being able to provide services to consumers in specialized vertical industries.

---

[3] After the Internet bubble burst.

As businesses become more dynamic and critical of the IT functionalities they purchase and use, the companies specifically in vertical industries like health care, finance, manufacturing, and government will be looking to vendors who have experience dealing with these specific industries. These businesses will look to vendors who are not of the general-purpose kind but who have specialized knowledge of their industry.

Companies within vertical industries will look for partners and providers of services who understand the needs of their respective industries. The companies with which they will do business will be business-oriented rather than product-oriented in nature. Financial companies will look to partners who are experts in changes in Securities and Exchange Commission regulations like the Sarbanes-Oxley Act. Health care industry customers will look for partners who are experts in the Health Insurance Portability and Accountability Act. Retail industry companies will look for experts attuned to the seasonal demands of their industries. Providers of human resource services that transcend other vertical industries will look for partners who are experts in different vertical industries to provide them with more specialized services.

Further, customers will look to vendors who have experience dealing with other companies that are the same size as their own companies (size specialization). Size specialization is why most large companies today have formed an organization within their companies to deal solely with small- to medium-sized businesses.

As utility computing becomes more mainstream, companies that are already providing, and those still looking to provide, utility services for infrastructure and applications will need to provide more specialized services in addition to other nonspecialized services if they want to grow. The need to specialize will come from customers demanding a higher level of service as well as better performance from their computing resources.

12.4 CHANGING ROLES OF SOLUTION VENDORS

As many businesses continue to analyze and reengineer their organizations for better performance, the reengineering process will come with corresponding changes to IT infrastructure. Solution vendors will be changing their roles from selling product-specific solutions to selling more service- and business-oriented solutions. Business and technical consultants will have to adapt and learn each other's roles. Both will have to rely on each other's abilities to bring about a solution that best fits the customer's requirements.

Traditionally, business analysts (BAs) have been seen as skilled individuals who work with users and determine their needs in relation to computing functionalities. BAs facilitate the definition and creation of a requirements document based on business needs of the company. This document is handed to an application architect (AA) who interprets the business requirements and translates them into application architecture requirements. These requirements are then implemented either by in-house application developers or through the purchase of customized enterprise application solutions. The application is run on an infrastructure that has been defined by another individual, the Infrastructure Architect (IA). The IA may have designed an architecture based on peak capacity demands, which by now we know can lead to underutilized resources.

In the future, we will see more collaborative efforts between previously disconnected professionals as described above. A new type of consultant called the IT architect (ITA) will emerge to oversee and bring together the business and technical requirements within a company. The ITA's role will be to oversee the collaboration between the BAs, AAs, and IAs. New data, which includes usage patterns, will be added to the list of things to be considered. By looking at both functional and usage requirements, a design for an on-demand IT infrastructure can be implemented to eliminate problems such as underutilized resources and low return on investments.

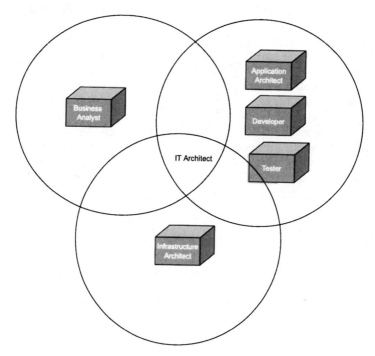

Figure 12.2 The IT architect brings together previously disconnected parties to facilitate better flow of information.

Figure 12.2 shows the job of an ITA, which is to oversee and bring together different professionals to work toward an IT infrastructure implementation that is based on functional business requirements and usage patterns. From a broader perspective, the diagram may represent customers, ISVs, managed hosting providers, and value-added resellers (VARs). In the diagram, the customer who has a list of requirements is represented by the BA; the ISV that offers an SaaS solution is represented by the group that includes the application architect, developer, and tester; and the managed hosting provider is represented by the IA. In the middle of the diagram is the solutions vendor, or VAR, which is represented by the ITA. The solutions vendor (a.k.a., the ITA) is responsible for finding the best solution to the customer's set of requirements by bringing together a portfolio of service offerings from both hardware and software service providers. As SaaS and utility hosting providers look for new ways to promote business, they will look to VARs to help bring in new customers. In return, VARs will be able to generate revenue from software and hardware utility offerings by providing their own services around such offerings. [4].

12.5 VENDORS', PROVIDERS', AND CONSUMERS' NEXT STEPS

Vendors, providers, and consumers of utilitylike products and services will have key business decisions to make. These decisions will dictate the development, implementation and wider acceptance of utility computing in the next few years. While large amounts of investment have already been made by hardware and software vendors and utility providers within the infrastructure and application space, there is no doubt that more money will need to be invested to improve and market existing technology.

In the last few years, hardware vendors have sold enterprise servers that can be partitioned to run separate operating system environments. This partitioning technology, otherwise known as virtualization, allows the server to have higher utilization rates than its predecessors. Hardware vendors have successfully introduced and sold this new technology to customers classified as *early adopters.* These same vendors need to develop new marketing strategies to sell these technologies to a broader set of adopters in a much wider range of industries.

Established software application vendors that sell traditional licensed software applications will need to decide whether to invest capital in a new business model called SaaS. In addition to investing in the new business model, they will need to learn how to operate as a SaaS application provider. One option that some traditional ISVs have taken is to partner with a company that already has a reputation for helping ISVs establish a SaaS business. An established SaaS partner may provide help ranging from application transform into a SaaS to hosting the application in a utility infrastructure.

Software vendors also have their work cut out for them. Providing an option for the customer to "buy" application capabilities on demand will require business process and mind-shift transformation. Software executives will need to adopt an attitude that a SaaS business model will not only open new markets for their product but also prevent competitors from luring away loyal customers. The short-term outlook will be challenging for vendors who want to enter the SaaS application arena–nevertheless, they need to put a stake in the ground and proceed with a strategy that will not only be good for their businesses but good for their present and future customers.

Infrastructure and SaaS providers will need to implement and provide services that consumers will find secure and disaster-proof. Security and protection of vital data will always remain a concern for consumers. It will be more of a concern within a utility computing environment since servers and applications can potentially be shared by different customers at the same time. Providers will need to convince consumers that their data is as secure within a shared environment as in a nonshared environment. Today, a service-level agreement is a way to guarantee that service is always available at acceptable levels. However, most SLAs may not guarantee continued service in cases of catastrophic disasters, natural or man-made. Utility computing providers have a responsibility to their consumers to provide a plan for disaster recovery in these cases.

As new ideas for innovation in technology will always come from customers and not from technology companies, consumers have a chance to continue to define and refine their requirements so that vendors and service providers will be able to give them what they need. Ideally, new technology will come in the form of a solution to a problem that a customer is having. This new technology is then refined to provide a 100% solution to the problem.

Companies looking to implement utilitylike solutions can choose to implement them gradually. First, they can consolidate servers by migrating to new servers that implement virtualization technology. They can meter usage of hardware resources to produce utilization measurements that can be used to trigger automatic allocation or deallocation of resources as needed. Second, software applications that do not hold any strategic value to the business can be outsourced as SaaS applications. Later on, as their business functionalities become more standardized and as they get more accustomed to the use of utility-provided applications, they can start thinking of outsourcing more of their other noncore business functionalities.

Rapidly changing business and economic conditions will continue to drive business need for more responsive, adaptive, and flexible IT infrastructures and applications. The demand for quick and cost-effective access to the latest technologies will continue to grow. While a lot of business functionalities are still highly customized to a specific company, there is a trend to move them into more standardized functions, paving the way for utility-type offerings. Both providers (including vendors) and consumers of utility computing can coexist in a symbiotic relationship following Oliver Williamson's transaction cost economics [5], where both can match each other's needs.[4]

---

[4] Consumers can use the services of utility providers to help cut costs and outsource noncore functions. Providers can help consumers through standardized utility-type services.

12.6 ADVANCING UTILITY COMPUTING

In *Diffusion of Innovations* [6], Everett Rogers describes the way in which an idea or innovation disseminates into the marketplace. According to Rogers, the adoption of innovation happens in stages—awareness, interest, evaluation, trial, and adoption. Adopters of new innovation go through each stage, and depending on their ability to adopt new innovation, they are categorized as innovators, early adopters, early majority, late majority, and laggards. Figure 12.3 shows a density representation of each category within a bell curve.

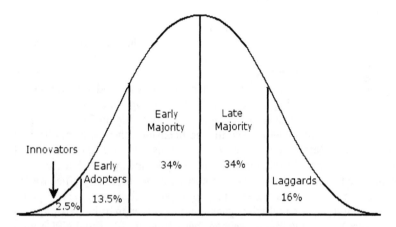

Figure 12.3 Bell curve representation of adopters of innovation.

As new innovation is introduced, innovators and early adopters are the first to adopt the new innovation. Over time, the adoption cycle accelerates with early majority and late majority adopting the innovation.

Today, Rogers' research and work has found itself in technology adoption studies. In his book *Crossing the Chasm* [7], Geoffrey Moore draws from Rogers in stating how and why technology companies succeed. Moore states, "The point of greatest peril in the development of a high-tech market lies in making the transition from an *early market* dominated by a few *visionary* customers to a *mainstream market* dominated by a large block of customers who are predominantly *pragmatists* in orientation." Moore represents the technology adoption life cycle as presented in Figure 12.3. The figure represents different types of customer that vendors of new technology sell to. After the introduction of a new technology, vendors will typically find their first customers in the innovator and early adopter types. Over time, as the market matures for the new technology, the next types of customers will buy the technology. Although not obvious, each type of customer represents a new challenge for the marketers and vendors of these new technologies. As these vendors go through the different market makeups and characteristics of their customers, they become more challenged by the fact that later customers require more and more good references proving that the new technology actually works.

Moore describes a transitional gap between the early adopters and the early majority markets as "the chasm." Moore explains that early majority customers are harder to please than early adopter customers. Early majority customers require proof that the new technology will give them a 100% solution to an existing problem. Anything less than 100% would make them unhappy, and they will tell others about their experience. So what is a 100% solution? Moore refers to it as the whole product, which he further clarifies is the minimum set of products and services necessary to fulfill a customer's requirements and give them a reason to buy the product.

Today, utility computing vendors and providers are crossing this chasm. Vendors have already successfully sold the technology to the early adopters. Now, it's time to sell to the early majority. Whatever methods vendors and providers use to cross this chasm, one thing is clear—there needs to be more cooperation between hardware and software in areas such as licensing and integration for vendors to sell utility computing successfully to the next type of customers.

In the licensing area, virtualization technology and multichip CPU packaging have created complex and sometimes confusing licensing schemes from different middleware vendors. Before, a server might have consisted of a fixed number of physical CPUs, which could run an instance of an operating system. For example, a server configured as a four CPU server requires a customer to pay a license fee based on running the middleware application on a four-way server. With virtualization technology or multichip packaging, a server may have 4 physical CPUs but be capable of running somewhere between 4 to 40 virtual CPUs with potentially more than one instance of the operating system (OS). Due to differences in CPU configuration, middleware vendors have changed their licensing structures to accommodate the use of the middleware within a virtualized, multichip, and multi-OS environment. This puts a burden on customers to make certain that using virtualized and multichip technology does not put them in a situation where they inadvertently violate software licensing agreements. This may be hard to do since the hardware configuration is now more dynamic in nature. Licensing structures for middleware applications need to accommodate a dynamic hardware environment. One solution might be for middleware vendors to adopt an on-demand licensing scheme that is well integrated with virtualized hardware technology. In this scheme, licensing fees change dynamically as the underlying hardware configuration changes. Another solution might be for middleware vendors to adopt a usage-based licensing scheme where license fees are charged based on middleware application usage and not based on hardware configuration. For this to happen, hardware and middleware software needs to be more tightly integrated. This brings us to the next issue, which is integration.

Today, most software applications are not fully aware of the new technology available in today's enterprise servers. Today, hardware capable of deallocating resources dynamically can create problems for software applications. Some enterprise software applications are programmed to query underlying hardware resources when they first start up and assume these hardware resources will be there when needed. This may have been true before the introduction of virtualization technology. Companies running these types of applications on servers that are dynamically configured every so often may get a big surprise when their application suddenly fails days after they have reconfigured their servers. Enterprise software applications need to be modified so that they know when resources have been deallocated in order for them to adjust resource needs. The reverse is also true in that software applications need to be modified so that they can predict when they are about to run out of resources and let the underlying hardware know that it needs to allocate more as soon as possible. For these modifications to happen, software vendors will need to work more closely with hardware vendors. Software vendors have the responsibility of incorporating the needed changes to their software, while hardware vendors have the responsibility to develop user-friendly APIs that software vendors can use easily with new hardware capabilities.

Utility computing is a technology that requires customers to make a paradigm switch in how they acquire IT resources. Enterprise servers, which were once mostly static in configuration, can now be shared and dynamically partitioned, resulting in better utilization rates and lower cost of ownership. Traditional licensed software now has versions that can be bought on a usage basis. As we see more hardware and software vendors setting their sights on developing utility-type products and services, we will also see both hardware and software vendors work more closely with each other, integrating their products better to develop the 100% solution the next type of customer is looking for.

12.7 CLOSING NOTES

This book described an overall view of utility computing as it stands today. It presented different strategies for and ideas about improving today's utility computing technologies in ways that can result in better products and offerings in the future. This book painted a broad picture of utility computing and the utility model in three areas–hardware infrastructure, software application, and business services. As utility computing vendors and providers switch their customer focus from the early adopters to the early majority, the emphasis of their efforts must be on developing solutions that have tighter integration between hardware and software components. Not only are early majority customers looking for more affordable solutions, but they also want solutions that are more reliable and easier to use.

In the past 40 years, we have seen changes in market structures that have rendered existing technologies obsolete. For example, mainframes[5] lost popularity in favor of minicomputers, and minicomputers in turn lost appeal in favor of personal computers. In the past 10 years, we have been in the midst of a changing market structure of global proportions. The emergence of the Internet has brought about changes in delivering information and products. The economic problems of the late 1990s and early 2000s, following the burst of the Internet bubble, have made organizations more cautious and, as a result, more demanding about the return on their IT infrastructure investments. In light of these market changes, innovative technologies like grid computing, virtualization,[6] and software delivered as a service have been developed to create a different way of delivering IT–as a utility, just like water and electricity.

Delivering IT like a utility, utility computing requires a paradigm shift for hardware and software vendors and customers. For hardware and software vendors, the shift will come from selling hardware and software that offers more performance year after year to selling hardware and software that can be bought on demand. For both types of vendors, revenue will come from sustained usage of their products and not from large, one-time, upfront hardware and software deals. Profit margins will be lower than they have been.

For customers, the shift will come from departmental and organizational changes in the form of relinquishing control of their own IT infrastructures to sharing the infrastructure with other organizations within the company or with other companies. This type of arrangement, in the long run, will save the company money, which can be invested in other parts of the organization.

Utility computing is a disruptive technology.[7] Vendors and providers need to take note of this technology. Many hardware and software companies, large and small, have made the mistake of not paying close attention to subtle market changes being served by disruptive technologies. As a result, most of them do not exist anymore. Can you afford not to pay attention to utility computing?

References

[1]   Tapper, D., "Utility Computing: A Look at Demand Side Needs for On-demand Computing Services," *IDC*, March 2003, #28864.

[2]   Ross, J, G. Westerman, "Preparing for Utility Computing," *IBM System Journal*, Vol. 43, No. 1, 2004, p. 7.

---

[5] Although mainframes never became obsolete and in some cases are still relied on by large companies requiring robust and reliable servers, the majority of companies today favor and use personal computer technology for day-to-day operations.

[6] Virtualization technology as applied to modern-day enterprise servers, storage, and networks.

[7] Disruptive technology as defined by [8].

[3]   Scannel, E., "IBM's Corgel: Software as a Service Is Coming," *InfoWorld*, June 2, 2004, available at www.infoworld.com/article/04/06/02/HNcorgelqa_1.html.

[4]   McCabe, L., "Software as a Service Vendor: Strategies for Building Productive Channels," Summit Strategies, March 2004.

[5]   Lacity, M., and R. Hirschheim, *Information Systems Outsourcing: Myths, Metaphors and Realities*, New York, John Wiley and Sons, 1993.

[6]   Rogers, E., *Diffusion of Innovation*, Free Press, 5th Edition, August 2003.

[7]   Moore, G., *Crossing the Chasm: Marketing and Selling Technology Products to Mainstream Customers*, New York, HarperBusiness, 1991.

[8]   Christensen, C., *The Innovator's Dilemma*, Cambridge, MA, Harvard Business School Publishing, 1997.

Appendix A

Self-Assessment for Software Utility Applications

This self-assessment puts the software utility application (SUA) attributes into perspective so that an application architect can quickly review the readiness of the application into becoming an SUA. While this self-assessment focuses mainly on the technical aspects of transforming to a software utility application, it must be used in conjunction with a business rules approach. [1],[2] The technical attributes of an SUA mentioned in this book serves as a guide to influence business processes but not to drive them. Ultimately, the rules of the business drive the technical requirements for transforming into a software utility application.

For each of the technical attributes mentioned, think of a business process within the company that is affected by the attribute. As an example, for the "metering" attribute, what business rules or processes need to be examined in order to make sure the metering metrics are in line with the business objectives of the company? Another example is the "update and notification" attribute. What business rules and processes will affect the type of update and notification policy implemented?

For every attribute, ask what business rules or processes are influenced by it. Then, ask what business rules or processes need to be considered to drive the technical attributes to a complete set of technical requirements for the development team to implement.

The examples above give the reader a high-level understanding of how to use this self-assessment in conjunction with a business rules approach. Business rules and processes drive technical requirements, while technical attributes influence business processes only when the business requires them.

A.1 ANATOMY OF A SOFTWARE UTILITY APPLICATION

The successful SUA requires several attributes in order to exploit the utility environment fully. Transforming an existing, nonutility application is not a trivial matter. Both business rules and technical attributes need to be considered before actual implementation.

This section introduces the attributes needed by an SUA. They are classified according to their suggested stages of implementation. The classifications begin at stage one and go up to stage three. These stages are meant to provide guidance to the application owner as to which attributes, when implemented, will help the application reap the full benefits of the utility infrastructure, as well as provide a sustainable quality of service in a flexible hosting environment.

Stage one attributes are attributes that need to be implemented so that the application can be hosted in a data center and accessed over the Internet. Stage one attributes also contribute to a sustainable and acceptable quality of service.

Stage two attributes are classified as strategic and targeted for evolution and growth of the SUA. They are needed to make the application more user friendly for administrators and subscribers. As the application becomes more popular, manageability of subscribers becomes an issue. Use of the application needs to be monitored to prevent abuse, and a more sophisticated billing system needs to be implemented. As such, these attributes will need to be implemented before such problems occur—within four to eight months of the SUA availability.

Stage three attributes are classified as integral to the evolution of future technologies. With sustainable quality of service in mind, stage three attributes aim to contribute to the robustness of the application; use of Grid technology and autonomic behavior fall into this category. The suggested implementation time frame is 12 months and beyond after the SUA first becomes available.

In the following discussion on SUA attributes, the self-assessment presents the ISV with a series of questions answerable by a yes or no. At the end of each topic, the ISV can assess its application as (1) ready, (2) almost ready, or (3) not ready for that particular attribute.

The objective of the questions asked is to help the ISV assess its application for hosting readiness as an SUA. It is recommended that the ISV ask itself the business process that affects the decision to implement the attributes.

At the end of the self-assessment, the application owner will have a fair idea of what attributes are needed by the application. The self-assessment provides guidelines for the application owner in getting the right help for each identified attribute if needed.

A.2 SUA ATTRIBUTES (STAGE 1)

A.2.1 Suitability for Hosting

The suitability or amenability of an application to be hosted is the minimum requirement for hosting on any hosting center. Simply put, satisfying this requirement creates the basis for administrating the application either remotely by the application owner or locally by the hosting provider's system administrators. It also ensures that critical data is backed up and safe in case of a catastrophic failure. It ensures that the application has the necessary support structure to allow it to serve its purpose with minimum interruptions to its users.

Self-assessment Questions:

File Backup

Certain business data must be protected in case of storage failure or erroneous modification (user error). Logs or journals might have to be backed up to satisfy legal or business requirements. The application owner is charged for the amount of data that is transferred or stored.

Can you identify critical files that need to be backed up?   **Yes   No**

Remote Administration

The hosting center allows encrypted connections to pass through to a customer-designated machine by using a virtual private network (VPN). With the VPN connection, the application owner can administer the application remotely. The application could also provide administrative functions using a browser (completely Web enabled).

Can the application be remotely administered? **Yes   No**

Browser Interface

Browsers provide a universal and flexible access interface to Web-based applications. Besides that benefit, it eliminates development support for multiple desktops.

Is the application accessed through a browser interface? **Yes   No**

Access to Legacy Applications

Some applications may need to have access to legacy data and applications.

Does the application provide a way to integrate with legacy data and applications if needed? **Yes   No**

Security for Internet

Does the application have enough security to be delivered on the Internet? **Yes   No**

Circle One

READY   ALMOST READY   NOT READY

A.2.2 Use of a Utility Hosting Center

Two main hosting infrastructure models are traditional nonutility and utility hosting centers. Understanding both infrastructure models and their capabilities is essential for deciding where best to host an application. Traditional nonutility infrastructures cater to customers who would rather own their own dedicated servers and run dedicated/sell-as-a-license-type applications. The utility hosting center caters to customers who prefer to run their applications in a shared utility infrastructure. Resources such as CPU, storage, and network are provided in a utility like manner. The applications they run may also have some characteristics of a utility.

Self-assessment Questions:

Use of Traditional Hosting

Will the application be hosted in a traditional nonutility hosting environment? **Yes   No**

Use of Utility Hosting Center

Will the application be boarded in a UHC? **Yes   No**

Circle One

READY   ALMOST READY   NOT READY

A.2.3 Use of Virtualized Resources

Virtualization is a technology used in a utility hosting environment to respond to demand for server, storage, and network resources. The ISV's application must not have any hardware or platform-specific dependencies to be able to use virtual services.

Self-assessment Questions:

Hardware Dependency

If the application code does not have any dependencies on underlying hardware implementation, the answer here is yes.

Does the application use any application extensions or functions that depend on the underlying hardware? **Yes   No**

Testing on Virtualized Environment

If the application runs on a Windows environment and it has been successfully tested on a virtual environment like VMware, then the answer here is yes.

Has the application ever been run on a virtualized environment? **Yes No**

Benchmarking

If the application has been run in a virtualized environment within a hosting facility and the application owner has data that helps in the creation of a capacity planning guide, then the answer here is yes.

Has the application ever been benchmarked in a virtualized environment within a hosting facility? **Yes   No**

Circle One

READY   ALMOST READY   NOT READY

A.2.4 Multitenancy

A multitenant application can share one application instance among several businesses or enterprise customers. The one-to-one, single-tenant application is mostly sold as a stand-alone application. It is installed in a dedicated hosting center or on the customer premises and is used within the enterprise. A multitenant, one-to-many application needs a more robust level of security and requires more isolation but can be shared among multiple companies. Multitenancy is a desirable property for an SUA because it can offer significant cost savings on license fees as well as infrastructure and support costs.

Self-assessment Questions:

Multitenant and Data Separation

Will the application support multiple companies (or organizations or enterprise customers) in a single installation instance? **Yes   No**

Hierarchical-type Access

A multitenant application should have a hierarchical access structure to prevent users from accessing parts of the application for which they are not authorized. For example:

- End user access (lowest-level access)
- End user authentication through passwords with syntax enforcement and expiration policies
- Organization administrator access (medium level)
- Application administrator access (top level or superuser)

Does the application have a hierarchical access structure? **Yes   No**

Process-to-Process Communications

Most applications are modeled after a distributed-type model for scalability. Applications are partitioned according to their functions, and each of the partitioned functions may be installed on separate machines within the application environment. The application as whole will communicate using process-to-process communication and transmit data on network ports using a known communications protocol. These network ports must be made more secure. An example might be to authenticate the communicating process using digital certificates. Logs must also be kept to see if there are any malicious login attempts to exploit the communications channel.

Does the application have a process-to-process security policy in place? **Yes   No**

Malicious User Protection

Applications must be secure such that users are not allowed to issue commands to the operating system or break out to an operating shell. Applications must be aware of potential buffer overflow in the application and protect themselves from such buffer overflow exploits.

Does the application have malicious user protection policies in place? **Yes   No**

Audit Trails

Most applications already do some type of limited logging. Usually applications will log an error or a type of condition that the application flags as an essential activity to log. These types of logging are essential for problem determination but it lacks the ability to audit user activities if needed. A policy needs to be put in place to log user activities that are deemed necessary for future user auditing.

Does the application have an audit trail process in place? **Yes   No**

Data Separation

The application or database implementation should not allow any type of user of one company to view, query, back up, or restore data belonging to another company.

Do the application and database implementations keep the data of one company separate from that of another? **Yes   No**

Database Queries

A multitenant application should not permit a customer to use a database query tool to see data belonging to another customer.

Does the application prevent the use of direct queries to the database through database-provided tools? **Yes   No**

Database Tables

An application could implement multitenancy by keeping all of its enterprise customer data in one big database table. In this case, if there are no tools or application support to separate the data of one customer from that of another during a backup, then it may be impossible to restore a given customer's data without affecting other customers.

Does the application or database architecture allow managing of organization A's data without affecting customer B's data? **Yes   No**

Stateful Sessions

An application could use session tokens or cookies to track a user session. These tokens or cookies may persist on the client or server machine. The application should securely terminate the session by invalidating tokens or cookies so they cannot be reused to grant access to unauthorized users.

Does the application implement safe and secure stateful sessions?
Yes   No

Circle One

READY   ALMOST READY   NOT READY

A.2.5 Software Maintenance and Upgrade Policy Plan

Applying maintenance, upgrades, and fixes to an application in a shared environment has more risk than when the application is not shared. Upgrading the application to a newer level or installing a software fix is "business as usual" in a dedicated (nonshared) environment. In a shared application environment, however, some additional steps may have to be in place because each company sharing the application may have varying levels of expectations of application availability. An inadequate or nonexistent policy plan for software maintenance and upgrades can bring widespread customer dissatisfaction due to corrupted or bad data caused by a bug or flaw in the application.

Self-assessment Questions:

Upgrade and Bug Fix Policy

Do you have a policy in place for maintaining and upgrading your application and environment? **Yes   No**

If you do not have a policy plan, skip the rest of the questions.

Contingency Plan

Does your policy plan include how to back out of a fix or an upgrade?
Yes   No

Staging (Preproduction) Environment

Does the policy plan include procedures to have the upgrade or the fix tested in a staging (preproduction) environment in the utility hosting center? **Yes   No**

Customer Notification

Does the policy plan include notifying customers, as well as the hosting provider's support personnel (if needed), in a timely fashion?
Yes   No

Third-party Product Upgrades

Does the policy plan include procedures on upgrading or applying maintenance to third-party products used by the shared application?
Yes   No

Policy to SLA Relationship

Does your policy plan track closely to service level agreements presented to the customer? **Yes   No**

Circle One

READY   ALMOST READY   NOT READY

A.2.6 Application Scalability

Scalability is an application attribute that describes the variability of user response time when a fixed amount of resources are added to support a linearly increasing set of users.

Resources can be hardware in terms of CPU or memory, while a software resource can be in the form of another application server or database instance. The extra resource is added to support an increasing number of users so that response time is not impacted.

Horizontal scalability is defined as the ability to add application or middleware instances and/or servers when demand rises. Vertical scaling is defined as the ability to use features provided by the infrastructure, such as single sign-on, directory services, or digital certificate services, as needed to handle diverse business demand.

Self-assessment Questions:

Scaling in All Tiers

Is the application multitiered and does it allow additional resources be put in place in any tier without affecting other tiers? **Yes   No**

Load-balancing

Does the application have internal or external load-balancing capabilities?
Yes   No

Peak Demand Policy

A utility application should have a means of preventing degradation of service due to peak demand usage. CPU monitors can send alerts to systems administrators, who can initiate provisioning additional resources when necessary.

Does the application have a policy to provision for peak demand such that it prevents the degradation of quality of service? **Yes   No**

Capacity Planning Guide

Does the application provide a hardware capacity planning guide based on performance or statistical models? **Yes   No**

Hosting Benchmarks

A capacity planning guide should be supported by benchmark data in a hosting environment.

Has the application ever been benchmarked while running in a hosting environment? **Yes   No**

Circle One

READY   ALMOST READY   NOT READY

A.3 SUA ATTRIBUTES (STAGE 2)

A.3.1 Portal

This attribute looks at the application's adaptability to be integrated into a community portal where the users or administrator of the application can log on, discover relevant services to which they are entitled, access the application, or view the application/service usage and billing information.

Self-assessment Questions:

User Profile Views

Users and administrators need to have access to their own account views of usage, billing, and profiles.

Does the application have a Web-based portal that allows users to view and manage their account profiles? **Yes   No**

Customized Views

Different subscribers will have different needs for viewing and accessing user account and information.

Does the application allow subscribers to customize or personalize their view of the front-facing Web page for the application? **Yes   No**

Branding

Different enterprise companies may wish to display their own company logos for their users.

Does the front-facing web page of the application provide rebranding capability for enterprise customers?   **Yes**   **No**

Circle One

READY   ALMOST READY   NOT READY

A.3.2 User Provisioning Services

One of the goals the SUA should strive for is to present a universal user-friendly environment to subscribers as well as administrators. Subscribers are given the ability to self-manage and view their accounts and passwords after enrolling. Offering such capabilities transfers some of the administrative burden from the ISV to its customers, which can lower user and management cost and deliver value to their customers.

Company administrators can also be allowed to authorize administrative functions for the company they administer for. This will also alleviate ISV administrative work for each individual company.

Here are some desirable application provisioning functionalities:

- Ability to delegate a hierarchy of user administrators to administer the application
- Ability for an organization to subscribe to the application
- Ability to create secure administration domains so that no unauthorized personnel can access other organizational domains that they should not have access to
- Ability to store user password and profile information for users
- Ability to grant and restrict subscribers to their respective entitlements
- Ability to enforce user password policies
- Ability to authenticate and authorize subscribers on a single-sign-on basis
- Ability to grant or restrict access to subscribers depending on time of day, priority, or business functions
- Ability to grant or restrict access to different modules of the application
- Ability to log information for user administration needs

Self-assessment Questions:

Functional Capabilities

Do you want your application to have some or all of the capabilities previously mentioned?

Yes   No

Circle One

READY   ALMOST READY   NOT READY

A.3.3 Application Provisioning Service

Automatic provisioning for needed resources is a function offered by the application provisioning service. It communicates with the hosted ISV application to determine if there are adequate resources for new application users. Other capabilities include the following:

- Creating a new instance of an application;
- Configuring access control for the application instance;
- Initiating request to add user-specific parameters to the ISV application;
- Granting application access;
- Logging all activities

Self-assessment Questions:

Functional Capabilities

Do you want your application to have some or all of the capabilities previously mentioned? **Yes   No**

Circle One

READY   ALMOST READY   NOT READY

A.3.4 Customer Care

Application help and support are functions needed by any software provider. The SUA provider needs to offer these services for subscribers to use in reporting, viewing and tracking reported problems.

Self-assessment Questions:

Does your application have a customer care service? **Yes   No**

Circle One

READY   ALMOST READY   NOT READY

A.4 SUA ATTRIBUTES (STAGE 3)

A.4.1 Application Metering Capability

Metering capability allows an application to monitor usage. Certain parts of the application can be monitored to produce usage and profiling information. Usage information can be fed to a billing system in order to bill subscribers for usage of the application at a more granular level. Profiling information can give the application owner the means to improve the quality, performance, and features of particular parts of the application.

Self-assessment Questions:

Metering Capability

Does the application owner wish to include a metering capability?
Yes   No
Skip the rest of the questions if the answer is NO.

Relevance of Metering Data

When including metering capability, some things to think about are what to meter and whether that metered data is relevant to the billing model.

Is the metered data relevant to the overall billing model?   **Yes   No**

Interface to Metering Service

Can the application communicate through Web services to interact with other third-party metering services? **Yes   No**

Interface to Third-Party Billing Engines

Can the application's metering engine interface with third-party billing engines? **Yes   No**

Circle One

READY   ALMOST READY   NOT READY

A.4.2 Application Billing Service

The simplest strategy for billing in a shared-application environment is to charge subscribers a set monthly fee. For the most part this monthly fee may have been derived through some empirical means and multiplied by a coefficient factor to make sure the application owner profits from the whole operation.

While this billing strategy works most of the time, it leaves a lot to be desired. Although all subscribers may pay the same monthly rate, some may be using more resources than others. This can lead some subscribers to inadvertently abuse the applications to the detriment of other subscribers.

Billing for actual application or service usage time is the recommended way of operating as an SUA. This approach, together with the metering attribute mentioned previously, enables the application to bill for the correct amount of time.

Even if the application owner does not make a choice to bill for application usage time, it may still be beneficial to use a billing service because it can offer more specialized expertise in the billing arena than the abilities the application owner has in-house. This leaves the application owner with the ability to focus more on his or her core competency.

The questions that follow bring to the attention of application owners some thoughts on why an application billing service may be important to their applications. If you do not wish to have a billing service, please skip to the next attribute.

Self-assessment Questions:

Billing Functionality

Do you want to include a billing functionality in your product?   **Yes**
No

Skip the rest of the questions if the answer is NO.

Pricing Structure

An application may offer several levels of functionalities. You may wish to charge differently for the different functionalities, as well as for its levels. A billing application may help in this situation.

Does the application need the capability of offering different pricing structures for varying uses of the application?   **Yes No**

Rating

You may want to rate your application's subscribers according to their use of a function. This could lead to discounts being given to certain groups of target customers.

Does the application have rating capabilities?   **Yes No**

Invoicing

A billing service may also include the ability to invoice customers for different services used, in a timely fashion. This may also be tied to some form of a portal for customers to use in viewing their monthly statements.

Does the application have customer-invoicing capabilities? **Yes No**

Interface to Metering Engine

Data that goes to the billing engine can be imported from different sources. One of them is a metering engine.

Does the billing engine allow data to be imported from different sources?
Yes No

Interface to Credit/Collection Service

An interface to a credit and collection service needs to be considered. Third-party credit and collection services can enhance the service delivery of the application service.

Does the billing service allow interface to third-party credit and collection services? **Yes   No**

Circle One

READY   ALMOST READY   NOT READY

A.4.3 Packaged for Automatic Installation and Provisioning

Automatic installations are part of an automated provisioning system. They allow the infrastructure of the application to shrink and grow as needed. Mutual cooperation between the application and the infrastructure is needed to ensure successful autoprovisioning.

Self-assessment Questions:

Unattended Installation

To support autoprovisioning, the application must be "packageable" to provide unattended installation. For example, a Windows 2000 application can use InstallShield with the necessary response files. An AIX or Linux application can be packaged with the scripts necessary to untar the install images and place them in the appropriate directories. Postinstallation customization and configuration must also be packaged or kept to an absolute minimum.

Can the application be packaged for unattended installation? **Yes   No**

Installation Tool

The specific version of the installation tool (i.e., InstallShield) must be supported by the target operating system on which it will run.

Has the current version of the installation tool been tested on the operating system platform on which it will run for both install and uninstall operations? **Yes   No**

Postinstallation

Postinstallation activities might consist of creating database schemas and populating the tables, configuring user profiles, or tailoring other specific application parameters. The postinstallation process should be as automated as possible.

Can the postinstallation process be automated or scripted to support autoprovisioning? **Yes   No**

Deinstallation of an Application or Its Components

The deinstallation of an application may be required. If the application takes advantage of a newly autoprovisioned resource such as a new server, it may need to save some configuration or user files before the resource is taken away by "reverse autoprovisioning" (shrinking of resources because utilization of the resource goes below a threshold).

Does the application have deinstallation capabilities? **Yes   No**

Circle One

READY   ALMOST READY   NOT READY

A.4.4 Service-Oriented Architecture (SOA) Based on Web Services

As a SUA provider, you may wish to subscribe to other external services or providers of services based on SOA. These external services may be provided by the infrastructure or other SUAs. If you do not have plans to subscribe or provide any services within the infrastructure, please proceed to the next attribute.

A.4.4.1 Subscriber of Services[1]

If you want your application to communicate with external common services offered within the infrastructure (such as those offered through the software utility application framework (sasf) described in Chapter 7), you will have to do so using Web services technology. This includes the use of XML, SOAP, and UDDI.

---

[1] If your application will not use external services functions or communicate with external common services, skip this section.

Self-assessment Questions:

Interfacing to sasf

Is the application capable of communicating with the sasf using Web services technology? **Yes   No**

Interfacing with Common Services

Is your application capable of communicating with external common services using Web services technology?
Yes   No

External Web services interface

Has your application been tested to communicate with external Web services?
Yes   No

A.4.4.2 Provider of Services

Transforming an application into an SUA may include exposing any of its functionality for use by other applications on a subscription basis. This requires the SUA to adhere to the basic premise of service-oriented architecture.

Web Services Functions

Does your application plan to expose any of its functionalities as Web services? **Yes   No**

sasf Testing

Have the Web services exposed by your application ever been tested in an sasf environment? **Yes   No**

UDDI Repository

Does your application publish its services in a UDDI repository? **Yes No**

Circle One

READY   ALMOST READY   NOT READY

A.4.5 Single Sign-on

Sometimes an application may offer different services within itself and access to it may require subscribers to log in more than once. Single sign-on capability eliminates multiple sign-on requirements.

Self-assessment Questions:

Multiple Logins

Does your application require multiple logins to access different parts of it?   **Yes   No**

Does your application have single sign-on capability? **Yes   No**

Circle One

READY   ALMOST READY   NOT READY

A.4.6 Application Self -Monitoring

An application that monitors itself is akin to one having its own autonomic abilities. The application may choose to monitor some key resources or application heuristics that it relies on to function correctly. If it senses that something is about to go awry or that a threshold is reached, the application may choose to write a message to a log file, send an alert to an SNMP agent, or take some self-corrective actions, if necessary.

Self-assessment Questions:

Alerts

Does your application send out alerts to administrators when it needs attention? **Yes No**

Thresholds

Does your application monitor certain thresholds for resources or application usage for sending alerts to administrators? **Yes No**

Data/Transmission Integrity

Several Internet protocols offer stateless transmission of data. Data transmitted can get lost without anyone knowing about it until it is too late. Are there areas in your application that rely on stateless and asynchronous data transfers? If yes, do you have ways to assure data is not lost? **Yes No**

Autonomic Behavior

Does your application use some heuristics to monitor and correct itself when needed? **Yes No**

Circle One

READY   ALMOST READY   NOT READY

A.5 OTHER CONSIDERATIONS (BUSINESS-TYPE NEEDS)

Below is a list of other attributes that SUAs need to think about:

- Entitlement;
- License agreement;
- Service level agreements (SLA);
- Integration with other applications;
- User/enterprise qualification (credit check, valid legal entity);
- Trial subscriptions;
- Resource provisioning;
- Offer catalog (UDDI, Web applications, nonexclusive rights to a given function);
- Ordering (via sales force, via Web site).

A.6 BECOMING AN SUA

A.6.1 Instructions

After answering the self-assessment questions above, the application owner will now have a better understanding of what the current application needs in order to become an SUA. The next step is to identify the type of work necessary to achieve this goal.

To get started, go through the list of attributes and pick one.

1. If you have circled "ready" for one picked, then there is nothing to do for that attribute.
2. If you have circled "not ready" or "almost ready," decide whether to implement it. If you decide not to implement it, proceed to the next attribute (if there are more) and repeat step 1:
3. If you decided to implement the attribute, decide whether the application change for this attribute can be made in-house or if external help is needed. If the attribute can be changed in-house, then proceed to the next attribute (if there are more) and repeat from the start.
4. If you decide to get external help, go through the list of self-assessment questions. Decide what kind of help is needed for this particular attribute. The types of help and a brief description of each are listed in Section A.6.2.
5. After selecting the help that is needed, mark the kind of help that is needed for the attribute for each stage in the checklist. For example, if for attribute 1, you discovered from the flowchart that you needed hosting consulting, you would put an "X" in the box where attribute 1 and hosting consulting intersects.

It is left to you to decide whether the type of work necessary for each attribute can be done in-house or must be outsourced to external consulting firms. If the type of work necessary is to be outsourced, you need to know the types of consulting services that are available. The next section describes the different types of services.

A.6.2 Types of Consulting Services

Architectural Consulting:
- *Infrastructure architecture consulting*: Consists of identifying the infrastructure footprint of the application;
- *Application architecture consulting*: Consists of identifying the architecture of application partitioning;
- *Deployment unit consulting*: Consists of placement of the deployment units on the infrastructure nodes.

Development Consulting:
- Provides necessary development tools (IDEs, toolkits);
- Educates on Web service architectures, such as SOAP, WSDL, and UDDI;

- Educates on service-oriented architecture;
- Educates on how to utilize sasf and common services;
- Identifies modules in the application in which the APIs need to be integrated;
- Converts application to ones that are SOA-based using Web services if necessary.

Hosting Consulting:

- Provides consulting on a backup/restore strategy and a recovery strategy;
- Provides consulting on application packaging changes for autoprovisioning (application provisioning);
- Provides consulting on the creation of any needed configuration files, including instructions;
- Provides remote-access and administration tools, and educates on how to use them.

Application Transformation Program (ATP) Consulting:

- Provides a product testing environment;
- Provides assistance in performance analysis.

A.6.3 Process Flow Diagram

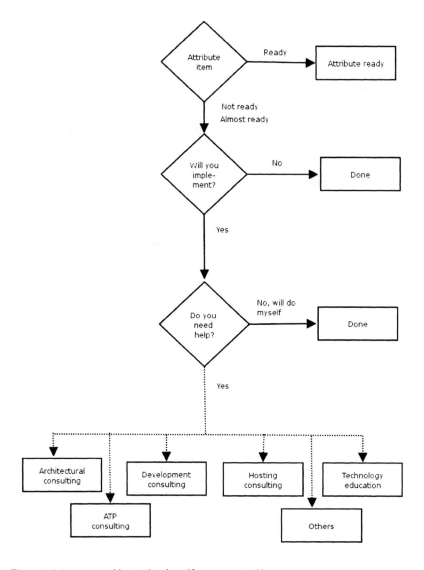

Figure A.1 A process guide to using the self-assessment guide.

A.6.4 Checklist for Stage 1 Attributes

	Architectural Consulting	Development Consulting	Hosting Consulting	ASP Consulting	Technology Education	Others
Suitability to be hosted						
On-demand infrastructure use						
Autoprovisioning packaging						
Multitenancy						
Software maintenance						
Scalability						

Figure A.2 A sample checklist for stage 1 attributes.

A.6.5 Checklist for Stage 2 attributes

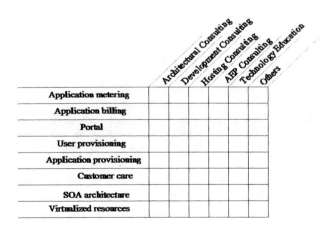

	Architectural Consulting	Development Consulting	Hosting Consulting	ASP Consulting	Technology Education	Others
Application metering						
Application billing						
Portal						
User provisioning						
Application provisioning						
Customer care						
SOA architecture						
Virtualized resources						

Figure A.3 A checklist for stage 2 attributes.

A.6.6 Checklist for Stage 3 attributes

	Architectural Consulting	Development Consulting	Hosting Consulting	ATP Consulting	Technology Education	Others
Single sign-on						
Application self-monitoring						
License agreements						
Service level agreements						
Trial subscriptions						
Resource provisioning						
User/enterprise qualifications						
Offer catalog						

Figure A.4 A checklist for stage 3 attributes.

A.7 WHERE TO START

To get an idea on what it takes to transform their enterprise application into a software utility application, we will take the example of the mythical company Alamo presented in Chapter 10 of the book. Alamo application architects will have to go through a set of self-assessment questions for each attribute. Although there is a brief description for each attribute, the questions in each bring other details related to the attribute to the application architects attention.

As an example, Alamo's application architecture is sold as a stand-alone, licensed product, as well as installed and administered on the customer's premises. The architect reads the first attribute, "Suitability for hosting".

Going through each of the self-assessment questions, the architect answers the following questions as shown:

File Backup
Can you identify critical files that need to be backed up? **Yes** (**No**)

Remote Administration
Can the application be remotely administered? **Yes** (**No**)

Security for Internet
Does the application have enough security to be delivered on the Internet?
(Yes) No

Here are the explanations for the answer choices.

File Backup—In the above example, the architect already knew which essential files to back up in case of a catastrophe.

Remote Administration—The application did not have the capability to be administered remotely, since this was a stand-alone application installed on a customer's premises. So in this case the architect circles No.

Security for Internet—Since the product was already Web-based, it is understandable that the designers of the application designed it with encryption technology for Internet access. So the architect answered yes to this question.

At this point the remote administration issue is brought to the attention of the application engineers. Since they know their application best, and they have the people to do it, they recode their application to have remote administration accessible through the Internet with the same security functions they implemented for user application access.

Next, multitenancy is one attribute that the application architects have always been curious about. They proceed to read through the description. After reading the description the architects are convinced that to offer a service the application needs to be rearchitected to support multiple companies with a single instance of the application. They also learned that being able to support multiple companies in a single install instance would save the company money in terms of what they have to pay for hardware, support maintenance, and third-party licensing fees.

Here are the architect's answers to the questions:

Multitenant and Data Separation
Does the application allow multiple companies to use it in a shared manner?
Yes (**No**)

Hierarchical Type Access
Does the application have hierarchical type of access that prevents unauthorized access to any part of the application by any type of user that does not have such access rights?   **Yes** (**No**)

Data Separation
Does the database implementation of the application separate data of one company from another? **Yes** (**No**)

Database Queries
Does the application direct queries to the database through database-provided tools? **Yes** (**No**)

Database tables
Does the application or database architecture allow managing of organization A's data without affecting customer B's data? **Yes** (**No**)

Stateful Sessions
Does the application implement safe and secure stateful sessions?
Yes (**No**)

Versioning policy
Does the application have a versioning policy? **Yes** (**No**)

Here is the explanation for the answers above:
Since the application was designed to be a stand-alone enterprise solution, nothing in the design allowed it to be used by multiple companies at the same time. In this case the answer to all of the questions was no.

The architect may refer to the section titled "Becoming an SUA" after answering the questions for this attribute or he or she may continue to the next attribute. The "Becoming an SUA" section describes what to do next after answering the self-assessment questions for each attribute. It also describes the services that external consulting firms can provide if the architect decides they need external help to architect or implement a solution.

As the flowchart indicates, if the application is not ready for a particular attribute (for this example, multitenancy), then the architect needs to decide if the attribute needs to be implemented or not. If it is to be implemented, the architect then needs to decide whether the company has enough experience and expertise to rearchitect the application. If there are areas the application owner is not comfortable with he or she may decide to get help from external consultants. The application owner decides which kind of help he or she needs. Each attribute may need architectural or development needs or other types of services provided by the external consultant. After deciding which help is needed for an attribute, the architect marks an "X" on the checklist provided for stage 1.

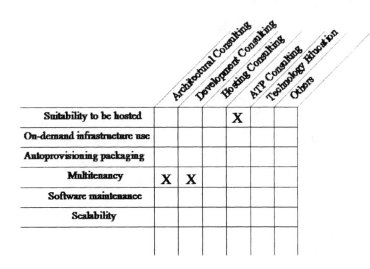

	Architectural Consulting	Development Consulting	Hosting Consulting	ATP Consulting	Technology Education	Others
Suitability to be hosted				X		
On-demand infrastructure use						
Autoprovisioning packaging						
Multitenancy	X	X				
Software maintenance						
Scalability						

Figure A.5 A checklist as marked by the application architect on what type of consulting the organization will need to enable them to become an SUA.

By the time the architect finishes answering all questions and marking X's on the grid, he will have a clear understanding of what changes need to be done to the application.

The previous scenarios are examples of how to use this workbook. The objective of the workbook is to help application owners transform their applications that can be hosted in a utility hosting center. It lists all the design considerations that an application owner needs to be aware of so he can plan for it. It helps the application owner decide which expert help he already has and which he will need externally.

It is up to the application owner to decide which attributes are really needed for his application. Implementing all the attributes is best to reap the full benefits of being an SUA. Implementing some is also an option. Whatever the application architect decides, the self-assessment guide brings to the attention of application owners what it really means to become an SUA.

References

[1]   Morgan, T., *Business Rules and Information Systems*, Boston, MA, Addison-Wesley Professional, March 2002

[2]   Halle, B., *Business Rules Applied*, Wiley, September 2001.

List of Acronyms

ATP	Application Transformation Program
API	Application Programming Interface
ARM	Application Response Monitoring
BPEL	Business Process Execution Language
CIM	Common Information Model
CPU	Central Processing Unit
DCML	Data Center Markup Language
DMTF	Distributed Management Task Force
GGF	Global Grid Community
HTTP	Hypertext Markup Language
IETF	Internet Engineering Task Force
JCP	Java Community Process
MDA	Model-Driven Architecture
MOWS	Management of Web Services
MUWS	Management Using Web Services
OMG	Object Management Group

267

OS	Operating System
PC	Personal Computer
RAS	Reusable Asset Specification
SaaS	Software as a Service
sasf	Software Application Services Framework
SLA	Service Level Agreement
SOA	Service-Oriented Architecture
SOAP	Simple Object Access Protocol
SPML	Service Provisioning Markup Language
SUA	Software Utility Application
UDDI	Universal Description, Discovery, and Integration
UHC	Utility Hosting Center
W3C	World Wide Web Consortium
WSDL	Web Services Description Language
WSDM	Web Services Distributed Management
WSI	Web Services Interoperability
WSRF	Web Services Resource Framework
XML	Extensible Markup Language

About the Author

Alfredo (Freddie) Mendoza is an IT specialist in the ISV Business Strategies and Enablement Group within the IBM Systems and Technology Division with more than 19 years of application architecture and management experience. He currently works with independent software vendors to port and migrate their applications into IBM cross-platform operating system offerings. Prior to his current position, Mr. Mendoza worked in IBM's Global Services and AIX Kernel development organizations and as an independent consultant for different software-development organizations. Mr. Mendoza has authored and coauthored several patent invention publications on thread management and software algorithms. He is the author of *Unix to Linux Porting* and coauthor of "Design of an Enablement Process for On-Demand Applications" in the utility computing issue of the *IBM Systems Journal*.

Index